This book describes and evaluates the literature on exchange rate economics. It provides a wide-ranging survey, with background on the history of international monetary regimes and the institutional characteristics of foreign exchange markets, an overview of the development of conceptual and empirical models of exchange rate behavior, and perspectives on the key issues that policymakers confront in deciding whether, and how, to try to stabilize exchange rates. The treatment of most topics is compact, with extensive references to the literature for those desiring to pursue individual topics further. The level of exposition is relatively easy to comprehend; the historical and institutional material (part I) and the discussion of policy issues (part III) contain no equations or technical notation, while the chapters on models of exchange rate behavior (part II) are written at a level intelligible to first-year graduate students or advanced undergraduates. The book will enlighten both students and policymakers, and should also serve as a valuable reference for many research economists.

Exchange rate economics

CAMBRIDGE SURVEYS OF ECONOMIC LITERATURE

Editor
Professor Mark Perlman, University of Pittsburgh

The literature of economics is expanding rapidly, and many subjects have changed out of recognition within the space of a few years. Perceiving the state of knowledge in fast-developing subjects is difficult for students and time-consuming for professional economists. This series of books is intended to help with this problem. Each book gives a clear structure to and balanced overview of the topic, and is written at a level intelligible to the senior undergraduate. They will therefore be useful for teaching but will also provide a mature yet compact presentation of the subject for economists wishing to update their knowledge outside their own specialism.

Exchange rate economics

Peter Isard

International Monetary Fund, Washington

CAMBRIDGE
UNIVERSITY PRESS

Published by the Press Syndicate of the University of Cambridge
The Pitt Building, Trumpington Street, Cambridge CB2 1RP
40 West 20th Street, New York, NY 10011–4211, USA
10 Stamford Road, Oakleigh, Melbourne 3166, Australia

First published 1995

Printed in Great Britain at the University Press, Cambridge

A catalogue record for this book is available from the British Library

Library of Congress cataloguing in publication data

Isard, Peter.
  Exchange rate economics / by Peter Isard.
      p.   cm.
  Includes bibliographical references and indexes.
  ISBN 0 521 46047 6. – ISBN 0 521 46600 8 (pbk.)
  1. Foreign exchange rates.   2. Foreign exchange rates – Econometric
models.   I. Title.
  HG3851.I8   1995
  332.4'56 – dc20   95-8063   CIP

ISBN 0 521 46047 6 hardback
ISBN 0 521 46600 8 paperback

SE

To Maggie

Contents

Figures

Tables

Preface

Economists have written extensively about exchange rates, particularly during the past two decades. This book tries to describe and evaluate the literature in a way that will enlighten both students and policymakers, while also serving as a valuable reference for many research economists. Prospective readers should note three characteristics. First, the book provides a wide-ranging survey, with background on the history of international monetary regimes and the institutional characteristics of foreign exchange markets, an overview of the development of conceptual and empirical models of exchange rate behavior, and perspectives on the key issues that policymakers confront in deciding whether, and how, to try to stabilize exchange rates. Second, the treatment of most topics is compact, with extensive references to the literature for those desiring to pursue individual topics further. Third, the level of exposition is relatively easy to comprehend; the historical and institutional material (part I) and the discussion of policy issues (part III) contain no equations or technical notation, while the chapters on models of exchange rate behavior (part II) are written at a level intelligible to first-year graduate students or advanced undergraduates.

My perspectives on exchange rate economics have been fostered by professional experience in two of the leading research-oriented policy environments for international economists: the International Finance Division of the Federal Reserve Board from 1972 until 1985, and the Research Department of the International Monetary Fund since 1985. Among the people with whom I have had the privilege of working closely at times, and to whom I am especially indebted for insights on topics covered in this survey, are Michael Dooley, Robert Flood, Morris Goldstein, Dale Henderson, Michael Mussa, and Ralph Smith.

I also am grateful to many other people for making this book possible, and for feedback on its contents. Special thanks go to Hali Edison, for reading earlier drafts of all the chapters, identifying deficiencies, and offering numerous constructive suggestions; to Rosalind Oliver, for outstanding work and patience in typing and repeatedly revising the manuscript and carefully shepherding it through its various transformations; and to my wife, Maggie, and children, Ben and Harsha, for endowing me with happiness and inspiration and bearing with my prolonged state of writer's distraction.

Most of the views expressed in the book can be found elsewhere in the literature. Those that are controversial do not necessarily reflect the views of the Management or Executive Directors of the International Monetary Fund. I take full blame for any erroneous or misleading material, as well as any major sins of omission.

1   Introduction

Exchange rate economics was revitalized in the early 1970s. The catalyzing event was the crumbling of the postwar international monetary system, under which countries had for the previous quarter century kept their exchange rates fixed within narrow ranges, with only occasional adjustments. Subsequently, except within Europe, the major industrial countries have maintained flexible exchange rate arrangements, and market pressures have been allowed to generate large fluctuations in currency values. This has given economists a new set of phenomena to explain.

In a fundamental sense, however, the renewed interest in exchange rate economics has also reflected the fact that exchange rates are important. Changes in exchange rates have pervasive effects, with consequences for prices, wages, interest rates, production levels, and employment opportunities, and thus with direct or indirect implications for the welfare of virtually all economic participants. Accordingly, large and unpredictable changes in exchange rates present a major concern for macroeconomic stabilization policy.

To many economists and policymakers, the extent to which exchange rates have fluctuated since the early 1970s has indeed been quite surprising. Typically, exchange rates between the major currencies have changed by several percent per month, while changes of 10 percent or more in a matter of weeks have not been uncommon. This can be seen in figures 1.1 and 1.2 and table 1.1, which focus on exchange rates between the world's three most widely traded currencies – the United States dollar, the German mark, and the Japanese yen.

Figures 1.1 and 1.2 distinguish between short-term and longer-term fluctuations. Short-term variability, characterized by month-to-month percentage changes, increased dramatically following the shift from fixed to flexible exchange rates in the early 1970s (figure 1.1).[1] During the period 1974–94, the absolute values of month-to-month percentage changes averaged about $2\frac{1}{2}$ percent for each of the three key-currency exchange rates

---

[1] Prior to 1971, the only two occasions of large month-to-month changes were the realignments of the mark in March 1961 and September–October 1969.

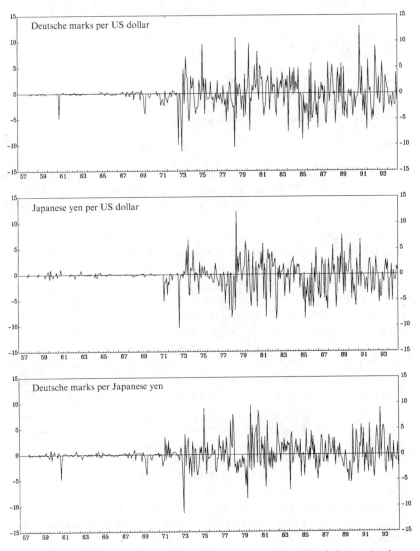

Source: Based on end-of-month data from International Monetary Fund, *International Financial Statistics.*

Figure 1.1 Short-term variability of key-currency exchange rates, 1957–94, percentage change from previous month

Table 1.1. *Perspectives on exchange rate variability, 1974–94*

	Average absolute values of month-to-month percentage changes		
	1974–83	1984–94	1974–94
Nominal exchange rates			
Deutsche marks per US dollar	2.38	2.78	2.59
Japanese yen per US dollar	2.38	2.45	2.41
Deutsche marks per Japanese yen	2.43	2.22	2.32
Consumer price indices			
United States	0.66	0.32	0.48
Germany	0.37	0.22	0.29
Japan	0.59	0.25	0.41
Stock-market price indices			
United States	2.92	2.49	2.70
Germany	—	3.76	3.75[a]
Japan	2.24	3.68	3.00
Commodity price indices			
Agricultural raw materials	2.52	1.89	2.19
Minerals and metals	2.47	2.71	2.59
Food	3.25	2.09	2.65
Gold	5.58	2.40	3.92
Petroleum	5.18	6.27	5.75

Note:
[a] 1984–94.
Sources: International Monetary Fund, *International Financial Statistics*, except for equity price indices, which are from Data Resources Inc. The equity price indices are the Dow Jones index, the Frankfurt Commerzbank index, and the Nikkei 225 average.

(table 1.1). To put this number into perspective, these exchange rates varied month-to-month roughly five times as much during 1974–94 as the prices of consumer goods and services in the United States and Japan, and eight times as much as consumer prices in Germany. At the same time, however, the key-currency exchange rates have exhibited somewhat less month-to-month variability than major stock-market price indices, and comparable or lower variability than the prices of many primary commodities.

Over intervals longer than a month, the successive month-to-month changes in exchange rates have often offset each other.[2] Nevertheless, the

[2] From end-of-year to end-of-year during the 1974–94 period, the percentage changes in the mark/yen exchange rate were only about twice as large in average absolute value as the month-to-month percentage changes, while year-to-year percentage changes in the mark/dollar and yen/dollar rates had average absolute values about four times those of the month-to-month percentage changes.

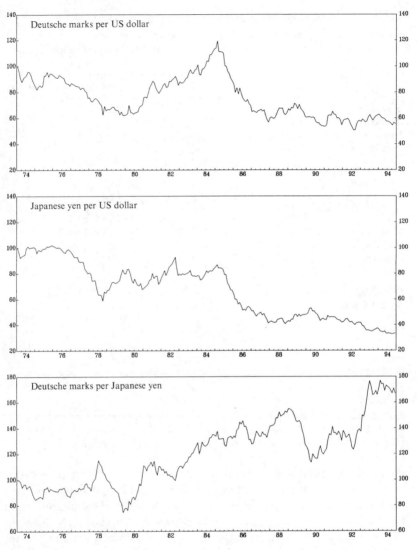

Source: Based on end-of-month data from International Monetary Fund, *International Financial Statistics.*

Figure 1.2 Key-currency exchange rates, 1974–94 (January 1974 = 100)

cumulative changes in these exchange rates over the past two decades have been large (figure 1.2), and on some occasions the deviations of exchange rate from their longer-term trends have seemed to defy rationality. The most outstanding example was the dramatic appreciation of the dollar against the mark from end-1980 to early 1985, which doubled the purchasing power of the dollar and greatly increased the propensity of US residents to take European vacations and shopping trips. The rise of the dollar was followed by an even sharper fall through early 1987.

Given the pervasive effects that changes in exchange rates can have on economic conditions, policymakers naturally want to understand what can feasibly be done to limit exchange rate variability, and with what consequences. Economists, stimulated by the policy issues, have engaged in extensive conceptual and empirical research aimed at explaining the behavior of exchange rates since the early 1970s. To date, however, these research efforts have met with only limited success. Meanwhile, the policy issues have evolved as lessons have been learned from, and new questions raised by, the experience of attempting to maintain macroeconomic stability in an evolving world economy.

This book provides a broad survey of exchange rate economics. Part I presents relevant historical and institutional background on foreign exchange markets and exchange rate arrangements. Part II, the core of the book, focuses on the behavior of exchange rates, describing the evolution of both conceptual models and empirical research, summarizing what has been learned to date, and pointing to some new directions in the literature. Part III provides policy perspectives on the key issues that arise in deciding whether to maintain fixed or flexible exchange rate arrangements and, more generally, in considering whether, and how, to try to stabilize exchange rates.

When attempting to explain changes in exchange rates from day to day and year to year, most experts traditionally point to the behavior of other macroeconomic variables. Normally, little attention is paid to the institutional characteristics of the environment in which exchange rates are determined – and rightly so, since such characteristics tend to change very gradually over time. Nevertheless, an awareness of certain institutional influences, and of how they have evolved, provides relevant perspectives in developing an understanding of exchange rate behavior. For this reason, historical and institutional background is provided in part I of the book, which is organized into two chapters. Chapter 2 focuses on relevant characteristics of foreign exchange markets and money, with particular attention to the features of modern foreign exchange trading. Chapter 3 describes the different types of exchange rate arrangements that countries may choose, and presents a brief history of the evolution of international monetary regimes over the past century.

The discussion of institutional considerations emphasizes that the behavior of exchange rates from transaction to transaction largely reflects the instincts of foreign exchange "dealers" in adjusting their bid and asked quotations in response to both the flow of trading and the flow of news and rumors. The review of historical experience suggests that exchange rate behavior depends importantly on the exchange rate arrangements and international monetary regimes that countries choose, and on the actions of policy authorities. Yet, despite the influence of marketmakers and policy authorities, the behavior of exchange rates is linked fundamentally to the behavior of other economic variables. Indeed, the rate quotations and market transactions of foreign exchange dealers, as well as the actions of policymakers, are generally responsive to current economic developments and to changes in the economic outlook. These perspectives are emphasized in part II of the book, which addresses the relationships between exchange rates and other economic variables.

Historically, economists have identified price levels, interest rates, and international payments balances as three classes of economic variables to which the behavior of exchange rates is linked particularly closely. Chapter 4 focuses on the relationships between exchange rates and ratios of national price levels, discussing the purchasing power parity hypothesis and the counterarguments, reviewing the empirical evidence, and summarizing the main implications for exchange rate models and policies. Chapter 5 considers the relationships between exchange rates and international interest rate differentials, discussing the covered and uncovered interest rate parity hypotheses, along with various possible interpretations of the empirical finding that interest rate differentials provide biased predictions of changes in exchange rates. Chapter 6 reviews the conceptual literature that had developed by the early 1970s on exchange rates and the balance of payments. This literature, which largely preceded the rational expectations revolution in macroeconomics, includes the static elasticities–absorption models of the current account, the early models of external-and-internal stabilization policy for the open economy (the Mundell–Fleming framework), and the early monetary and portfolio-balance forms of asset equilibrium models of the balance of payments under fixed exchange rates.

Beginning in the 1970s, conceptual models of exchange rate behavior emphasized that currency values, like stock market prices, tend to jump in response to new information about economic variables or events that may affect the economy. Chapter 7 focuses on several classes of forward-looking models that have been developed to capture the influence of news, and of revisions in expectations, on the dynamic behavior of exchange rates, including the phenomenon of exchange rate "overshooting." It also addresses the conceptual literature on exchange rate target zones.

Chapter 8 provides a short survey of the literature on the empirical performance of single-equation (or small-scale) structural models of exchange rate behavior since the early 1970s. It also considers the inferences that have been drawn about the effectiveness of exchange market intervention policies, and it briefly describes the treatment of exchange rates in large-scale macroeconometric models.

Chapters 9 and 10 discuss new directions in the analysis of exchange rate behavior. Chapter 9, which focuses on why, and when, exchange rates come under attack in fixed rate regimes, illustrates the perspectives that emerge from using a policy optimization approach to model the behavior of realignment expectations and the risk premium, and to analyze the effectiveness of exchange market intervention. Chapter 10 considers new directions in conceptual models of flexible exchange rates, including both models in which market participants are assumed to form rational expectations based on complete information, and models in which market participants either are not fully rational or have limited information.

Chapters 11 and 12, comprising part III of the book, turn to exchange rate policy. Chapter 11 discusses how the structural characteristics of economies, along with various other considerations, affect a country's optimal choice between fixed and flexible exchange rate arrangements. It also addresses the trend toward increased international capital mobility and its implications for the choice of currency arrangements, with particular attention to exchange arrangements during the process of transition toward a common currency for Europe. Chapter 12 focuses on several policy issues that bear importantly on exchange rate stability, regardless of whether countries adopt fixed or flexible exchange rate arrangements. Perspectives are provided on the importance of fiscal and monetary discipline as a precondition for exchange rate stability, on the pros and cons of placing restrictions on international capital movements, on the "capital inflows problem" and its policy implications, and on the role and limitations of international policy cooperation in stabilizing exchange rates.

Although the book does not contain a summary chapter, conclusions on the state of exchange rate economics can be found in the final sections of chapters 4 through 6 and chapters 9 through 12. In particular, chapters 4 through 6 provide concluding perspectives on the relationships between exchange rates and other economic variables, chapters 9 and 10 on new directions for modeling the behavior of exchange rates, and chapters 11 and 12 on exchange rate policies and the prospects for exchange rate stability.

Part I

Historical and institutional perspectives

2 Foreign exchange markets and the marketability of money

This chapter provides historical and institutional perspectives on foreign exchange markets and the monetary instruments that are traded in them. The first section traces the evolution of markets for exchanging one money for another. The second section addresses the conceptual issue of why money is valuable. The third section focuses briefly on the implications of various legal restrictions that are sometimes placed on the convertibility of money. The fourth and fifth sections, the greater part of the chapter, describe the modern foreign exchange market and the manner in which foreign exchange dealers determine the exchange rates that they quote to customers.

1 The evolution of foreign exchange markets

Markets for exchanging different monetary instruments have ancient origins. Coins made of gold and silver have particularly long histories as monetary units, and arrangements for trading the coins used by different societies were perhaps the earliest foreign exchange markets. Specific references to the practice of exchanging coins at rates reflecting their different metallic contents have been found in scattered documents from Egypt, Mesopotamia, and the Greek city states.[1]

The advent of paper instruments as means of payment marked a watershed in the evolution of international trading arrangements and foreign exchange markets. With the growing importance of bank deposits as part of the money supply in Europe, it became customary during the Middle Ages for merchants in major trading centers to make payments by assignment on their bank accounts.[2] International banking developed simultaneously with local banking following the introduction of the bill of exchange, "a powerful innovation of the Italians in the thirteenth century."[3] This profound transformation in settlement instruments provided a major stimulus to the volume of trade between different

---

[1] Bingham (1992).   [2] Spufford (1986, pp. 28–30).   [3] Kindleberger (1984, p. 39).

commercial centers.[4] By the early fourteenth century, with the widespread acceptance of paper instruments as means of payment, merchants no longer needed to finance trade by transporting large quantities of precious metals, which were bulky and relatively vulnerable to theft.

In the early stages of international trade, merchants typically sold goods in a town for local money, using the proceeds to buy goods in the same market.[5] Over time, some towns began to organize international trade fairs, where merchants from different places could exchange their wares. A fair might last for several weeks, providing merchants with a number of days to arrange their purchases and sales, after which the officials of the fair would supervise a multilateral net-settlement process. The officials would validate the payments due to and due from each merchant, and where feasible, settlement obligations would be canceled against each other to reduce the need for actual payments. Most actual payments came to be handled through bills of exchange.

Bills of exchange were primarily drawn against banks located in one of several dozen major trading cities in Europe, which were also the principal financial centers. In general, bills of exchange did not bear interest, which was forbidden by the Church in Rome. They were payable on sight, normally in gold or silver that had been placed on deposit and, in theory, remained in the reserve holdings of banks. The acceptability of pieces of paper as means of payment was linked to the presumption that the paper could ultimately be converted into gold or silver.

Since merchants had strong incentives to avoid transporting large quantities of gold or silver, the expansion of trade at international fairs gave rise to secondary markets for buying and selling bills of exchange. Dealers emerged. A merchant from Florence could pay for goods from Bruges with a bill of exchange drawn against a bank in London, which the merchant from Bruges could either keep or sell to a dealer.

Nothing in the system required the residents of any trading place to balance their purchases and sales *vis-à-vis* any other center. Dealers in bills of exchange, however, were reluctant to accumulate large holdings of claims on any particular trading place. Accordingly, the relative prices at which bills of exchange could be purchased or sold tended to fluctuate within limits in response to developments in the balance of trade. As payments imbalances accumulated, the exchange rates (explicit or implicit) between bills drawn on banks at different trading places tended to rise or fall. When the price of a bill of exchange fell sufficiently, the option of selling the bill on the secondary market became less attractive than the alternative of presenting the bill to the obligor, taking claim to silver or gold, and

---

[4] Spufford (1986, p. 30).
[5] See Kindleberger (1984, chapter 3) for a more extensive discussion.

incurring the costs and risks of transporting bullion. Allegedly, the quantities of silver and gold transported between trading centers did not decline with the growing use of bills of exchange to make foreign payments, but the volume of silver and gold shipments expanded much less rapidly than the volume of merchandise trade.[6]

In recent decades, the institutional characteristics of markets for exchanging different monetary instruments have been influenced by another profound transformation in the means of settling transactions. With the revolution in telecommunications and computer technologies, the practice of using paper instruments to settle international transactions – one of the major economic innovations of the Middle Ages – has for most purposes become obsolete. Today, international payments can be made very rapidly and inexpensively through the transmission of electronic payments messages.

The institutional characteristics of international financial markets have also changed importantly since the Middle Ages in at least two other respects. First, the volume of international trade payments as a share of international financial transactions has declined dramatically. In this sense, the composition of the supply and demand orders that are placed in foreign exchange markets has changed substantially. Second, it is no longer customary for financial instruments to take the form of legal obligations to deliver gold or silver. The convertibility characteristics of the monetary instruments traded in foreign exchange markets have thus also changed.

2   What makes money marketable?

Over the centuries, many different types of monetary instruments have been used to settle domestic and international transactions. In primitive societies, the articles adopted as money have included stones, beads, shells, whales' teeth, furs, cloth, and grains – among others.[7] Even in modern times, items such as cigarettes have served as money where national currencies were either scarce (for example, in prisoner-of-war camps) or rapidly losing purchasing power under conditions of hyperinflation.[8]

The attractiveness of any particular item as a monetary instrument depends, *inter alia*, on whether it can function conveniently as both a medium of exchange and a store of value, in addition to serving as a unit of account. Primitive moneys have tended to be objects that were nonperishable, relatively small, and easy to carry.

Historically, the instruments that have served as money have often had intrinsic usefulness in production or consumption. In such cases, the value

---

[6] Kindleberger (1984, p. 33).   [7] Einzig (1949).   [8] Steiger (1992).

of money has derived partly from the fact that it could be eaten, smoked, or transformed into clothing or other useful products. In many cases, however, the acceptability of money has been acquired partly or wholly from a social convention:

Somehow the members of a society agree on what will be acceptable tender in making payments and settling debts among themselves. General agreement to the convention, not the particular medium agreed upon, is the source of money's immense value to the society.[9]

Indeed, in modern societies, monetary instruments generally have no intrinsic usefulness in production or consumption, and derive their acceptability solely from national legislation defining them as legal tender.

Notably, when doubts emerge about the future legal acceptability of any particular form of money, its rates of exchange against other forms of money can change dramatically. During the period leading up to a currency reform, the monetary unit that is being withdrawn from circulation thus sometimes depreciates substantially.[10] This is particularly likely when market participants anticipate that the government may seek to "default" on part of its outstanding monetary liabilities by placing quantitative limits on the volume of monetary conversions, or by conducting the conversions at a "confiscatory" exchange rate.

3   Restrictions on the convertibility of money

Just as the source of money's value depends fundamentally on its general acceptability as legal tender, both the level and the stability of a currency's exchange rates against other currencies can be sensitive to any restrictions that are placed on the range of transactions for which its use is permissible. In reality, many countries maintain restrictions on the convertibility of their currencies. Such convertibility restrictions take several forms. In some instances, bank deposits or other monetary assets may be frozen, thereby limiting, among other things, the convertibility of domestic money into goods. This was the case, for example, in the former Soviet Union prior to the political dissolution and economic reforms of the early 1990s. A more prevalent practice, however, is to place restrictions on the convertibility of domestic money into foreign money.

Restrictions on the convertibility of domestic currency into foreign currency are often based on the purpose for which the currency conversion is desired. Such restrictions may also be based on the residency or citizenship of the party seeking to undertake the currency conversion. Many countries, for example, restrict the extent to which domestic residents

---

[9] Tobin (1992, p. 770).   [10] Garber and Spencer (1994).

are legally permitted to purchase foreign exchange for purposes of building up financial or physical asset holdings in other countries. In addition, many countries still maintain restrictions of some form on the extent to which it is legally permissible to convert domestic money into foreign exchange for purposes of financing merchandise imports or making payments for other current international transactions (such as interest payments to nonresidents or payments for travel expenses).[11]

Throughout most of this book, the primary focus is on the behavior of exchange rates between the currencies of major industrial countries. Moreover, except in chapter 3, attention is devoted mainly to the period since the early 1970s, which marked the breakdown of the exchange rate system that had been established after World War II. For the major industrial countries, restrictions on convertibility for purposes of financing international trade had been abolished by the early 1970s, and during the following two decades restrictions on convertibility for international capital transactions were progressively eliminated. As discussed in chapter 11, it is widely perceived that the behavior of exchange rates has been affected quite significantly by an increase in the international mobility of capital, which has been associated, *inter alia*, with the removal of convertibility restrictions.

4 The modern foreign exchange market

The market for conducting foreign exchange transactions today is arguably the largest and most technically advanced market in the world.[12] Unlike markets where people get together to conduct business, the foreign exchange market operates through a phone and computer network of "over-the-counter trading" among dealers dispersed around the globe. Most foreign exchange transactions are arranged from the offices of major commercial banks. Modern technology allows traders to communicate rapidly with each other, primarily via computer terminals, telephones, and telexes. Moreover, because the business hours of major trading centers overlap around the world, traders with access to telephones or other rapid communication facilities can conduct business 24 hours a day (except on weekends or holidays). Banks in Australia and the Far East begin trading in Sydney, Tokyo, Hong Kong, and Singapore about the time that the trading day ends in San Francisco and Los Angeles. As trading closes in the Far East, banks in Bahrain and other Middle East centers have already been open for several hours, while the trading day is just beginning in London,

[11] International Monetary Fund (1994, summary table, line E1, pp. 588–94).
[12] See Walmsley (1992), Grabbe (1991), and Riehl and Rodríguez (1983) for extensive descriptions of the foreign exchange market and the characteristics of trading.

Frankfurt, Zurich, and other European centers. By early afternoon in Europe, active trading is underway in New York. By mid-day in New York, trading is beginning on the west coast of the United States.

Foreign exchange transactions may be associated with either international trade or international investment activities. Participants in the foreign exchange market comprise the commercial banks and brokers that serve as "dealers" in foreign exchange, other private financial institutions (including nondealing banks, securities' companies, pension funds, insurance companies, and mutual funds), nonfinancial businesses, individuals, public agencies, and central banks. Many nonfinancial businesses – such as corporations with international operations – conduct foreign exchange transactions in association with both trade and investment activities.

One of the most significant developments in foreign exchange markets in recent decades has been the growth of investment-related foreign exchange transactions relative to transactions related to exports and imports of merchandise. This trend has been associated with the increasing prominence of institutional investment funds and the international portfolio diversification that these funds have undertaken. The liberalization and modernization of financial markets in Japan and several major European countries during the 1980s, and the vastly improved access to information made possible by the revolution in telecommunications and computer technologies, have greatly facilitated the international diversification of financial portfolios. At the same time, the increasing institutionalization of savings (outside of banks) has rapidly expanded the amounts of funds under the management of institutional investors with internationally diversified portfolios.

Most large foreign exchange transactions involve transfers of funds between different bank deposits. Unlike the transactions conducted by tourists and business travellers, who typically exchange domestic banknotes for foreign banknotes, large-scale exchanges of domestic currency for foreign currency generally involve funds being deposited in a foreign-currency bank account and debited from a domestic-currency account. To a considerable extent, the attractiveness of exchanging domestic and foreign bank deposits reflects the convenience of conducting foreign exchange transactions through commercial banks. The central role that commercial banks play in domestic payments systems makes it natural for them also to perform a central role in arranging the foreign exchange transactions associated with international payments. Thus, with the increasing integration of international financial markets, the foreign exchange market and domestic money markets have become interlocked. Most commercial banks are prepared to handle foreign exchange transactions for their customers, although many rely on large correspondent banks in money market centers to execute the transactions. Among the banks that maintain active foreign exchange operations, many have established branches in major trading centers throughout the world.

Banks generally conduct foreign exchange transactions (whether for their own accounts or for customers and correspondents) in either of two ways: through direct dealing with other banks that are actively engaged in foreign exchange trading, or through foreign exchange brokers. Each method has some advantages and some disadvantages. In direct dealing, the bank is generally assured of making a transaction, but in some circumstances it may take less time and effort to find an attractive exchange rate by dealing through a broker who maintains information on the bid and asked rates of various market participants, and who specializes in matching buyers and sellers.

Surveys conducted by central banks and monetary authorities in 26 countries during April 1992, as compiled by the Bank for International Settlements (BIS), estimated that the amount of money traded in the global foreign exchange market was equivalent to 880 billion US dollars a day.[13] This turnover volume was 42 percent larger than the estimated size of the global foreign exchange market in April 1989, which in turn had roughly doubled from three years earlier. The bulk of the turnover reflected transactions between dealers – mainly banks. But foreign exchange brokers were apparently involved in arranging about one-third of the global turnover volume. About half of the global turnover in April 1992, and nearly 60 percent of inter-dealer business, reflected cross-border transactions – that is, transactions between parties residing in different countries.

The composition of foreign exchange market activity in April 1992 is shown in table 2.1. By geographical location, almost 30 percent of trading was conducted in the United Kingdom, nearly 20 percent in the United States, and more than 10 percent in Japan. The four next largest trading centers – Singapore, Switzerland, Hong Kong, and Germany – together accounted for roughly 25 percent of the total.

The foreign exchange market has several different segments, reflecting the different types of transaction that take place. There are four basic types of over-the-counter contracts: spot transactions, outright forwards, swaps, and options. In addition, trading in standardized foreign exchange futures contracts and options contracts takes place on organized exchanges outside the over-the-counter foreign exchange market.

[13] Bank for International Settlements (1993). This estimate of global net turnover was adjusted for virtually all double counting of trades reported by both parties to the transactions, as well as for estimated gaps in reporting. Moreover, the data reported for April 1992 reflect turnover during "a fairly normal month;" in mid-September 1992, when trading became extremely active in markets for many European currencies, turnover volumes were reported to have reached as much as two or three times their normal levels.

Table 2.1. *Shares of global foreign exchange market activity, April 1992*[a]

By geographical location	
United Kingdom	27
United States	17
Japan	11
Singapore	7
Switzerland	6
Hong Kong	5
Germany	5
All others	22
By type of transaction	
Spots	47
Forwards	46
Outright forwards	(7)
Swaps	(39)
Futures	1
Options[b]	5
By currency	
US dollar	82
Deutsche mark	40
Japanese yen	23
Pound sterling	14
Swiss franc	9
All others	32
Memorandum item: composition of forward contracts by maturity	
Up to seven days	64.3
Eight days to one year	34.5
Over one year	1.2

Notes:
[a] In percent.
[b] Includes both over-the-counter and exchange-traded options.
Source: Bank for International Settlements (1993, tables IIIa, V, VI, 5–A).

The spot market is the segment in which the two parties to a transaction arrange to conduct the exchange of currencies within a relatively short-term horizon. More precisely, in a spot transaction, the agreed payment date or "value date" for debiting and crediting deposit balances is normally two business days after the transaction is arranged, although banks often trade for "next day" value.[14] The lag allows time for banks to confirm the details of transactions and properly execute the fund transfers. By contrast, in an outright forward transaction, payment based on an agreed exchange rate takes place on a specified date more than two business days in the future. The maturity of a forward contract may be a few days, weeks, months, or even years.[15]

A forward transaction provides a way for an individual or a business to arrange in advance to buy foreign exchange for the purpose of making a future international payment, or to sell foreign exchange that will be available in the future. A large proportion of outright forward transactions are undertaken to hedge currency exposures arising from international trade. In purchasing or selling the foreign exchange forward, the exchange rate can be agreed upon today. By contrast, under the alternative of waiting to purchase or sell the foreign exchange spot at the time it is needed or available, the individual or business would remain uncertain about the exchange rate until the spot transaction took place.

The third basic type of transaction – a swap – constitutes a simultaneous purchase and sale of a specified amount of foreign exchange for two different value dates. In a swap transaction, the amount of foreign exchange purchased spot (or at a near-term forward date) is simultaneously sold forward (or at a more distant forward date). Swaps can provide an attractive vehicle for corporations or institutional funds to make temporary investments in a currency. Swaps also provide a mechanism for a bank to accommodate the outright forward transactions executed with its customers, and more generally, to modify the maturity profile of its outstanding spot and forward contracts.

In practice, swap transactions are much more customary than outright forwards and almost as prevalent as spot transactions; indeed, the April 1992 survey revealed that spot transactions accounted for just under half of all foreign exchange trading, with swap transactions accounting for

[14] Grabbe (1991). To be eligible as a value date, a day must be one on which money markets are open for business in the home countries of each currency involved in the transaction; when a day is ineligible, the value date is normally the next eligible business day. In North America, spot exchanges in US dollars against Canadian dollars or Mexican pesos are conventionally for next day value.

[15] In assembling time series data for empirical research on exchange rate behavior, it is useful to know that the value dates for one-month to twelve-month forward maturities are normally on the same day of the month as the spot value date. For example, if the spot value date is April 20, the three-month forward value date would normally be July 20. When this procedure leads to a date on which one of the relevant markets is closed, the value date is shifted forward to the next eligible day, unless it would carry the value date into the next month, in which case the value date is shifted backward to the next eligible day. See Grabbe (1991).

roughly 40 percent and outright forwards for 7 percent (table 2.1). The maturities of most forward contracts – including the forward legs of swap transactions – are quite short. In April 1992, nearly two-thirds of all forward contracts had maturities of seven days or less, about one-third had maturities of eight days to one year, and only 1.2 percent had maturities in excess of one year.

In parallel with the expansion of spot, swap, and outright forward transactions, trading in standardized exchange-traded foreign currency futures and options contracts, and in over-the-counter foreign exchange options, has been growing rapidly in recent years. As in markets for commodity futures, trading in foreign currency futures takes place through open auction on the floors of central exchange houses, with buyers and sellers placing orders through brokers or exchange members. Futures contracts have standard sizes, which vary among the different currencies traded, and are available for only a few value dates a year.

Although futures contracts provide an additional mechanism for buying and selling currencies, most participants in futures markets are motivated to bet on the direction in which exchange rates will move over the period preceding the value date, without ever making or taking delivery of foreign currencies. In most cases a futures contract is thus effectively canceled before the value date arrives through the practice of entering an equal and opposite futures contract for the same value date. Because currency futures prices move over time in close parallel with exchange rates, a trader who opens and subsequently cancels a futures contract can profit from correctly anticipating the direction of exchange rate movement.

Foreign currency options are contracts that give their owners the right, but not the obligation, to deliver or receive a specific amount of foreign currency at a specific "exercise" price. Options are classified according to whether they are rights to buy (call options) or sell (put options), and also according to whether they can be executed only on a prespecified date (European options) or at any time prior to a specific date (American options). Options can be written on spot exchange or on foreign currency futures, and in a variety of forms. Foreign currency options are traded in standardized forms on several exchange-based markets, and are also traded over-the-counter in the interbank market, where they can be customized in any manner agreed by the contracting parties. Over-the-counter options – which account for roughly 80 percent of combined trading in the two types of options – can thus be drawn up for any amount, maturity date, and exercise price.

Although the expansion of trading in foreign currency futures and options in recent years is a significant development in the continuing evolution of international financial markets, an understanding of these derivative contracts is not central to understanding the behavior of exchange rates. Accordingly, the subjects of foreign currency futures and options are not discussed further in this book.[16]

5 Exchange rate determination: the myopic perspective

Before launching a broad analysis of exchange rate determination, it is useful to consider the myopic perspective of how foreign exchange dealers determine the exchange rates that they quote to customers. The myopic perspective captures the movement of exchange rates from transaction to transaction.

Except when specified otherwise, this book focuses on the behavior of spot exchange rates. As noted earlier, the market for spot foreign exchange is a global, 24-hour, over-the-counter market in which most transactions are arranged from the offices of major commercial banks. Worldwide, 30 to 50 of the largest banks, along with a handful of the largest securities houses, serve as "marketmakers" in the major currencies,[17] standing ready throughout their business days to quote prices at which they are willing to buy or sell foreign exchange to other market participants. Unlike a foreign exchange broker, who matches buy and sell orders from different parties, a marketmaker is prepared to take either side of a foreign exchange transaction itself. A marketmaker deals in "two-way prices," simultaneously quoting the bid price at which it is willing to purchase a foreign currency and the offer or asked price at which it is willing to sell.[18]

In practice, most marketmakers quote exchange rates and conduct trades in terms of a "vehicle" currency. A customer seeking to transact with a New York bank to exchange Swiss francs for Dutch guilders will be quoted a "cross" exchange rate derived from the relevant bid or offer rates for exchanging each currency directly against the US dollar. Consistently, the exchange will be executed in effect as two separate transactions involving the US dollar. This practice saves time and other trading costs by reducing the amount of information that must be processed. When n currencies are being traded, the vehicle currency system requires information on $n-1$ exchange rates, whereas a system in which each currency is traded directly against every other currency requires information on $n(n-1)/2$ exchange rates. Trading in vehicle currencies also automatically prevents a marketmaker from creating profitable triangular arbitrage opportunities for

[16] See Walmsley (1992), Grabbe (1991), and Goldstein et al. (1993) for a more extensive introduction to these subjects.   [17] Goldstein et al. (1993, p. 5).

[18] The number of marketmakers has declined in recent years, partly reflecting mergers of some large banks, but also reflecting reduced profitability as the improvement and spread of communications technology has eroded the information advantage enjoyed by marketmakers.

customers to exploit. When there is no direct exchange rate between the Swiss franc and the Dutch guilder, and only the cross-rate derived from the exchange rates of the two currencies against the US dollar, there is no possibility for customers to profit by arbitraging discrepancies between the direct exchange rate and the derived cross-rate.

Most foreign exchange trading today involves the US dollar. In April 1992, the US dollar figured on one side of over 80 percent of total global foreign exchange turnover (table 2.1). After the US dollar, the most widely traded currencies were the German mark and the Japanese yen, which were involved, respectively, in 40 percent and 23 percent of all foreign exchange transactions, followed by the British pound and the Swiss franc, which were involved in 14 percent and 9 percent, respectively.

Marketmakers do not charge fees for ordinary foreign exchange transactions. Rather, they seek to cover the costs of their operations by setting their asked prices at a spread above their bid prices. In a hypothetical sequence of offsetting purchases and sales of foreign currency at constant bid and asked prices, marketmakers would cover their costs by selling foreign currency for more than they paid for it.

In practice, of course, bid and asked prices do not stay constant. However, under normal market conditions, competition among marketmaking banks often results in bid–asked spreads that are uniform among most marketmakers and relatively stable over time. Thus, when asked how it quotes spot Deutsche marks, a marketmaker in New York might answer 1.6340–50, meaning its bid price for dollars (offer price for marks) is 1.6340 marks per dollar, while its offer price for dollars is 1.6350. At the same point in time, another marketmaker might provide a slightly higher or lower two-way price, but one that would normally involve the same spread of 0.001 marks per dollar. Each marketmaker generally changes its price continuously throughout the day, but without often changing the spread. Spreads tend to widen at the times of day when trading volumes are relatively low, and also during periods of relatively high uncertainty about future exchange rate movements. Similarly, spreads tend to be larger (as percentages of exchange rates) in markets where trading volumes are smaller and uncertainties higher.

After announcing its two-way price, a marketmaker may be "hit" on either the bid side or the offer side. In practice, a marketmaker that continued to announce the same price would be unlikely to receive a sequence of offsetting hits, since the prices of other marketmakers would typically be moving in one direction or the other. A marketmaker that failed to follow a general upward movement in the mark/dollar rate would be offering to sell dollars relatively cheaply and would likely find itself building up a relatively large position in marks. Similarly, a marketmaker that failed to lower its mark/dollar rate with other marketmakers would be offering a relatively attractive bid price for dollars and would likely acquire a relatively large position in dollars. Neither outcome is desirable. No marketmaker wants to find itself holding a currency position that has depreciated relative to its acquisition cost. In practice, foreign exchange traders are often directed to adjust their net long or short positions in foreign currencies during the trading day to comply with risk management procedures specified by their supervisors. Such procedures are intended to limit the exposure of bank capital to the risk of valuation losses associated with exchange rate changes.

Although marketmakers are cautious in exposing their capital to risks, their ultimate objective in trading foreign exchange is to earn profits by anticipating the direction in which interbank exchange rate quotes are headed. Traders are continuously re-evaluating their views on where the market is headed, partly based on the flow of trading and the minute-to-minute dynamics of exchange rate changes, and partly based on the flow of news and rumors about economic statistics, policy announcements, and various other events.

From this perspective, the hour-to-hour and day-to-day behavior of exchange rates is largely determined by the instincts of interbank traders. Exchange rate quotations reflect their expectations, based on both the flow of trading and the flow of news and rumors. Whatever traders respond to in making decisions – whether signals obtained from "technical analysis" of recent exchange rate movements, or news about particular economic fundamentals – is likely to be reflected in the behavior of exchange rates over short intervals of time.[19]

---

[19] Interviews of market participants conducted by national authorities during 1992 suggested that technical analysis and economic fundamentals play complementary roles in shaping decisions that affect exchange rates; see Group of Ten Deputies (1993, annex I, paragraph 20). Technical analysis to infer future price movements from past price developments – whether based on charts or on more formal statistical techniques – played a prominent role in determining the timing of transactions and in the design of very short-term trading strategies. At the same time, fundamentals were said to be much more important than technical analysis in long-term strategic position taking. See also Taylor and Allen (1992).

3   Exchange rate arrangements and international monetary regimes

Every country that has its own currency must decide what type of exchange rate arrangement to maintain. In academic discussions, the decision is often posed as a choice between a fixed or a flexible exchange rate. In reality, however, there are different varieties of fixed and flexible arrangements, providing a range of alternatives.

The different alternatives have different implications for the extent to which national authorities participate in foreign exchange markets. When the authorities choose to fix the exchange rate of their country's currency against another currency, or against a composite of other currencies, they make a commitment to intervene in the markets themselves, transacting to buy or sell their currency whenever necessary to keep the exchange rate from changing. By contrast, when the authorities abstain completely from intervening in exchange markets, they are choosing to let their exchange rate float freely. In practice, by controlling the extent to which, and the conditions under which, they intervene in exchange markets, national authorities may attempt to manage their exchange rate with essentially any degree of flexibility they desire. Normally, the type of exchange rate arrangement that a country chooses has a major influence on the way its exchange rate actually behaves.

Why then do exchange rates often "misbehave"? Why is it that national authorities often complain about the instability of exchange rates when it appears to be within their power to keep exchange rates stable? The abstract answer is that the actions required to keep exchange rates stable can sometimes involve very high costs. A deeper understanding is provided in part III of this book, which focuses on exchange rate policies. Before that, part II describes what economists have learned about the behavior of exchange rates. And as relevant background for both part II and part III, this chapter presents a description of alternative exchange rate arrangements, a short history of the international monetary regimes that have transpired over the past century, and some statistical comparisons of the behavior of exchange rates and macroeconomic performance indicators under different exchange rate arrangements and international monetary regimes.

1   Alternative exchange rate arrangements

In practice, countries rarely seek to keep their exchange rates rigidly fixed. To do so would be almost an impossible task in a country where residents had the freedom to exchange currencies with each other. At any announced exchange rate parity, rarely would an hour pass during which the amounts of a currency offered for sale at the announced parity exactly matched the amounts demanded. In situations of excess supply, some sellers would normally be willing to lower their offer prices, just as buyers would normally be willing to raise their bid prices in periods of excess demand. Thus, to keep the exchange rate rigidly fixed, the national authorities would have to participate in the foreign exchange market continuously to buy as much of their currency as market participants might otherwise offer to sell at rates below the announced parity, and to sell as much of their currency as market participants might otherwise seek to buy at rates above the parity.

Instead, countries that adopt fixed exchange rate arrangements generally provide for a limited degree of flexibility by defining fluctuation ranges or bands around the central parities. Exchange rates are allowed to fluctuate within the bands in response to the buy and sell orders of market participants. But to prevent exchange rates from trespassing the limits of the bands, national authorities are committed to intervene when necessary through purchases of whatever amounts of their currencies market participants could not otherwise sell at rates above the lower limits, or through sales of whatever amounts of their currencies market participants could not otherwise purchase at rates below the upper limits.

By the same token, countries rarely allow their exchange rates to float freely. In most countries with floating currencies, the national authorities follow exchange market developments closely throughout every trading day, sometimes intervening to purchase or sell currencies on their own account for the purpose of limiting the extent to which the excess demands or supplies of market participants cause exchange rates to fluctuate.

Each year, the International Monetary Fund publishes an annual report describing the exchange arrangements and exchange restrictions of its member countries.[1] The reports reveal that different varieties of fixed and flexible exchange arrangements are attractive to different countries. Thus, the 1994 report, which covered 180 countries, listed 77 cases of fixed exchange rates, 12 cases of exchange arrangements allowing "limited flexibility," and 91 cases of "more flexible arrangements."[2] In the fixed

---

[1] See International Monetary Fund (1994). A table classifying countries by their exchange rate arrangements is also provided in the monthly editions of the IMF's *International Financial Statistics*.

[2] These data refer, in most cases, to the exchange arrangements prevailing as of December 31, 1993. The countries include the 178 member countries of the Fund as of end-1993, plus Hong Kong and Aruba and the Netherlands Antilles.

group, 24 countries pegged their currencies to the US dollar; 14 to the French franc; 9 to other individual currencies; and 30 to a composite of currencies, of which 3 were pegged to the SDR.[3] The 12 cases of limited flexibility included the 8 countries participating at end-year 1993 in the Exchange Rate Mechanism (ERM) of the European Monetary System (EMS), along with 4 Middle Eastern countries whose currencies were pegged to the SDR, but with scope to fluctuate within wide margins extending $7\frac{1}{4}$ percent on each side of their central parities. The 91 cases of more flexible arrangements included 34 countries that maintained official central parities but adjusted them on a regular basis (in many cases daily); such arrangements are often called "crawling pegs" or "gliding parities." The other 57 countries with more flexible arrangements maintained independently floating currencies with no official parities.

Figure 3.1 contrasts the degrees to which selected exchange rates have fluctuated since March 1979, when the ERM went into operation. The figure shows month-to-month percentage changes for three different cases: the exchange rate between the currencies of France and Germany, two participants in the pegged arrangements of the ERM; that between Austria and Germany, which has not been governed by any formal obligations, but which the Austrian authorities have sought to keep stable; and that between Germany and the United States, which has been left to float. Notably, the exchange rates between the two pairs of European currencies fluctuated much less widely than the mark/dollar rate, consistent with the different degrees of formal or informal policy commitments to maintain stable exchange rates.

Additional evidence that the degree of exchange rate variability reflects the nature of policy commitments to maintain stable exchange rates is provided by the dramatic increase in the month-to-month variability of key-currency exchange rates during the early 1970s (recall figure 1.1, p. 2). That period marked the breakdown of the "Bretton Woods system" of international monetary arrangements, which had been established when the Articles of Agreement of the International Monetary Fund were adopted in 1944. Germany and Japan were not original members of the IMF, but joined in 1952. Under the Bretton Woods system, the yen and the mark were each pegged to the US dollar, with fluctuation margins of 1 percent on each side of the central parities. Although the central parity of the mark was revalued upward by 5 percent in March 1961, and by another 9.3 percent in September–October 1969, exchange rate variability was generally limited until 1971, when exchange market pressures led Germany

---

[3] The SDR, an abbreviation for "special drawing right," is a composite of five currencies (US dollar, Japanese yen, German mark, UK pound, and French franc) created by the International Monetary Fund.

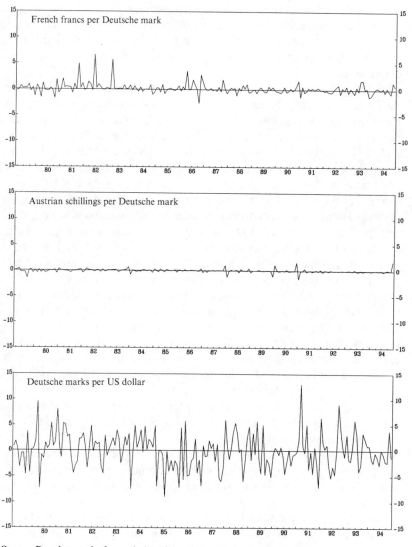

Source: Based on end-of-month data from International Monetary Fund, *International Financial Statistics.*

Figure 3.1 Short-term variability of selected exchange rates, March 1979–December 1994 (percentage change from previous month)

and Japan to float their currencies, beginning in May and August, respectively. By early 1973, the major countries had decided not to reestablish fixed parities between the mark, the yen, and the dollar, and an era of much greater short-term variability of exchange rates had commenced.

Notably, the operation of fixed exchange rate arrangements by individual countries, and of international systems of exchange rate pegs, has normally been associated with occasional adjustments of exchange rate parities. For example, the central ERM parity between the French franc and the Deutsche mark was changed six times between March 1979, when the ERM began to operate, and the end of 1994; and indeed, the cumulative net change in the franc/mark parity during that period exceeded the net changes in the schilling/mark and mark/dollar exchange rates (figure 3.2), neither of which was formally pegged. Generally, adjustments of exchange rate pegs are associated with economic or political developments that would move a floating exchange rate in the same direction. The type of exchange arrangement thus influences the behavior of the exchange rate, but more fundamental influences are also at work.

Subsequent chapters will discuss these fundamental influences, with particular emphasis on developments in inflation rates, interest rates, and international payments imbalances. Other things being equal, a country that experiences more rapid inflation than its trading partners will tend to experience downward pressure on the foreign exchange value of its currency as inflation erodes the price-competitiveness of the goods and services it produces. Similarly, a country that lowers its interest rates relative to those of other countries will tend to experience a decline in the demand for its currency, *ceteris paribus*, leading to a depreciation of its exchange rate. And a country that experiences an adverse shift in its balance of international payments for goods and services (perhaps because export revenues are affected by a bad harvest or a decline in export prices) will also tend to encounter downward pressure on the foreign exchange value of its currency.

Subsequent chapters will stress, in addition, that the correlations between exchange rates and other economic variables can depend to a considerable extent on the manner in which national policy authorities act, or are expected to act, in responding to and attempting to guide economic developments. Similarly, the behavior of exchange rates reflects the prevailing international monetary system, narrowly defined as the system of rules and institutions that countries have adopted for purposes of jointly monitoring and managing the exchange rates between their currencies. The priorities or perceived priorities of national economic policymakers, and the degree of consistency between the policy priorities of different coun-

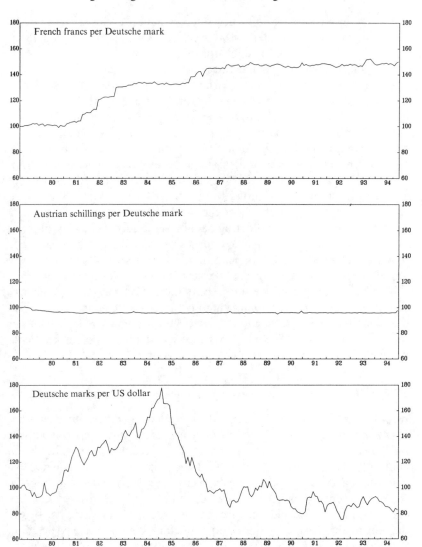

Source: Based on end-of-month data from International Monetary Fund, *International Financial Statistics.*

Figure 3.2 Selected exchange rates, March 1979–December 1994
(March 1979 = 100)

tries, can have a major influence on economic developments and the behavior of exchange rates. Moreover, as policy priorities and international monetary rules and institutions evolve over time, so do the relationships between exchange rates and other economic variables.

The economic history summarized in the remainder of this chapter provides perspectives on various factors influencing the behavior of exchange rates, and on the importance of the policy environment; readers with little interest in these historical perspectives can move on to chapter 4. In reviewing the relevant history, it is convenient to focus sequentially on the different international monetary regimes that have evolved over time, starting with a section on the international gold standard regime that prevailed for a third of a century leading up to World War I. Subsequent sections cover the interwar experience with four short-lived regimes – a system of relatively free floating, a gold-exchange standard of fixed exchange rates, an uncoordinated hybrid system, and a system of managed floating – along with the experience under the Bretton Woods system of adjustable pegs during the quarter century following World War II. Little is said in this chapter about the more recent international monetary regimes – the system of generalized floating among the major nonEuropean currencies since the early 1970s, and the European Monetary System that has prevailed since 1979. These regimes receive attention later in the book, particularly in chapters 11 and 12.

2   The international gold standard regime, 1880–1914

A country establishes a gold standard when it fixes an official price or "mint parity" for gold in terms of its currency unit and stands ready to convert freely between domestic money and gold at the official par value. From about 1880 until the eve of World War I, most major countries adhered to a gold standard.[4] England had established a gold standard during the eighteenth century, which was abandoned in 1797 but revived in 1819. Germany moved to a gold standard in the early 1870s and was joined before the end of the decade by the Latin Monetary Union (France, Belgium, Switzerland, and Italy), Holland, the Scandinavian countries, and the United States. Austria–Hungary adopted a gold standard in 1892, followed by Russia and Japan in 1897.

In addition to the interconvertibility between domestic money and gold at a fixed official price, in most major countries the gold standard regimes that prevailed during the late nineteenth and early twentieth centuries had two basic features: private citizens were free to import and export gold; and

---

[4] Kindleberger (1984), Yeager (1976).

the stocks of national banknotes and coinage in circulation were backed with gold reserves.[5] The freedom of private citizens to buy or sell gold and ship it between countries had the effect of establishing a system of fixed exchange rates between national currencies. At the same time, the "rules" linking the quantity of domestic money in circulation to a country's gold stock may have helped to sustain the fixed official prices of gold.[6]

Notably, the international gold standard regime provided scope for market exchange rates between currencies to fluctuate within limited ranges around the central rates implied by the official gold parities. The widths of these ranges reflected the margins that had to be available on exchange transactions to make it worthwhile for arbitragers to incur the costs of transporting and insuring gold. Thus, for example, the dollar/pound exchange rate was not constrained from fluctuating in the market to levels somewhat above or below the central rate implied by the official gold parities for the two currencies. But it tended to remain within the "gold points": it generally did not fall further than the lower gold point at which private citizens, instead of selling pounds to purchase dollars in the exchange market, could exploit the opportunity to obtain more dollars by purchasing gold at the official price in Britain, incurring the costs of shipping it to the United States, and selling it there at the official dollar price; and similarly, the dollar/pound exchange rate generally did not rise above the upper gold point. Remarkably, the exchange rates of the gold standard countries stayed within their relatively narrow fluctuation ranges

without the support of exchange restrictions, import quotas, or related controls, which were virtually unknown even for currencies on paper or silver standards. Only a trifling number of countries were forced off the gold standard, once adopted, and devaluations of gold currencies were highly exceptional.[7]

The manner in which the gold standard first evolved in Britain during the eighteenth century "was largely inadvertent, rather than the outcome of design."[8] At the end of the seventeenth century, silver coins were disappearing from circulation. An attempt was made to remedy the problem through the Great Recoinage of 1696, during which old silver coins were turned in and reminted into heavier ones. When that proved unsuccessful in arresting the outflow of silver from Britain, a commission was established to study the situation. The commission determined that the mint price of gold relative to that of silver was higher in England than abroad. Consequently, it recommended a reduction in the price of gold. The recommendation was

---

[5] Eichengreen (1985, pp. 3–4).
[6] The extent to which countries actually adhered to the "rules" is a matter of debate. See
    Yeager (1976, pp. 332–4) and references cited therein.   [7] Bloomfield (1959, p. 9).
[8] Kindleberger (1985, p. 57).

carried out in 1717 by Sir Isaac Newton, Master of the Mint. In the event, however, gold kept flowing into Britain, silver supplies to the mint remained meager, and the shortage of silver coins became more serious. Although the shortage of silver can be regarded to have established an effective gold standard from 1717, Britain did not officially demonetize silver until 1774.[9]

In the United States, the gold standard also arose inadvertently from the demise of a bimetallic system. The Coinage Act of 1792 defined the dollar as the basic monetary unit, established a bimetallic standard under which both gold and silver were legal tender, and fixed the mint prices of the two metals to imply an official exchange rate of 15 ounces of silver per ounce of gold.[10] Soon thereafter, the market exchange rate in the United States rose toward the rates prevailing on world markets, which were close to the official French ratio of $15\frac{1}{4}:1$. This curtailed deliveries of gold to the US mint, since gold could be sold elsewhere at more attractive terms. The situation was reversed, however, after the official US ratio was raised to 16:1 in 1834. Gold coinage subsequently increased and coinage of silver waned. In 1873, after longstanding disuse of silver, the legal authority for coinage of silver at the mint was discontinued. Thus, when the United States returned to a metallic standard in 1879, nearly two decades after convertibility had been suspended during the Civil War, the only practical option was to establish a monometallic gold standard.[11]

Unlike the initial moves to gold standards in Britain and the United States, the restoration of the British gold standard in 1821 was motivated by sophisticated economic analysis. The suspension of convertibility a quarter century earlier, viewed as a "temporary" action at the time, had come after rumors of an impending French invasion had provoked a bank run. The rush to withdraw deposits had drained Bank of England notes from the reserves of the banking system. In turn, conversions of bank notes had put pressure on the country's gold reserves until, in 1797, the Bank Restriction Act officially forbade the Bank of England from redeeming its notes in gold.

The suspension of convertibility was followed by a series of debates about monetary theory and policy – conventionally referred to as the "Bullionist Controversy."[12] Reflecting these debates, the *Bullion Report*, issued in 1810 by a select committee of Parliament, emphasized that the issuance of bank notes, unless constrained to a rate that met the requirements of convertibility, could become a recipe both for inflation and for the depreciation of sterling against foreign currencies. The experience since

---

[9] Kindleberger (1984, p. 59).   [10] Bordo (1992a, p. 209).
[11] Jastram (1977, p. 139).
[12] See Laidler (1992) for a discussion of the Bullionist Controversy and the return to convertibility.

1800 seemed to confirm this analysis, and the Report, whose authors worried about the Bank's capacity to conduct policy competently in the absence of "rules" linking the supply of money to the stock of offical gold holdings, recommended that convertibility be restored within two years at the 1797 parity. At the time, however, Britain was still in the midst of a major war with France, and sterling was significantly depreciated relative to that parity. A return to convertibility might have constrained the government's ability to finance the war. Moreover, a return to the old parity would have resulted in prices of British goods that were substantially higher than the prices of similar foreign goods in both domestic and foreign markets; this, in turn, would have threatened substantial declines in domestic output and employment and required a significant fall in Britain's domestic price and wage levels to restore her international competitiveness. Fortunately, Parliament had the wisdom to reject the Report's proposal. As it turned out, British price levels fell significantly after the end of the war, and in 1819, with only a minor amount of domestic price deflation still needed to make the 1797 parity effective, a law was passed requiring the Bank of England to make its notes convertible again by May 1821.

These historical perspectives point to some of the possible advantages and disadvantages of a gold standard system. The main attraction of an international gold standard regime – when private citizens are free to buy and sell gold, and when supplies of domestic money are linked by "rules" to the stocks of national gold holdings – is its potential to promote an environment of stable exchange rates and stable domestic price levels. A major limitation is the possibility that a country will adopt an official gold parity at which the goods and services it produces cannot compete successfully with similar products from other countries, in which case the dislocations experienced by domestic firms and workers are likely to be severe. Indeed, this lesson was driven home by the experience between the two world wars, as discussed in the next section.

The fact that the prewar international gold standard survived as long as it did calls for an explanation. Obviously, a gold standard system can become unsustainable if national gold reserves become depleted. Similarly, systems of fixed exchange rates with formal intervention margins can lose their sustainability if the policy authorities do not remain willing and able to buy or sell currencies when necessary, or to take other actions that are effective in keeping exchange rates within the prespecified currency bands. Sustainability thus requires a mechanism that operates effectively to prevent countries from depleting their holdings of gold or foreign exchange reserves, or from losing their ability to acquire gold or foreign currencies through borrowing.

Under an international gold standard regime, an outflow of gold from any participating country, when it arises, may be curtailed either through an automatic adjustment mechanism or through discretionary policy adjustment, such as a discretionary increase in domestic interest rates that encourages market participants to hold assets other than gold. Regardless of the nature of the adjustment process, however, sustainability depends critically on whether market participants have confidence that the adjustment process will be effective. Without a high degree of confidence that the adjustment process will successfully curtail the drainage of gold, market participants would have incentives to launch a speculative attack, selling the depreciating currency for gold, thereby accelerating the depletion of official gold reserves, and thus undermining the sustainability of the gold standard.

During the eighteenth century, economists had argued that outflows of gold would be curtailed automatically by a so-called "price–specie–flow mechanism."[13] In its streamlined form, the conceptual model of this mechanism had three components. First, a country's price level was viewed as positively related to the domestic money supply. Second, the domestic money supply was positively related to the country's official stock of gold, with sales and purchases of gold by the monetary authorities providing the primary mechanism for contracting and expanding the supplies of currency and bank reserves. Third, a country's trade balance was regarded as inversely related to its price level (relative to foreign price levels). An outflow of gold would thus reduce the domestic money supply and cause the domestic price level to fall, which would lead to an improvement in the trade balance and thereby counteract the gold outflow. Similarly, a rise in the domestic price level (relative to foreign price levels) would lead to a deterioration in the trade balance, which would induce an outflow of gold, thereby reducing the domestic money supply and acting automatically to reverse the initial rise in the price level.

By the late nineteenth century, the concept of the price–specie–flow mechanism had been supplemented by the recognition that short-term capital flows could also play a part in the adjustment mechanism, reinforcing the effects of trade balance adjustment. In particular, insofar as a contraction of official gold holdings and the domestic money supply would normally give rise to an increase in short-term interest rates, it would also normally attract an inflow of funds from abroad, offsetting the initial outflow of gold.

In practice, the process of adjusting to economic disturbances during the gold standard era was much less automatic than economic theory

---

[13] See Bordo (1992b), who notes that the price–specie–flow mechanism, while given most prominence by Hume (1752), was first analyzed by Cantillon (1755).

suggested.[14] Moreover, the economic environment during the decades prior to World War I was by no means tranquil. Disturbances to financial markets were commonplace, and deficits in the balance of trade periodically posed a potential threat to the national gold stocks of Britain, the United States, and other countries. With Britain at the center of the system and London the financial capital of the world, the Bank of England took on a prominent role in responding to pressures on the international monetary regime. But the Bank of England and other central banks relied heavily on discretionary responses to economic developments:

at no time . . . did central banks mechanically obey rules of the game, automatically restricting credit in response to gold outflows and loosening it in response to inflows.[15]

For the Bank of England, the late nineteenth century provided a valuable experience in learning to influence domestic monetary conditions through the discretionary use of the instruments over which it had direct control. Beginning in the early 1870s, it began to use its discount rate – the "Bank Rate" – in new ways. In late 1871, for the first time, it stopped simply adjusting the Bank Rate to follow the market interest rates established by discount companies.[16] In 1874, it raised the Bank Rate to resist a potential outflow of gold at a time when following the market would have required a reduction in the Bank Rate. Gradually, the Bank developed devices for achieving more effective control over money market conditions through short-term lending and borrowing operations. During the period 1890–1914,

the market and the Bank taught one another the theory of centralized money-market control by the use of these devices and the Bank gained, by convention, a fair degree of control over the market when the foreign balance required it.[17]

The Bank of England, in the light of its competence in managing money market conditions, deserves considerable credit for defusing the pressures that periodically emerged on the exchange rate system. But as economic historians have emphasized, the longevity of the international gold standard reflected much more than the market analysis and operational capabilities of the monetary authorities in England and other countries.

In a fundamental sense, the relatively long life of the system of fixed exchange rates under the gold standard regime reflected the credibility of the authorities' commitments to keep the system in place.[18] The credibility of such commitments in part reflected the "reputations" that core countries

[14] Bloomfield (1959), Eichengreen (1992).   [15] Eichengreen (1992, p. 65).
[16] Scammell (1965).   [17] Scammell (1965, pp. 111–12).
[18] Eichengreen (1992, chapter 2).

had gained for never changing their gold parities following temporary suspensions of convertibility during major wars.[19] In addition, credibility reflected both the absence of serious domestic political opposition to the gold standard and the presence of substantial international cooperation in acting to support individual countries during times of crisis.

Political opposition to the gold standard was particularly weak in the core European countries – Britain, France, and Germany.[20] Unemployed workers were in no position to rebel against the effects of the credit stringency that the authorities sometimes imposed in response to undesired gold flows. And producers that competed with imports – in particular, French and German farmers – were protected from strong competition by the presence of tariff barriers.

International cooperation played an important role by signaling to market participants that individual countries – especially those at the core of the system – were not limited by their own reserve holdings in resisting attacks on their gold parities.[21] The Bank of England stood ready to relinquish gold when it was needed in the United States; the Bank of France, the Reichsbank, and the Russian Government at times came to the aid of the Bank of England; and on another occasion, Germany received assistance from England and France.[22] By helping each other resist pressures on their gold parities, the major countries strengthened the credibility of their commitments to defend the international gold standard regime. As a result, market participants gained confidence that the authorities were indeed committed and able to defend the core of the system. The effects of this confidence influenced the behavior of market participants in ways that tended to keep short-term private capital flowing in stabilizing directions, thereby mitigating the pressures on the gold standard system.

3   The wartime and interwar regimes

During and between the two world wars, the international monetary system evolved through a sequence of short-lived arrangements as stability proved elusive.[23] Between 1921 and 1925, exchange rates among the major currencies were left to float freely, with virtually no central bank intervention. From 1925 to 1931, exchange rates were predominantly fixed through the restoration of gold standards in a number of countries and the introduction

---

[19] Bordo (1993a). This applied to the suspensions of convertibility by England during the Napoleonic Wars, by the United States during the Civil War, and by France during the Franco–Prussian War.   [20] Eichengreen (1992, p. 30).

[21] Eichengreen (1992, p. 31).

[22] The fact that the core countries generally abided by balanced budget objectives may have had an important influence on the willingness of other countries to come to their assistance in times of need; see Eichengreen (1995a).   [23] Eichengreen (1989).

of gold-exchange standards elsewhere. After 1931, when countries began to abandon gold, the system evolved into an uncoordinated hybrid regime; and after 1936, with the Tripartite Monetary Agreement between Britain, France, and the United States, it evolved into a regime in which the management of exchange rates became coordinated.

Arrangements during World War I

The breakdown of the international gold standard did not come abruptly, but by late July 1914 the strains on the system had greatly intensified. The impending war had heightened the perceived riskiness of holding various types of financial claims, which brought frantic attempts to adjust financial portfolios toward relatively safe assets. Investors hastened to sell securities, causing stock exchanges to close in the United States, England, and other European countries. With transatlantic gold shipments at risk from hostile cruisers on the seas, some Europeans who sought to convert the proceeds from sales of US securities in New York had to pay as much as 7 dollars in exchange for 1 pound – well above the parity of $4.87 per pound implied by official gold prices. The disparity between market exchange rates and the official rate was reduced, however, after the Bank of England agreed on August 12 to accept gold deliveries in Canada.[24] Although the international gold standard did not completely dissolve, the era had effectively ended. Gradually over the next few years, countries imposed official or *de facto* restrictions on both the convertibility of paper money into gold and the free international movement of gold.

The introduction of convertibility restrictions helped to limit exchange rate fluctuations. At the end of 1915, the pound had depreciated by about 3 percent from its prewar dollar parity, and the French franc by a little more than 10 percent.[25] In January 1916, the pound/dollar rate was pegged at $4.76; and from April 1916, with some assistance from the US Treasury, the exchange rate between the pound and the French franc was also stabilized through official support operations.[26] The support operations that maintained the wartime parities were terminated in early 1919.

Free floating

Although the United States returned to a full gold standard in June 1919, the dollar was the only currency for which gold convertibility was restored. Thus, no effective constraints were imposed on the exchange rates between

---

[24] Yeager (1976, p. 310), Kindleberger (1984, pp. 291–2).
[25] Board of Governors of the Federal Reserve System (1943, pp. 670 and 681).
[26] Yeager (1976, p. 311).

currencies. The years that ensued were characterized by the virtual absence of official intervention – a relatively free floating exchange rate regime – until Britain returned to the gold standard in 1925.[27]

The period of free floating brought large movements in exchange rates between the key currencies. By late 1920 the pound had fallen to a level more than 25 percent below its wartime peg against the dollar – a trough from which it had recovered considerably by mid-1922, and fully when the British gold standard was restored in April 1925. Meanwhile, the French franc by the end of 1920 had plunged to a level nearly 70 percent below its early 1919 exchange rate against the dollar – a trough from which it recovered only partially, and for no longer than a few years.

In sharp contrast with the period of the prewar gold standard, the postwar period began with large divergences in the macroeconomic conditions of the key-currency countries and substantial differences in their economic policy priorities. This, and the hostile feelings created by the war, made international policy cooperation difficult. In general, countries sought to return to the gold standard eventually, but only the United States was prepared to do so immediately. Influential British economists argued that the restoration of the gold standard was a necessary condition for financial stability, but they also stressed that balanced government budgets had to come first, along with actions to insulate central banks from pressures to provide credit to government agencies.[28]

The task of establishing macroeconomic stability proved difficult. Currency supplies and price levels had risen during the war years by comparable amounts in the United States and Britain, by about twice as much in France, and by significantly more in Germany.[29] Following the signing of the Armistice Convention in November 1918, the release of pent up demands generated booming economic conditions, both in Western Europe and in the United States. Employment expanded rapidly. Prices and wages accelerated. Toward the end of 1919 and into the following year, central banks reacted by raising their discount rates: in Britain, from an October rate of 5 percent to 6 percent in November and 7 percent in April; in the United States, from 4 percent in October to 4.75 percent in November, 6 percent in January, and 7 percent in May; and in France, from 5 percent in October to 6 percent in April.[30] Wholesale prices peaked during the spring of 1920 and then fell sharply over the next year in Britain, France, and the United States. Economic activity also fell sharply, especially in Britain. Subsequently, prices stabilized in Britain and the United States, while inflation re-ignited in France.

---

[27] Eichengreen (1989, pp. 15–16).   [28] Eichengreen (1989, p. 127).
[29] Yeager (1976, p. 312).   [30] Tsiang (1959, p. 253).

The German experience was far worse. By end-1921, wholesale prices were 35 times their prewar level; a year later, nearly 1500 times.[31] One of the classic hyperinflations of history was underway, along with similar experiences in Austria, Hungary, Poland, and Russia.

The inflation that sprang up in Central and Eastern Europe was seeded in the physical devastation and financial strains that resulted from the war. The countries of continental Europe had seen their productive capacities sharply reduced and possessed limited financial resources. Moreover, in the light of the credit risks, there was limited scope to borrow abroad and large debts to be paid. In addition to debts incurred during the war, the terms of surrender included an agreement that the defeated powers were to pay reparations. The amounts were left to be determined by a reparations commission, which announced its decisions in April 1921. Initially, the United States insisted on prompt repayment of the war loans it had made to its European allies, and also adopted a hard-line position on reparation settlements by Germany. Not surprisingly, the European countries turned to deficit spending to meet their excess demands for foodstuffs and raw materials, and to finance the capital goods imports needed for reconstruction.

Although the prevailing macroeconomic conditions precluded an early return to an international gold standard, countries considered steps to promote international monetary stability and economic recovery in Europe. A series of international monetary and financial conferences took place in the early 1920s, motivated in part by common interest in rebuilding the international economy. Beyond that common interest, however, the three leading countries had very different economic policy objectives.[32] At the time of the Genoa Conference of 1922, the Americans and the British agreed that recovery required a revitalization of foreign trade, whereas the French were strongly opposed to initiatives for easing protectionist barriers against imports. The British and French favored reducing reparations through renegotiations facilitated by concessions from the United States on the war debts of its allies, but the Americans were strongly resistant to making such concessions.

Although conflicting national interests precluded significant cooperative actions to help rebuild the economies of the war-ravaged countries, a set of resolutions emerged with the aim of easing the transition back to gold.[33] The Genoa resolutions encouraged countries that had experienced sustained inflation to avoid the output costs associated with restoring prewar price levels by returning to gold at depreciated parities. They also urged

---

[31] Yeager (1976, p. 313).
[32] Eichengreen (1989, pp. 125–7).   [33] Eichengreen (1989, pp. 128–9).

governments to reduce the need for monetary gold by holding official reserves in the form of foreign currency balances rather than gold.[34]

A gold-exchange standard

The British announced their return to the gold standard at the end of April 1925.[35] During the previous year, after difficult negotiations, a package of policy measures known as the Dawes Plan had been agreed to by the major countries.[36] The measures included an easing of German reparation payments along with the issuance of a new German currency, the Reichsmark, which was pegged to gold. In addition, a successful international effort was launched to raise private-sector funds for the purpose of lending Germany the money to pay reparations.

In October 1924, a new British government came to power, with Winston Churchill as Chancellor of the Exchequer. The pound had strengthened almost to the level of its prewar parity, and the law that had been protecting the gold reserves of the Bank of England was due to expire at the end of 1925. Churchill received conflicting opinions from the various experts he consulted on the wisdom of returning to gold. Ultimately, he followed the advice of experts within the Treasury and the Bank of England, also giving weight to the notion that returning to gold would retain for London "the central position in the financial systems of the world."[37] Another consideration that influenced the decision was the awareness that a number of other European countries were planning to restore their gold standards; Sweden had already returned to gold in March 1924.[38]

By the end of 1925, nearly three dozen currencies, in addition to the US dollar, were either formally pegged once again or had been stabilized *de facto* for a full year.[39] For many of the countries, the adoption of new statutes, encouraged by the Genoa resolutions, permitted central banks to hold foreign exchange instead of gold in their legal reserves, thereby establishing a "gold-exchange standard."[40] Notably, the official parities at which countries stabilized their currencies reflected national decisions and did not adequately reflect the different degrees of inflation that had occurred in the different countries; the ramifications would be remembered in reforming the international monetary system after World War II.[41] Some

---

[34] Another mechanism for economizing on gold was the substitution of bank notes and deposits for gold coins in circulation.   [35] Kindleberger (1984, pp. 329–45).

[36] Kindleberger (1984, pp. 302–4).

[37] From Churchill's Budget Speech of April 28, 1925, as cited in Kindleberger (1984, p. 341).

[38] Clarke (1967, pp. 80–1).   [39] Brown (1940, Vol. I, pp. 393–4).

[40] Nurkse (1944, pp. 28–30), who emphasized that the gold exchange system had been practiced in many cases before 1914 and was by no means invented in Genoa.

[41] Yeager (1976, p. 330).

countries had difficulty competing with foreign producers at the new exchange rates and, in the light of pressures on their gold reserves, had to keep their monetary policies tighter than would have been appropriate for their domestic economies alone. Other countries experienced large capital inflows under the new exchange rates and built up large official holdings of international reserves.

The Bank of England confronted a number of challenges in preparing for the return to gold and in conducting monetary policy subsequently.[42] During the year preceding the restoration of the gold standard, the British authorities made efforts to muster US support for the stabilization of sterling, reflecting concerns that existing British gold reserves might prove inadequate. Lines of credit from the Federal Reserve, and from a private syndicate headed by J.P. Morgan & Co., were negotiated with little difficulty. In the months immediately following the return to gold, however, the Bank of England maintained a tight monetary policy and a considerable volume of bullion began to flow into its reserves, obviating the need to draw on the credit lines.

The stance of British monetary policy during the next several years partly reflected a "competitive struggle for gold" among central banks,[43] which was associated with heavy flows of capital into Germany and France, particularly during the period 1926–28. Capital flows into Germany, induced to a large extent by the rapid economic recovery, created concerns at the Reichsbank about the threat to monetary control. Until 1926, the Reichsbank had acquiesced in accumulating the sterling balances brought by the capital inflow, but it then began to convert these balances into gold.

Similar developments were occurring in France. Successful fiscal stabilization measures taken in July 1926 by the newly formed Poincaré government had induced a huge influx of capital through mid-year 1927. The French authorities, unable to agree upon the exchange rate at which the franc should be stabilized, let their currency appreciate moderately and then pegged it *de facto* in December 1926, at about the same level at which it would subsequently be stabilized *de jure* in June 1928. In the first half of 1927, following the *de facto* stabilization, the Bank of France, which had accumulated large reserve holdings of sterling, began to convert these balances into both dollars and gold, while also converting dollar balances into gold. One of its aims was to induce an increase in British interest rates, which it hoped would discourage the capital flows into France.

With Britain in a vulnerable position, diplomacy came to the fore.[44] The

[42] Clarke (1967, pp. 81–105).
[43] Clarke (1967, pp. 108–23). The phrase comes from Eichengreen (1989), who cites (p. 129) similar terminology in the resolutions of the 1922 Genoa Conference.
[44] Clarke (1967, pp. 118–19).

Bank of England emphasized Britain's domestic economic difficulties to French officials, arguing that tightening its monetary policy would aggravate those difficulties unacceptably. If pressed too far, Britain's only alternative would be to abandon the gold standard. Apparently, the British authorities threatened also to turn up the pressure on France to repay its war debts. In the end, the impasse was broken partly by a degree of accommodation on both sides, and partly by the intervention of the United States, which agreed to sell some of its own gold to France for sterling.

The successful resolution of this episode did not end the struggles of sterling. Moreover, these struggles continued to have spillover effects on other countries. It has been widely suggested, in particular, that the desire to ease the strain on Britain's gold reserves had an influence on monetary policy in the United States during the second half of 1927, and that the departure of US monetary policy from the course most consistent with domestic needs in turn unintentionally fueled the boom and crash on Wall Street.[45] More generally, the attempts to adhere to restored gold standards that had limited credibility under the prevailing economic conditions, exacerbated by inadequate and in some cases ill-conceived efforts at international cooperation, have been blamed for playing a major role in generating the Great Depression, which in turn catalyzed the political transformations that led to World War II.[46]

Britain left the gold standard in September 1931. The collapse of several large banks in Austria and Germany had precipitated runs on a number of currencies, including the pound, as holders of financial assets became wary. Britain was only one of several dozen countries to abandon gold between 1929 and 1933. The United States left the gold standard unequivocally in April 1933, less than two months after the inauguration of President Franklin Roosevelt, whose views on economic policy were radically different than those of his predecessor.

An uncoordinated hybrid system

Britain's departure from the gold standard in September 1931 was "unexpected."[47] Once unpegged, sterling depreciated substantially, falling 25 percent against the dollar in the first week of floating. In December, its average exchange value against the dollar was 30 percent below the pre-September parity.

Both official and private holders of sterling assets experienced large declines in the gold values of their holdings, which may have made them

---

[45] Yeager (1976, p. 336).
[46] See Eichengreen (1992) and the review by Cooper (1992).
[47] Clarke (1967, p. 218).

more reluctant to retain balances of other currencies. Moreover, gold could no longer be obtained in London. Consequently, bullion began to drain from the reserve holdings of the United States, which remained on a gold standard. This led the Federal Reserve to consider actions to push up interest rates. Strong opposition was expressed by some,[48] based on the depressed condition of the US economy and the strength of the underlying US balance of payments position. Nevertheless, the rules of the Federal Reserve System restricted the types of assets that could be used as backing for central bank liabilities, and concerns to adhere to the existing rules and stop the gold drain were given priority over concerns about the domestic economy. Accordingly, the Federal Reserve decided to raise its discount rate sharply during October 1931.

With hindsight this is universally regarded as a serious mistake in monetary policy which deepened the depression in the United States and in the entire world outside the sterling bloc.[49]

With the world economy depressed, countries perceived advantages in strengthening the international competitiveness of their products by depreciating their currencies. Thus, when sterling appreciated in the early months of 1932, the British government responded by establishing an Exchange Equalization Account to manage the exchange rate – in particular, to resist the appreciation. In the same spirit, the United States, after abandoning gold in April 1933, resisted international political pressures to limit the dollar's depreciation until, in January 1934, Roosevelt announced a return to a fixed gold parity at 35 dollars an ounce. At that price, the dollar, in terms of gold, was 40 percent cheaper than its pre-1933 parity. Notably, during the autumn of 1933, the United States had probed whether the British were interested in stabilizing the dollar/pound exchange rate, only to find that the Bank of England was not ready to contemplate such an objective.[50]

Managed floating

France had remained on a gold standard at the parity officially established in 1928. Following the formation of a Popular Front government in the spring of 1936, pressures on the franc mounted and the authorities contemplated a devaluation. The Americans and the British were concerned that the franc might be devalued excessively; the French had reason to fear foreign retaliation. Negotiations led to the Tripartite Monetary

---

[48] Despres (1973, pp. xi–xii).   [49] Kindleberger (1984, pp. 380–1).
[50] Kindleberger (1984, p. 388).

Agreement of September 1936. As part of the Agreement, the franc was devalued by roughly 25 percent.

The Tripartite Agreement established a process of coordination between the three major countries and a system of managed floating.[51] Although no formal coordination mechanism was specified in the Agreement, arrangements for day-to-day collaboration among monetary authorities in managing exchange rates were soon worked out. The monetary authorities consulted daily to agree on appropriate levels for exchange rates and to decide on a common currency in which intervention would be conducted. When the parties agreed on both the exchange rate levels and the intervention currency, they further specified a price at which each central bank would exchange foreign currency for gold at the close of the business day.

Beyond efforts to coordinate day-to-day actions in exchange markets, the Tripartite Agreement did not constrain the three countries from pursuing independent policies aimed at domestic economic objectives. Formal coordination of monetary and fiscal policies was not taken explicitly into consideration.

Arrangements during World War II

The outbreak of World War II in 1939 ushered in a period of tight exchange controls. Exchange rates continued to be officially managed, with the pound rigidly pegged at 4.03 dollars. Given the scale and desperate nature of European needs for imported supplies, however, prevailing exchange rates would not have been sustainable without large-scale American assistance under the Lend-Lease Act of 1941.

The total outflow of Lend-Lease aid from the United States, net of eventual repayments, amounted to 37 billion dollars at a price level considerably lower than today's. Thirty-eight countries were recipients of this aid, with about 65 percent channeled to the British Empire, 23 percent to the Soviet Union, and 7 percent to France and her possessions.[52]

4   The Bretton Woods system, 1946–71

Plans for a new international monetary system began to take shape during the war. In hopes of avoiding the international economic disorder that had followed World War I, the British and American authorities during the early 1940s assembled groups of government and academic experts to begin articulating ideas and negotiating rules and institutions for postwar

---

[51] Eichengreen (1989, pp. 144–5).   [52] Yeager (1976, p. 378).

monetary and financial relations.[53] The agreements that emerged were adopted by 44 nations at a conference in Bretton Woods, New Hampshire, during July 1944. The new international economic order was formally launched with the declaration of fixed exchange rate parities by 32 countries in December 1946.

Ideologically, the Bretton Woods agreement reflected a middle ground between the philosophies of *laissez faire* and interventionism. The negotiations sought to forge a coalition between those parts of the political establishments that lobbied strongly for free trade and those that sought arrangements to foster full employment and economic stabilization.[54] One of the objectives was to reach an agreement that countries with depressed economies would not resort, as they had in the 1930s, to "beggar-my-neighbor" devices such as import restrictions or competitive devaluations. The outcome was a managed multilateral system that left individual countries with considerable policy autonomy but subjected their exchange rate practices and international trade and payments restrictions to international agreement.

Two new international organizations – the International Monetary Fund (IMF) and the International Bank for Reconstruction and Development (the World Bank, IBRD) – were created at the Bretton Woods conference. The IMF was designed to promote international monetary cooperation and an orderly exchange rate system, and to provide short-term financial assistance to meet temporary balance of payments needs. The World Bank was established to finance reconstruction and development.[55] The Articles of Agreement of the IMF defined a system

[53] Ikenberry (1993), Solomon (1982). Williams (1947) contrasts the strategy for economic reconstruction after World War II with the approach taken after World War I. Eichengreen and Kenen (1994) and Volcker and Gyohten (1992) credit the leadership role played by the United States during and after World War II, in contrast with US isolationism after World War I, as a major factor in the design of relatively successful rules and institutions; they also suggest that success was facilitated by the fact that most of the negotiations involved only two countries.   [54] Ikenberry (1993, pp. 157–8).

[55] See Bretton Woods Commission (1994) for historical perspectives and an appraisal of the two organizations on the occasion of their 50th anniversary. The Bretton Woods conference also generated plans for an International Trade Organization (ITO) to establish rules, eliminate restrictions, and settle disputes relating to international trade. The ITO was never established, because the US Congress did not approve its charter. In the late 1940s, however, the United States and many other countries adopted as treaty obligations the set of rules that had been developed for the ITO. The treaty was known as the General Agreement on Tariffs and Trade (GATT), and an informal secretariat for the GATT was created to provide a forum for addressing issues relating to international trade. During the 1980s and early 1990s it became increasingly evident that flaws in the institutional structure of the GATT impeded further progress in trade liberalization, and in December 1993, negotiations were completed to establish a new World Trade Organization (WTO), which came into existence on January 1, 1995.

under which: each member country was to fix, at a level approved by the IMF, a par value for its currency in terms of either gold or a currency fixed to gold; each country was to keep its exchange rate within 1 percent of its par value, but retained the right to adjust its central parity, upon securing the concurrence of the IMF,[56] if ever a "fundamental disequilibrium" developed in its balance of payments; the IMF was to make credit available to members for the purpose of financing temporary and cyclical balance of payments deficits, subject to quantitative credit limits and to conditions linking the provision of credit to the implementation of policies aimed at correcting payments imbalances; each country, after a transitional period, was to eliminate restrictions on currency convertibility for purposes of making payments for imports and other current account transactions; and countries were permitted, if not encouraged, to impose restrictions on undesired international capital flows.

The resulting system of exchange rates in effect established an international gold–dollar standard. The United States was the only country to peg its currency to gold; most other currencies were pegged to the US dollar. The US par value was left at 35 dollars per ounce of gold, where it had been since 1934. The United States was also the only industrial country prepared at the outset to forgo transitional arrangements and accept the obligation of avoiding restrictions on convertibility for current account payments.[57] Under a policy adopted in 1934, however, the United States sold gold only to foreign central banks and governments (and to licensed private users of gold for the industries and arts).[58]

Once the new international monetary system was in operation, most of the growth over time in official international reserve holdings took the form of dollar-denominated claims on the United States. By the end of the 1950s, US liabilities to foreign monetary authorities had reached 10 billion dollars, about the same as official reserve holdings of British pounds, which had hardly changed during the previous decade.[59] US gold sales to foreign countries amounted to 5.7 billion dollars net during the period 1949–59.[60]

With the passage of time, the Bretton Woods era has come to be regarded as a period when both the world economy and the exchange rate system performed relatively well. The performance of the world economy during the Bretton Woods era, in comparison with the periods of other international monetary regimes, is summarized in tables 3.1 and 3.2. Table 3.1

---

[56] Concurrence was automatic if the proposed adjustment, together with all previous adjustments, did not exceed 10 percent of the country's initial par value.

[57] El Salvador, Guatemala, Mexico, and Panama also accepted this obligation at the outset.

[58] The IMF's charter gave each country the option of converting its currency either into gold or into the currency of the country seeking conversion; see Yeager (1976, p. 352).

[59] Solomon (1982, p. 29).   [60] Solomon (1982, p. 31).

Table 3.1. *Average growth and inflation rates during different international monetary regimes*[a]

	Gold standard 1881–1913	Interwar 1919–38	Bretton Woods 1946–70	Floating 1974–89
Growth of per capita real GNP				
United States	1.8	0.2	2.0	2.1
United Kingdom	1.1	1.2	2.1	1.5
Germany	1.7	2.6	5.0	2.2
France	1.5	1.3	3.9	1.7
Japan	1.4	2.0	8.1	3.5
Canada	2.3	0.2	2.5	1.6
Italy	1.0	0.9	5.6	2.5
Mean	1.5	1.2	4.2	2.2
Inflation[b]				
United States	0.3	− 1.8	2.4	5.6
United Kingdom	0.3	− 1.5	3.7	9.4
Germany	0.6	− 2.1	2.7	3.3
France	− 0.0	2.2	5.6	8.8
Japan	4.6	− 1.7	4.5	2.6
Canada	0.4	− 1.9	2.7	7.9
Italy	0.6	− 1.1	3.8	12.9
Mean	1.0	− 1.1	3.6	7.2

Notes:
[a] In percent per annum.
[b] Based on GNP deflators.
Source: Bordo (1993b, table 1.1).

compares the average annual rates of *per capita* real GNP growth and inflation, during four periods with different international monetary regimes, for each of the seven largest industrial countries. Table 3.2 provides summary statistics on the variability of real growth and inflation rates. For the group of seven countries as a whole, and for most of the individual countries, the Bretton Woods era was characterized by more rapid growth and less rapid inflation than the subsequent period of floating exchange rates, by faster and less variable growth than either the gold standard era or the interwar period, and by less variable inflation than the interwar period.

The degree of exchange rate stability during the Bretton Woods era, in comparison with other periods, is shown in table 3.3. Notably, both nominal exchange rates and real exchange rates (that is, nominal exchange rates adjusted by ratios of national price levels) were relatively unstable

Table 3.2. *Variability of growth and inflation rates during different international monetary regimes*[a]

	Gold standard 1881–1913	Interwar 1919–38	Bretton Woods 1946–70	Floating 1974–89
Growth of per capita real GNP				
United States	5.0	8.1	2.8	2.7
United Kingdom	2.4	4.5	1.8	4.2
Germany	2.9	8.5	3.3	1.9
France	4.6	7.2	2.2	1.5
Japan	3.8	6.1	2.7	1.1
Canada	2.8	8.8	2.6	2.6
Italy	4.1	4.7	3.3	2.2
Mean	3.7	6.8	2.7	2.3
Inflation[b]				
United States	3.1	7.6	2.6	2.4
United Kingdom	3.1	7.8	2.2	6.1
Germany	2.6	4.7	4.0	1.3
France	5.0	9.1	4.1	3.2
Japan	5.5	7.3	4.6	2.4
Canada	1.4	6.0	3.0	3.0
Italy	3.2	11.7	11.5	4.6
Mean	3.4	7.7	4.6	3.3

Note:
[a] Standard deviations of growth and inflation rates measured in percent per annum.
[b] Based on GNP deflators.
Source: Bordo (1993b, table 1.1).

during the first part of the Bretton Woods period and highly stable during the latter part.

Despite the relatively high variability of exchange rates during the early years of the Bretton Woods period, par value changes occurred infrequently. In September 1949, the United Kingdom and most other European countries, with encouragement from the United States, devalued their currencies by about 30 percent against the US dollar. In September 1950, after a 10 percent devaluation during the previous year, the par value of the Canadian dollar was suspended in favor of a floating exchange rate for a period that was to last nearly a dozen years, albeit with very moderate fluctuations in the exchange rate between the Canadian and US dollars. And during 1957–58, the French franc was devalued in two steps by a total of 29 percent.

The postwar period through 1958 was characterized by a high degree of

Table 3.3. *Variability of nominal and real exchange rates during different international monetary regimes*[a]

	Gold standard 1881–1913	Interwar 1919–38	Bretton Woods		Floating 1974–89
			1946–58	1959–70	
Nominal exchange raes[b]					
United Kingdom	0.2	6.8	3.6	1.4	10.1
Germany	0.2	3.9	2.4	1.3	9.3
France	0.3	17.8	4.4	1.1	10.7
Japan	2.9	6.7	22.0	0.2	8.8
Canada	0.0	2.6	2.2	0.8	3.7
Italy	1.4	13.6	14.1	0.2	10.9
Mean	0.8	8.6	8.1	0.8	8.9
Real exchange rates[c]					
United Kingdom	1.7	6.5	4.7	2.5	9.4
Germany	2.4	5.8	3.8	1.9	8.8
France	4.3	8.9	6.2	2.5	9.2
Japan	6.6	7.8	4.4	2.1	9.6
Canada	2.6	3.2	2.4	1.2	3.8
Italy	2.1	13.3	13.1	2.4	8.6
Mean	3.3	7.6	5.8	2.1	8.2

Notes:
[a] Average absolute percentage changes from year to year.
[b] In domestic currency units per US dollar, except for the United Kingdom, which is US dollars per pound.
[c] Nominal exchange rates divided by ratios of consumer price indices.
Source: Bordo (1993b, table 1.1).

international economic cooperation. The industrial structures and financial positions of Europe and Japan had been devastated by World War II. In such circumstances, the war-torn countries looked to the United States for food, manufactures, and financial assistance. The United States offered the European Recovery Program – better known as the Marshall Plan. In addition to providing financial grants and loans, America encouraged the European countries to expand exports to the United States and liberalize trade among themselves, while maintaining restrictions on imports from outside Europe. The devaluations of 1949 were part of the effort to stimulate the expansion of European production by promoting exports and discouraging imports from outside Europe.

Simultaneously with reconstructing and expanding their production bases, the European countries sought to rebuild their depleted stocks of international reserves. By 1958, most European countries felt sufficiently secure with their expanded reserve holdings to remove the transitional restrictions on the convertibility of their currencies for purposes of conducting current international transactions. Apart from Germany, however, they did not take the further step of removing convertibility restrictions on capital account transactions.[61]

The Bretton Woods period was also characterized, until the late 1960s, by a remarkably high degree of consistency between the economic policy priorities of the industrial countries. The pursuit of export-led growth by Europe and Japan was not incompatible with domestic policy objectives in North America. Moreover, the maintenance of price stability in the United States provided a nominal anchor for other participants in the fixed exchange rate system, thereby permitting Europe and Japan to keep their policies oriented more toward promoting growth, and less toward resisting inflation, than might otherwise have been appropriate.

This is not to say that all was well in the world economy and the international monetary system. By the mid-1960s, many European countries had succeeded in reducing unemployment to relatively low levels, and wage and price pressures were intensifying. Moreover, by late 1964, growing concerns about the international monetary system were being openly discussed.[62]

The policy-oriented literature of the 1960s characterized the prevailing international monetary system as incapable of resolving simultaneously the problems of liquidity, adjustment, and confidence. With the production of new gold inadequate to meet the increasing demand for official reserves in a growing world economy, and with gold and reserve currencies comprising the principal reserve assets in the international monetary system, the liquidity problem could be solved, or so it was perceived, in only two ways: by continuing to increase the liabilities of the reserve-currency countries, especially those of the United States; or by raising the purchasing power of gold. This choice presented the so-called "Triffin dilemma."[63] The first solution would lead to a persistent balance of payments deficit for the United States on an official settlements basis[64] which, in the view of many economists, constituted an adjustment problem.[65] The second solution,

---

[61] Solomon (1982, p. 24). The Japanese yen was not made convertible for current transactions until 1964.   [62] Argy (1981), Solomon (1982).   [63] Triffin (1960).

[64] A country's official settlements balance amounts to its current account balance plus its balance of capital flows excluding any changes in foreign official holdings of short-term claims on residents of the country. Thus, if a country in current account balance experienced a net increase in the short-term liabilities of its residents to foreign monetary authorities, mirrored by other short-term or long-term capital flows, its official settlements balance would show a deficit.

[65] Notably, some economists correctly argued at the time that a persistent US balance of payments deficit on an official settlements basis (in association with a continuing build-up of short-term liabilities of the United States to foreign monetary authorities) did not require

moreover, would undermine confidence in the reserve system. In particular, an increase in the official dollar price of gold – or even the contemplation of an increase – could induce attempts by foreign governments to convert their dollar reserve holdings into gold, and would also induce speculative investments in gold by private market participants. This would rapidly drain the gold reserves of the United States and destroy the ability of the US authorities to defend any fixed gold parity for the dollar.[66]

The principal mechanism proposed to resolve this dilemma was for the International Monetary Fund to create a new reserve asset. The formal creation of this asset – the special drawing right (SDR) – took place with the approval in May 1968, and legal adoption the next year, of the First Amendment to the Articles of Agreement of the IMF. The initial allocation of SDRs took place in three stages during 1970–72; subsequent allocations were to be considered periodically as the global need for reserves expanded over time. In the event, however, the presumption that the expansion of dollar reserve holdings required an increase in the international indebtedness of the United States – or simply in the short-term liabilities of US residents to foreign monetary authorities – soon proved invalid. By the end of the 1960s, a large international market, known as the Eurodollar market, had developed outside the United States for the dollar-denominated liabilities of governments and reputable private borrowers. Official holdings of prime-grade dollar-denominated assets could thus be accumulated by borrowing from private financial intermediaries whose activities did not create balance of payments adjustment problems.

As it happened, the United States allowed a genuine adjustment problem to develop in the late 1960s when it overheated its economy and fueled inflation by failing to push for a tax increase or expenditure cuts at the time that the fiscal implications of the Viet Nam War were first anticipated.[67] Eventually, monetary and fiscal policies were tightened, which did not stop the upward spiral of wages and prices, but did generate a sharp slowdown and subsequent contraction of the US economy. In those circumstances, short-term dollar interest rates declined considerably during 1970, while surging economic activity was pushing interest rates higher in Europe and Japan. The widening nominal interest rate differentials and continuing US

---

a continuing increase in the *net* international indebtedness of US residents (as would be reflected in a continuing US current account deficit), and thus did not really represent an adjustment problem; see Kindleberger (1965) and Despres, Kindleberger, and Salant (1969).

[66] During the 1960s, the United States and a number of other countries developed various policies to limit conversion of dollars into gold. These included the formation of the Gold Pool in 1961, the issuance of Roosa bonds, and the establishment of the Two-Tier Arrangement in 1968; see Solomon (1982) and Pauls (1990).

[67] Solomon (1982, pp. 100–9).

inflationary spiral eroded the attractiveness of dollar-denominated assets relative to both gold and assets denominated in other leading currencies. As a result, private capital outflows from the United States rose sharply, mirrored by an increase in foreign official holdings of short-term claims on the United States, and the foreign exchange value of the German mark (already raised by 9.3 percent in September–October 1969) came under strong upward pressure. Thus emerged the type of confidence problem that had been widely discussed by Triffin (1960) and others. In May 1971, the German authorities decided to abandon their official parity and let the mark float. A few other countries followed, but most European countries and Japan continued to maintain their fixed parities. Speculation against the dollar grew more intense. This led the US authorities, on August 15, 1971, to suspend the practice of converting dollars into gold for foreign monetary authorities.

The suspension of dollar convertibility marked the end of the Bretton Woods era.[68] Less than two weeks later, the Bank of Japan, after heavy official intervention to defend its yen/dollar parity, decided to let its currency float. By the end of August, nearly all countries had relinquished their commitments to defend par values. Following the Smithsonian Agreement reached in December 1971, the Group of Ten countries, in an attempt to restore the Bretton Woods system, established new par values and widened the fluctuation margins to $2\frac{1}{4}$ percent on each side of the parities. As part of the agreement, the US dollar was devalued by raising the price of gold from 35 dollars to 38 dollars per ounce, with the unwritten *quid pro quo* that the United States would not be pressed to restore the gold convertibility of the dollar at an early date.[69] The new par values, however, proved difficult to defend. In June 1972, the United Kingdom decided to float its currency; Switzerland followed in January 1973, and Japan and Italy in February. In March, six members of the European Community (Belgium, Denmark, France, Germany, Luxembourg, and the Netherlands) announced that they would keep their currencies pegged against each other but let them jointly float against other currencies.[70] This

---

[68] Notably, the collapse of the Bretton Woods system was not the result of reserve shortages. Had the United States imposed stronger self-discipline over its macroeconomic policies in the late 1960s, the Bretton Woods regime could have been prolonged without systemic reforms. From the obverse perspective, however, it is hard to conceive of systemic reforms that, on their own, could have generated significantly stronger macroeconomic policy discipline in the United States or other major countries. It would thus be misleading to suggest that international monetary reform or the SDR came "too late."

[69] Solomon (1982, p. 205).

[70] The evolution of European exchange arrangements since the early 1970s is discussed in chapter 11 (pp. 200–5).

essentially ended the period of transition to the era of "generalized floating."[71]

In retrospective analysis of why the world economy and the exchange rate system performed relatively well during the Bretton Woods period, economists have pondered how much the stability of the world economic environment was responsible for the relatively smooth operation of the exchange rate system, and how much the operation of the exchange rate system contributed to world economic stability.[72] They have also reflected on the factors that made postwar institutional arrangements relatively successful and adaptable,[73] while questioning the extent to which restrictions on international capital flows, which were liberalized only gradually during the 1960s, prolonged the lifespan of the Bretton Woods system.[74] The answers will undoubtedly be debated and refined for many years. It is clear, however, that the stability of the world economy and the relatively smooth operation of the exchange rate system reinforced each other. Together, the initial conditions of the world economy at the beginning of the Bretton Woods era, and the features of the exchange rate system that was put into place, were conducive to a prolonged period of economic cooperation and mutually supportive policies among the industrial countries, which in turn brought a relatively high degree of stability – in comparison with other periods of time – to both the performance of the world economy and the operation of the exchange rate system.

[71] Initially, the move to generalized floating was regarded as temporary, and in June 1974, the Committee on Reform of the International Monetary System (the Committee of Twenty), which had been established in 1972, issued a report that envisioned an eventual return to an adjustable peg system; see Committee on Reform ... (1974). In November 1975, however, the major industrial countries agreed at the Rambouillet Economic Summit to legitimize floating formally by amending the Articles of Agreement of the International Monetary Fund, and to "deepen, systematize, and broaden" daily consultation among their monetary authorities with regard to exchange market information. See Pauls (1990).

[72] Eichengreen (1993a). Despite rosy assessments today, the Bretton Woods system did not function as well as it might have, and arguments for flexible exchange rates intensified during the 1950s and 1960s; see chapter 11.

[73] Eichengreen and Kenen (1994).

[74] Krugman (1993c, p. 540) suggests that the Bretton Woods era was

a time when financial markets worked acceptably precisely because regulation and controls were sufficient to limit the moral hazard that has driven so much lucrative but destructive financial action ... [subsequently].

Part II

Models of exchange rate behavior

4 Exchange rates and national price levels

In attempting to understand the behavior of exchange rates, economists have focused historically on three classes of explanatory variables: national price levels, interest rates, and the balance of payments. Part II of this book begins with chapters on the relationships between exchange rates and each class of explanatory variable individually.

The perception that exchange rates are related to national price levels has been traced back to the sixteenth century, with particular attribution to the School of Salamanca in Spain.[1] The genesis of this perception was linked to the development of the quantity theory of money:

In places where money is scarce, goods will be cheaper than in those where the whole mass of money is bigger, and therefore it is lawful to exchange a smaller sum in one country for a larger sum in another ...[2]

Presumably, these theories were catalyzed by the effects on money supplies and prices of large inflows of gold and silver from newly-discovered America, which Spain was the first European country to receive.

Although economists during subsequent generations continued to endorse and further develop the concept of a link between exchange rates and national price levels,[3] it was not until 1918 that Gustav Cassel coined the term "purchasing power parity" and, through prolific writing on the topic, became inextricably linked with the notion that exchange rates should be closely related to the relative purchasing powers of national monetary units. In particular, reflecting on economic developments during World War I, Cassel wrote:

The general inflation which has taken place during the war has lowered this purchasing power in all countries, though in a very different degree, and the rates of exchanges should accordingly be expected to deviate from their old parity in proportion to the inflation of each country.

[1] Einzig (1970) and Officer (1982), who both cite Grice-Hutchinson (1952).
[2] Domingo de Bañez, written in 1594, as cited in Officer (1982, p. 32) and Grice-Hutchinson (1952, pp. 57–8).
[3] Haberler (1961, pp. 46–7) provides selected quotations from Hume, Ricardo, the Bullion Report, and Thornton. Officer (1982) provides a more extensive history.

At every moment the real parity between two countries is represented by this quotient between the purchasing power of the money in the one country and the other. I propose to call this parity "the purchasing power parity." As long as anything like free movement of merchandise and a somewhat comprehensive trade between the two countries takes place, the actual rate of exchange cannot deviate very much from this purchasing power parity.[4]

This chapter focuses on the purchasing power parity (PPP) hypothesis and related topics.[5] Over time, a distinction has been drawn between two alternative forms of PPP, which are described in the first section. The second section considers the arguments against PPP in both the short run and the long run. The third section discusses direct evidence on the time series behavior of real exchange rates – that is, nominal exchange rates adjusted by ratios of national price levels – and on the long-run relationship between nominal exchange rates and national price levels. It also reviews evidence that the short-term variability of real exchange rates is sensitive to the nominal exchange rate regime. The fourth section addresses what the evidence implies for macroeconomic doctrine. The fifth section considers the usefulness of PPP as a normative formula for determining an appropriate level for the exchange rate. The sixth section provides concluding perspectives.

1   The purchasing power parity hypothesis

PPP theory has two main variants. The absolute PPP hypothesis states that the exchange rate between the currencies of two countries should equal the ratio of the price levels of the two countries. Specifically,

$$S = P/P^* \tag{4.1}$$

where S is the nominal exchange rate measured in units of currency A per unit currency B, P is the price level in country A, and P^* is the price level in country B. The relative PPP hypothesis states that the exchange rate should bear a constant proportionate relationship to the ratio of national price levels; in particular,

$$S = kP/P^* \tag{4.2}$$

where k is a constant parameter. The logarithmic transformations of (4.1) and (4.2) have the form

---

[4] Cassel (1918, p. 413). In later writings, Cassel (1922) clarified that he viewed PPP as a central tendency, noting a number of factors that prevented PPP from holding continuously.

[5] See Dornbusch (1992b) for another general discussion. See Edison, Gagnon, and Melick (1994), Boucher Breuer (1994), and Froot and Rogoff (1995) for discussions of the econometric methodology and conclusions of the empirical literature on PPP.

$$s = \alpha + p - p^* \tag{4.3}$$

where s, p, p^* are the logarithms of S, P, P^* and $\alpha = 0$ under absolute PPP. Under either variant of PPP, a change in the ratio of price levels implies an equiproportionate change in the exchange rate, such that

$$\Delta s = \Delta p - \Delta p^*. \tag{4.4}$$

The relative PPP hypothesis has been regarded not only as a proposition in positive economics, but also as a policy guideline in normative economics. Indeed, interest in PPP has historically been heightened when normative guidelines were needed – that is,

whenever existing exchange rates were considered unrealistic and the search began for the elusive concept of equilibrium rates.[6]

Such times of elevated interest have included the period of the Napoleonic Wars and the Bullionist Controversy during the early nineteenth century, the years leading up to the restoration of gold standards in the aftermath of World War I, and the period after World War II during which the choice of exchange rate parities was debated. The merits of relative PPP as a normative policy guideline are considered on pp. 70–1.

As a proposition in positive economics, the PPP hypothesis does not make any general assertion about the direction of causation between exchange rates and national price levels. It is quite consistent with a process of two-way causation, with exchange rates adjusting to changes in the ratios of national price levels while inflation rates are simultaneously responsive to changes in exchange rates. Neither exchange rates nor national price levels are exogenous variables. Thus, the PPP hypothesis is a theory about the relationship between endogenous variables. It is not, by itself, a complete model of either exchange rates or national price levels.

To the extent that information on national price levels is readily available in the form of price indices but not as absolute price levels, absolute PPP may not be a useful operational hypothesis.[7] Most of the empirical literature, in any case, has relied on price indices in examining the validity of PPP, and has thus focused implicitly on the relative PPP hypothesis. This chapter does the same. The PPP hypothesis is frequently restated in terms of the real exchange rate (Q), defined as

$$Q = SP^*/P. \tag{4.5}$$

[6] Balassa (1964, p. 584).

[7] Although considerable effort has been devoted to collecting and analyzing information on absolute prices during the postwar period under projects sponsored by the Organisation for European Economic Cooperation and the United Nations (see Gilbert and Kravis [1954], Kravis, Heston, and Summers [1982], and Summers and Heston [1991]), such data are available with much lower frequency than price indices collected by national authorities.

Under this terminology, (4.1) and (4.2) each imply that the real exchange rate is time-invariant.

2   Arguments against PPP

The PPP hypothesis has confronted several types of counterarguments. Some of these contend that various economic forces cause large and prolonged fluctuations in real exchange rates over time. Such arguments imply that PPP is not valid in the short run, but do not necessarily reject its validity over the long run. Other counterarguments point to economic forces that generate changes in the relative prices of tradable and nontradable goods, and thus in real exchange rates, over the long run. Accordingly, the validity of the long-run PPP hypothesis may depend on whether it is taken to apply to the price levels of tradable goods alone or to general price levels for tradables and nontradables together.

As a basis for distinguishing among different types of evidence and lines of argument, it may be noted that the PPP hypothesis would be valid for the general price levels of any two countries under the following three conditions:

(i) if each tradable good obeyed the "law of one price," exhibiting identical prices (when translated into a common currency) in each country,

(ii) if factor price equalization and identical production functions brought the prices of nontradable goods into equality internationally, and

(iii) if each good received identical weights in the aggregate price indices of the two countries.

Similarly, when applied to the price levels of tradable goods alone, the PPP hypothesis would be valid under conditions (i) and (iii).

Perhaps the main reason to doubt the validity of PPP in the short run is the fact that, for relatively narrow categories of manufactured goods, the common-currency prices of products from different countries often show large and persistent divergences following changes in nominal exchange rates, contradicting condition (i) above.[8] With widespread product diversification, most manufactured goods face finite elasticities of demand and are priced under conditions of imperfect competition. Transportation costs, trade restrictions, and taxes may contribute to reducing demand elasticities and the degree of international competition.[9] Moreover, the presence of medium-term labor contracts keeps wages and unit production costs sticky.

---

[8] Isard (1977).

[9] Engel and Rogers (1994) provide evidence that, when exchange rates are flexible, the behavior of the relative common-currency prices of similar products, as reflected in consumer price data collected in different markets, is affected both by the distance between the markets and by whether the markets are located in different countries.

Thus, producers are often inclined not to adjust prices in response to exchange rate changes – and all the more so when they are uncertain whether the exchange rate changes will persist or will soon be reversed.[10] This implies that, in the short run, price and wage adjustment mechanisms do not validate the law of one price among similar manufactured products from different countries, which makes it difficult to point to an adjustment mechanism through which departures from PPP at the macroeconomic level are likely to be eliminated quickly.[11]

Even if PPP is not valid as a hypothesis about short-run behavior, the forces of international competition may generate convergence over time in the common-currency prices of similar tradable goods. Rejection of the law of one price in the short run is not sufficient to dismiss the proposition that real exchange rates fluctuate around time-invariant means or equilibrium values over the long run.

However, the proposition of long-run PPP – at least as it applies to general price indices for tradable and nontradable goods combined – has been challenged by arguments that dispute the validity of conditions (ii) and (iii) above. In particular, it has been emphasized that there are major differences in the production functions, consumer preferences, and factor endowments of different countries, and that such differences are likely to be reflected in international differences both in the relative prices of tradable and nontradable goods and in price-index weights. Over time, moreover, production technologies and consumption preferences are likely to undergo different changes in different countries, thereby generating different patterns of change across countries in the relative prices of tradable and nontradable goods, with associated changes in real exchange rates.

Balassa's (1964) appraisal of the PPP doctrine made an important contribution to the development of such arguments.[12] Citing empirical evidence provided by Gilbert and Kravis and associates,[13] Balassa emphasized that

---

[10] See Greenwald and Stiglitz (1993), for example, on the microfoundations of price and wage stickiness. Dixit (1989) and Krugman (1989a) argue that the stickiness in traded-goods prices in the face of exchange rate uncertainty can be understood in terms of the costs that firms have "sunk" into entering foreign markets. Giovannini (1988) compares the prices at which Japanese products have been sold domestically with their export prices to the United States, finding large and persistent deviations from the law of one price.

[11] As Krugman (1990) notes, the view that the goods produced by different countries are very imperfect substitutes is consistent with the fact that econometric models of the volumes of national imports and exports, aggregated over all goods, normally yield estimated relative price elasticities in the range of 1 to 2.

[12] An earlier discussion of parts of Balassa's appraisal can be found in Harrod (1939); and Marris (1984) notes that seeds of some of the arguments can be traced back to Ricardo (1951).

[13] For example, Gilbert and Kravis (1954).

If differences in tastes do not counterbalance differences in productive endowments, there will be a tendency in each country to consume commodities with lower relative prices in larger quantities.[14]

This implied that a given category of goods would tend to have different weights in the prices indices of different countries. Furthermore, there was empirical evidence of international differences in the relative prices of tradable and nontradable goods and services. In particular, the price of services tended to be relatively high in countries with relatively high income levels.[15]

As Balassa further emphasized, the degree to which exchange rates and national price levels diverged from PPP over any period of time generally depended on the extent to which changes in price indices were driven by monetary developments rather than structural factors. Consistently, subsequent empirical testing has shown that the PPP hypothesis may have considerable validity during hyperinflations or other periods of very large changes in price levels.[16] But given the competitive pressures within each country for workers with similar skills to receive similar wages in the tradable and nontradable goods sectors, international differences in rates of productivity growth in the tradables sector would tend, other things being equal, to generate different rates of change in the relative prices of tradables and nontradables in different countries.[17] Accordingly, even in the absence of divergent movements in the common-currency prices of tradables, and abstracting from discrepancies in price-index weights, international differences in productivity growth could generate a secular divergence from PPP. Moreover, as Samuelson (1964) emphasized, the phenomenon of large cumulative differences in productivity growth was a prominent characteristic of the postwar world – partly reflecting the rebuilding of war-ravaged economies, and at the same time reflecting "the reducing of the technological gap between America and the less-than-most-affluent nations."[18] Thus, the process of opening the world economy to foreign investment tended to unleash forces that discredited PPP as a long-run hypothesis applied to general price levels.[19]

[14] Balassa (1964, p. 587).
[15] See also Kravis, Heston, and Summers (1982), who stress the inadequacies of using market exchange rates to convert individual country GDP data into a common currency for purposes of comparing living standards internationally.   [16] Frenkel (1976).
[17] Such pressures on relative prices would not arise in an economy with no factor mobility between the tradable and nontradable goods sectors. See Rogoff (1992b) for an analysis of real exchange rate behavior in that case.   [18] Samuelson (1964, p. 153).
[19] See Kravis and Lipsey (1983) for further discussion of the nonmonetary determinants of national price levels. See Turner and Van 't dack (1993) for a recent study, including historical perspectives, on measuring international price and cost competitiveness. See Marsh and Tokarick (1994) for a theoretical and empirical assessment of different competitiveness indicators.

A second type of challenge to the long-run PPP hypothesis has come from evidence that countries appear to face large differences between the income elasticities of their imports and their exports. This apparent evidence, first emphasized by Houthakker and Magee (1969), raised the prospect that secular changes in real exchange rates would be necessary to prevent trade imbalances from growing perpetually larger relative to national output levels as the world economy expanded.[20] In reality, as Krugman (1990) has noted, countries for which income elasticities appear to be higher for exports than for imports also tend to be countries where income growth during the postwar period has been relatively rapid, which has dampened the effects of income growth on trade imbalances. For consistent reasons, moreover, the apparent discrepancies in income elasticities have been shown to evaporate in some subsequent empirical estimates of respecified trade equations.[21] Thus, the Houthakker–Magee challenge to long-run PPP seems to have lost its force.

3   Direct evidence

Direct evidence on the behavior of real exchange rates strongly confirms that PPP is not a valid hypothesis about the relationship between nominal exchange rates and national price levels in the short run. A snapshot of the evidence is provided by figure 4.1, which plots quarterly data for the period 1970–94 on bilateral real exchange rates between Japan and the United States and between Germany and the United Kingdom. Each panel of the figure shows five different measures of the real exchange rate, based alternatively on consumer price indices, GNP deflators, wholesale price indices, indices of normalized unit labor costs, and export price indices. For each pair of countries, and particularly for Japan and the United States, the five different real exchange rate indices have diverged significantly over time. The most relevant point here, however, is that each real exchange rate index has exhibited large and persistent deviations around its mean. Real exchange rates do not remain constant in the short run.

Random walk tests on real exchange rates

The weight of the evidence rejecting the validity of PPP in the short run has spawned a body of literature testing whether it is possible to reject the

---

[20] The subject of long-run constraints on trade or current account imbalances, and the implications for real exchange rates, are discussed in chapters 6 and 10.

[21] Helkie and Hooper (1988), Hooper and Márquez (1995). The respecification adds a foreign (domestic) capital stock variable to the domestic import (export) equation to capture changes over time in available supplies of the goods in question.

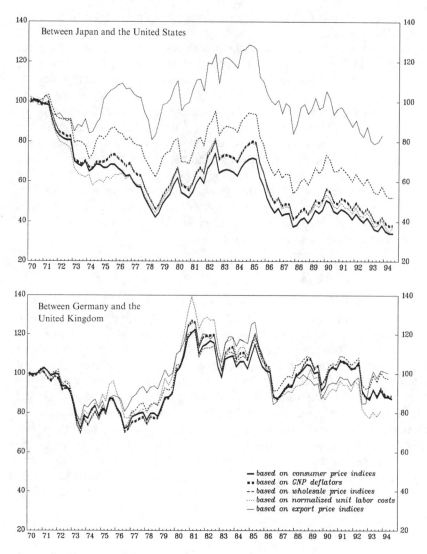

Source: Based on quarterly data from International Monetary Fund, *International Financial Statistics* and Research Department.

Figure 4.1 Real exchange rates, 1970–94 (1970 = 100)

hypothesis that the behavior of real exchange rates closely resembles a "random walk," with no tendency for changes in real exchange rates to reverse themselves over time. During the late 1970s and early 1980s, this hypothesis received support from a number of studies.[22] More recently, beginning with Edison (1981, 1987), it has been recognized that in a world of sluggish price-level adjustment, tests of whether changes in real exchange rates are persistent will fail to reject the random walk hypothesis unless they are applied to a long data series. Consistently, various studies focusing on long data periods and/or employing advanced econometric techniques have uncovered evidence that real exchange rates do indeed display tendencies to revert toward their means.[23] Moreover, cross-section data show very high correlations between changes in nominal exchange rates and relative national price levels over 10- or 20-year horizons.[24]

Evidence of mean reversion tendencies in real exchange rates, and of high cross-section correlations between changes in nominal exchange rates and relative national price levels over medium-term horizons, does not imply that real exchange rates have time-invariant means. In particular, such evidence does not undercut the theoretical arguments that Balassa (1964), Samuelson (1964), and others have put forth. Nevertheless, by clearly rejecting the random walk hypothesis over the medium run, the empirical evidence usefully puts to rest the highly implausible suggestion that the forces of international competition are too weak to prevent real exchange rates from rising or falling indefinitely.

Tests for long-run equilibrium relationships

Based on (4.3), one approach to testing the PPP hypothesis is to fit the regression hypothesis

$$s_t = \beta_0 + \beta_1 p_t - \beta_2 p_t^* + u_t \qquad (4.6)$$

where the β_j are the coefficients to be estimated, t is a time subscript, and u is an error term. Prior to the mid-1980s, the methods used to estimate (4.6) were ordinary and generalized least squares, with analysis centering on the hypothesis $\beta_1 = \beta_2 = 1$.

Around the mid-1980s, tests of PPP began to take new directions. Some economists began testing whether the secular behavior of nominal exchange rates relative to ratios of national price levels could be systemati-

---

[22] Roll (1979), Frenkel (1981), Adler and Lehmann (1983), Cumby and Obstfeld (1984). See also Hakkio (1984) for a multicurrency study that was more sympathetic to long-run PPP.

[23] Edison (1981, 1987), Frankel (1986), Huizinga (1987), Mark (1990), Abuaf and Jorion (1990), Grilli and Kaminsky (1991), Diebold, Husted, and Rush (1991), Glen (1992).

[24] Flood and Taylor (1995).

cally explained in terms of the Balassa–Samuelson effect[25] or some other structural process. Such tests for systematic long-run relationships were sometimes referred to as tests for long-run PPP, but in essence, the maintained hypothesis was that long-run PPP held only for the tradable-goods components of national price indices.

The second new direction has involved advances in econometrics for nonstationary time series, recognizing that classical hypothesis testing of (4.6) is inappropriate when the home and foreign price levels have time trends. These new tests for long-run relationships between nominal exchange rates and home and foreign price levels can be divided into different classes, reflecting differences in coefficient restrictions.[26] Some econometric studies have tested for the traditional form of PPP – that is, a long-run relationship under which changes in the home and foreign price levels are associated with "symmetric" and "proportional" effects on nominal exchange rates ($\beta_1 = \beta_2 = 1$). Other studies, however, have paraded as tests for long-run PPP without imposing the coefficient restrictions that would be implied (symmetry and proportionality) if real exchange rates had time-invariant long-run means. In the latter studies the interpretations of PPP thus represent weakenings of traditional or Casselian purchasing power parity.

The various tests for long-run equilibrium relationships have not led to unanimous agreement on how to interpret the evidence. Some economists argue that the Balassa–Samuelson effect may be relevant in the medium run, but that the dissemination of knowledge, along with the mobility of physical and human capital, generates a tendency toward absolute PPP over the very long run, abstracting from any cross-country differences in consumption patterns and price index weights.[27] In considering this paradigm of the very long run, however, it is worth noting that empirical support for long-run PPP is particularly weak for countries such as Japan and Argentina, where real incomes have undergone sharp changes relative to the real income of the rest of the world.[28]

The short-term variability of exchange rates

A number of issues relating to the short-term variability of exchange rates have received attention in the empirical literature. Among these are the questions of why the variability of real exchange rates depends on the nature of the nominal exchange rate regime, and whether the short-term

---

[25] Edison and Klovland (1987), Marston (1987). See Froot and Rogoff (1995) for an extensive and insightful discussion.
[26] Boucher Breuer (1994) provides a detailed review.
[27] Froot and Rogoff (1995).   [28] Froot and Rogoff (1995).

variability of exchange rates, conditional on the nature of the exchange rate regime, has increased over time.[29]

Evidence suggesting that real exchange rate variability is greater under floating rates than under fixed rate regimes has been provided by several studies.[30] Such evidence can be seen, for example, in figure 4.2, which shows again the striking difference in variability before and after the breakdown of the Bretton Woods system in the early 1970s. Two very different explanations have been offered. Mussa (1986) emphasizes that sluggishness in the adjustment of national price levels can help explain the lower variability of real exchange rates under regimes that commit the authorities to policies consistent with the maintenance of fixed nominal exchange rates. Stockman (1988) advances the alternative hypothesis that the regime-sensitivity of real exchange rate variability reflects regime-specific differences in the actual and expected policy responses to "real shocks," defined as shocks that affect the relative price of foreign goods in terms of domestic goods. Stockman essentially argues that the pressures on international reserves that real shocks tend to generate in a fixed nominal exchange rate regime create stronger policy concerns than the pressures on nominal exchange rates that real shocks tend to generate in a flexible rate regime; and that for this reason, countries with fixed nominal exchange rate regimes are more likely to impose trade restrictions, capital controls, or the equivalent taxes in response to real shocks, thereby dampening the impacts of such shocks on the real exchange rate.

Without necessarily taking a specific view on the question of why the nominal exchange rate regime affects the variability of the real exchange rate, several studies have suggested that the variability of real exchange rates, conditional on the nominal exchange rate regime, may have been lower in the past than it is today.[31] Such findings, however, appear to be somewhat distorted by the failure of the studies to adjust adequately for changes over time in the product coverage of national price indices. The issue is an important one in the light of the strong criticism by Keynes (1925) of PPP calculations based on the wholesale price indices that were constructed in the 1920s, which largely reflected the prices of raw materials rather than manufactures; see the discussion on pp. 70–1 below.

To the extent that it is valid, the suggestion that real exchange rate

---

[29] With respect to the behavior of real exchange rates for developing countries, attention has also been devoted to assessing the explanatory power of movements in the relative price of exports and imports (the "terms of trade"), operating on the real exchange rate through the opposite income effects of export and import price changes interacting with substitution effects; see De Gregorio and Wolf (1994) and references cited therein.

[30] Stockman (1983), Mussa (1986, 1990), Baxter and Stockman (1989).

[31] Grilli and Kaminsky (1991), Diebold, Husted, and Rush (1991). See also Frenkel (1978, 1981), Krugman (1978), Edison (1985).

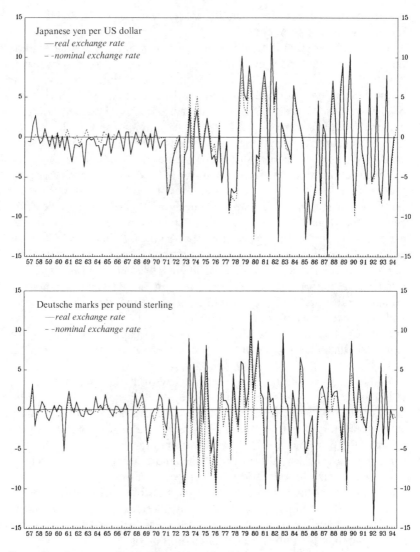

Source: Based on quarterly data from International Monetary Fund, *International Financial Statistics*, and Research Department; real exchange rates are based on consumer price indices.

Figure 4.2 Variability of nominal and real exchange rates, 1957–94 (percentage change from previous quarter)

behavior has varied substantially across historical periods, perhaps reflecting changes over time in the degree of international capital mobility,[32]
points to a possible source of bias in characterizing the influence of the
nominal exchange rate regime on the behavior of real exchange rates.[33]
Nevertheless, evidence provided by the experiences of Canada and Ireland
suggests that the nominal exchange rate regime does indeed have a strong
influence, independently of the historical period.[34]

4   Implications for macroeconomic doctrine

During recent decades, Keynesian economics has been vigorously con-
tested. A new classical school of thought has disputed the traditional
Keynesian paradigm of stickiness in the adjustment of nominal wages and
the prices of goods, while a neo-Keynesian school has sought to provide
rigorous microfoundations.[35] According to the new classical doctrine,
wages and goods prices respond flexibly to macroeconomic shocks, with the
implication that the price adjustment process – in the absence of imperfect
information or adjustment costs – would prevent nominal shocks to the
economy from affecting real economic variables.

As emphasized by Krugman (1990, 1993b), among others, the proposition that nominal shocks to the economy have no real effects is difficult to
reconcile with the evidence of strong correlations between nominal and real
exchange rates. The strong correlations are apparent, for example, in figure
4.2, which focuses on two selected pairs of nominal and real bilateral
exchange rates, revealing that there is very little in the behavior of nominal
exchange rates since the early 1970s that has not been associated with
parallel behavior of real exchange rates. Although these correlations could
be explained under the new classical doctrine if nominal shocks were
relatively rare (that is, if the behavior of real and nominal exchange rates
predominantly reflected the influence of real shocks), econometric studies
suggest that real and nominal shocks can each account for a substantial
share of the variance of exchange rates since the early 1970s.[36] Moreover,
even if one remains skeptical of the formal econometric results, anecdotal
evidence about factors contributing to episodes of exchange rate instability
during the past two decades casts strong doubt on the suggestion that most
of the behavior of nominal exchange rates has been attributable to real

[32] The influence of capital mobility on real exchange rate variability is discussed in chapters 10
and 11.   [33] Grilli and Kaminsky (1991).
[34] Mussa (1986), Baxter and Stockman (1989).
[35] Barro (1989) and the references cited therein provide perspectives on various aspects of the
new classical macroeconomics; Mankiw (1993) and the references cited therein, on the new
Keynesian economics.
[36] Bayoumi and Eichengreen (1994), Eichenbaum and Evans (1992), Clarida and Gali (1994).

shocks, and very little to disturbances associated with monetary policy or other nominal shocks.

The strong correlations between nominal and real exchange rates, in combination with formal and anecdotal evidence that nominal shocks have been prevalent, supports exchange rate models with sluggish price adjustment, such as the sticky-price monetary model discussed in chapter 7. The sticky-price view of the world, moreover, has important implications for exchange rate policy.[37] In particular, it supports the notion that a country can achieve a sustained depreciation of its real exchange rate – and thus a sustained improvement in its wage and price competitiveness – through a nominal depreciation of its currency. By the same token, it refutes the notion that no costs are incurred when countries make rigid commitments to a fixed exchange rate regime – or when they take the more extreme step of completely precluding nominal exchange rate changes *vis-à-vis* major trading partners by forming a common currency area.

5   Normative applications of PPP

When a country establishes or adjusts an exchange rate peg, it generally relies on some type of quantitative framework, such as the PPP formula, to help assess the appropriate level for the new parity. As discussed in chapter 10, a number of alternative assessment methods have been suggested in the literature,[38] and a strong awareness has developed of the limitations of relying entirely on PPP calculations. Nevertheless, the PPP framework continues to have widespread appeal as a starting point for such quantitative exercises.

In this connection, there are lessons to be learned from the most famous application – or misapplication – of the PPP formula. The occasion was the British return to the gold standard in April 1925. During the preceding year, deliberations had focused primarily on whether, and when, to re-establish a gold standard; the possibility of returning to gold at an exchange rate devalued from the prewar parity was debated less extensively.[39] Comparisons of British and American wholesale prices suggested that the ratio of national price levels had changed by only 2 or 3 percent since the prewar period, so that sterling would only be 2 or 3 percent overvalued if Britain returned to the prewar parity.[40] Furthermore, by early 1925, following the election to Parliament of an overwhelming Conservative majority in late October 1924, the pound had already appreciated into the neighborhood of the old parity.

[37] Krugman (1990).
[38] Artus (1978), Williamson (1983), Frenkel and Goldstein (1986), Bayoumi *et al.* (1994).
[39] Moggridge (1972, p. 84), Kindleberger (1984, pp. 337–41).
[40] Moggridge (1972, pp. 71, 89).

One of the most prominent opponents of a return to the prewar parity was John Maynard Keynes. Keynes argued that money wages and the cost of living were not adequately reflected by wholesale price indices as they were then constructed. In testimony given to a parliamentary committee, he suggested that sterling would be 12 percent overvalued at the prewar parity, based on a comparison of British and American retail prices.[41] The Chancellor of the Exchequer, Winston Churchill, included Keynes among the experts with whom he consulted. But Churchill either was not persuaded that British wages would have to be forced down, or misunderstood and underrated the consequences for unemployment and industrial strife. Subsequent to the decision to return to the prewar parity, in an essay castigating Churchill's advisors, Keynes noted that the prevailing wholesale price indices were

made up ... at least two thirds from the raw materials of international commerce, the prices of which necessarily adjust themselves to the exchanges ... [I]ndex numbers of the cost of living, of the level of wages, and of the prices of our manufactured exports ... are a much better rough-and-ready guide.[42]

In the event, the macroeconomic consequences predicted by Keynes proved to be correct.[43]

Economists today, when using the PPP methodology to help assess whether an exchange rate parity is sustainable, are still unable to agree on the most appropriate indices of prices or costs.[44] The more popular candidates include GNP deflators, consumer price indices, and indices of unit labor costs. What is different for the industrialized economies today, however, is that all these indices predominantly reflect the prices or costs of finished goods and services, unlike the particular wholesale price indices on which Churchill's advisors relied.[45]

6   Concluding perspectives

Much of the literature relating nominal exchange rates to national price levels has focused on the validity of the PPP hypothesis. A number of persuasive counterarguments have emerged to challenge this hypothesis on

[41] Moggridge (1972, pp. 43, 105–6). Throughout the deliberations over sterling's competitiveness, apparently no consideration was given to the exchange rates of the pound against currencies other than the US dollar.
[42] Keynes (1925, p. 11).
[43] Nurkse (1944, p. 128) notes that the British mistake was repeated by Czechoslovakia in 1934, when the exchange rate was devalued by 16 percent on the basis of inappropriate PPP calculations, such that another devaluation was required two years later.
[44] See Turner and Van 't dack (1993) for comparisons.
[45] Even so, Wren-Lewis et al. (1991) provide a study based on modern price indices that implicitly suggests the dangers of relying solely on PPP calculations.

conceptual grounds. Quite apart from the degree to which the hypothesis is valid, PPP suggests a relationship between endogenous variables and does not provide a complete model of the nominal exchange rate.

In general, the empirical evidence rejects PPP as a hypothesis about the short-run or medium-run relationship between nominal exchange rates and national price indices. The evidence on long-run PPP is still a matter of debate. Real exchange rates constructed from general price indices for tradables and nontradables combined have exhibited large and persistent fluctuations over the medium run and, in some cases, have exhibited significant long-run trends, particularly for countries in which real incomes relative to the rest of the world have exhibited significant trends. This being said, however, both theory and empirical evidence suggest that PPP has a high degree of validity for general price indices during hyperinflations or other episodes when changes in national price levels primarily reflect monetary causes rather than factors generating changes in intra-country relative prices.

The empirical evidence also suggests that the short-term variability of real exchange rates is sensitive to the nature of the nominal exchange rate regime. Along with other evidence, this presents a challenge for the new classical paradigm of macroeconomics, while providing support for the Keynesian view that nominal wages and prices respond sluggishly to economic shocks.

Rejection of PPP as a medium-run hypothesis by no means implies that the behavior of real exchange rates is a random walk, or that the behavior of nominal exchange rates is independent of the behavior of relative national price levels. To draw this false inference would be to suggest that the pressures of international competition have little direct or indirect influence on domestic price and wage setting. It would also suggest, other things being equal, that nominal exchange rates do not respond systematically to the large imbalances of trade in goods and services that can result from divergent trends in the price-competitiveness of different countries. From a policy perspective, the evidence against PPP over the medium run, together with the view that nominal wages and prices respond sluggishly to economic shocks, supports the notion that a country can achieve a sustained improvement in its wage and price competitiveness through a nominal depreciation of its currency, while refuting the notion that no costs are incurred when countries take the step of committing to a fixed exchange rate regime or forming a common currency area.

Most economists believe that the links between nominal exchange rates and national general price levels over the medium run – while not conforming to the PPP hypothesis – are nevertheless quite strong. Thus, as subsequent chapters emphasize, most single-equation reduced-form models of nominal exchange rates include national price levels, or their underlying determinants, as explanatory variables. Moreover, many large-scale macroeconometric models incorporate simultaneous two-way causation (direct or indirect) between nominal exchange rates and national price levels.

Given that international competitiveness is an important consideration in setting an exchange rate parity, PPP has found a place in normative economics as a quantitative framework that can help policymakers assess the appropriateness of exchange rates. If used intelligently, along with other approaches to assessment, PPP calculations can have significant diagnostic value.[46]

---

[46] Other approaches are discussed in chapter 10.

5   Exchange rates and interest rates

By the late nineteenth century, thanks partly to the experience gained in conducting British monetary policy during the gold standard era, it was common knowledge among policymakers that the behavior of exchange rates could be influenced through the adjustment of interest rates. By raising domestic interest rates, the foreign exchange value of the domestic currency unit could be strengthened. Likewise, by reducing domestic interest rates, the authorities could resist an undesired appreciation of the domestic currency.

The perception that exchange rates and interest rates were intimately related was reinforced as knowledge of the forward exchange market spread through practical banking circles during the second half of the nineteenth century.[1] The threads of a theory of forward exchange – explaining the difference between forward and spot exchange rates in terms of the differential between domestic and foreign interest rates – stretch back to Lotz (1889).[2] However, it was not until organized trading in forward exchange expanded rapidly following World War I that Keynes (1923) wove together the first systematic presentation.[3] Today, this theory is commonly referred to as the interest rate parity hypothesis.

The two main forms of the interest rate parity hypothesis – covered interest parity and uncovered interest parity – are discussed in the first section of this chapter. The second section surveys the empirical evidence on covered interest parity. The uncovered interest parity hypothesis, unlike covered interest parity, is formulated in terms of expected future exchange rates and cannot be convincingly tested in isolation, owing to the limited availability and questionable quality of data on exchange rate expectations. For the most part, uncovered interest parity has therefore been assessed jointly with the hypothesis that exchange rate expectations are rational and unbiased. The joint hypothesis – often called the efficient market hypothesis

---

[1] Einzig (1970, p. 214).   [2] Einzig (1970, p. 214).
[3] Keynes (1923), Einzig (1970, p. 275). The 1923 exposition was based to some extent on material published during 1922 in the Reconstruction Supplements of the *Manchester Guardian Commercial*.

– implies that interest rate differentials should be unbiased predictors of changes in exchange rates, which can be tested empirically. The third section describes the evidence on this efficient market or interest rate unbiasedness hypothesis. The fourth section considers several possible interpretations of the prediction bias and their implications for the validity of the uncovered interest parity hypothesis and the assumption that market participants have rational expectations. The fifth section discusses the data that are available from surveys of exchange rate expectations, and what these data suggest about the possible explanations of prediction bias. The sixth section provides concluding perspectives.

1 The interest rate parity hypothesis

Merchants engaged in international trade often enter into contracts to deliver or receive foreign currency at a future date. So do many investors with international portfolios. Such contracts expose the parties involved to the risks of losses or gains from changes in exchange rates during the periods before the foreign currency payments become due.

As noted in chapter 2, the forward exchange market provides a mechanism for eliminating the exchange rate uncertainty associated with future foreign currency payments. In particular, the forward market provides a way of arranging in advance to convert domestic currency into foreign currency, or vice versa, on the future payment date at a prespecified forward exchange rate.

In developing a theory of how the forward exchange rate behaves, Keynes focused on the variation over time in the difference between forward and spot exchange rates and sought to explain the causes. He reasoned that:

If dollars one month forward are quoted cheaper than spot dollars to a London buyer in terms of sterling, this indicates a preference by the market, on balance, in favor of holding funds in New York in the month in question rather than in London, – a preference the degree of which is measured by the discount on forward dollars.[4]

He then considered the factors that could be regarded as determinants of the market's preference for holding funds in one international center rather than another, listing the interest rate differential as "the most fundamental cause."[5]

Formally, the argument can be stated as follows. Suppose that r_t and r_t^* are the interest rates that can be earned between times t and $t+1$ on local currency investments in countries A and B, respectively. Also let S_t and F_t be

---

[4] Keynes (1923, p. 123).   [5] Keynes (1923, p. 124).

the spot and forward exchange rates between the currencies of the two countries, measured in units of currency A per unit currency B, with s_t and f_t denoting the logarithms of S_t and F_t. Note that one unit of currency B converted at the spot exchange rate and held in a currency A-denominated investment would accumulate to $S_t(1+r_t)$ units of currency A at time $t+1$. Alternatively, under a forward contract arranged at time t, the initial unit of currency B could be held in a currency B-denominated investment until time $t+1$ and then converted into $F_t(1+r_t^*)$ units of currency A. Accordingly, if the two investment opportunities were regarded as equivalent in all respects other than their currency denominations and interest rates, market pressures would tend to generate an equilibrium outcome with

$$F_t(1+r_t^*) = S_t(1+r_t). \tag{5.1}$$

This would imply[6]

$$\frac{F_t - S_t}{S_t} \approx f_t - s_t \approx r_t - r_t^*. \tag{5.2}$$

This relationship, whether described in the strict form of (5.1) or the approximate form of (5.2), is known as the covered interest parity (CIP) condition. It provides an expression for the forward premium or discount (that is, the proportionate difference between the levels of the forward rate and the spot rate, or the simple difference between the logarithms of the forward and spot rates) that merchants or investors would have to pay at time t to hedge or "cover" the exchange rate risk associated with a contract to receive or deliver foreign currency at time $t+1$.

The derivation of the covered interest parity condition is based on a comparison of two alternative ways of accumulating currency A at time $t+1$ from one unit of currency B at time t. A third alternative is to hold the initial unit of currency B in a currency B-denominated investment and convert into currency A at the spot exchange rate that prevails at time $t+1$, leading to an accumulation of $S_{t+1}(1+r_t^*)$ units of currency A. Under this third alternative, however, the investor remains uncertain about the exchange rate until the date of conversion arrives: the foreign exchange risk is left uncovered during the interval between time t and time $t+1$.

The hypothesis of uncovered interest parity (UIP) postulates that market forces equilibrate the return that investors expect to earn on the uncovered investment alternative to the return on the riskless option of converting into currency A initially.[7] In particular, if $E_t S_{t+1}$ denotes the expected value at

[6] Note that, for $1+r_t^*$ and $1+r_t$ close to 1, (5.1) implies
$$F_t/S_t = 1 + (r_t - r_t^*)/(1+r_t^*) \approx 1 + r_t - r_t^* \text{ and hence } f_t - s_t \approx r_t - r_t^*.$$

[7] The conceptual framework from which this hypothesis emerges as a special case is generally referred to as the international asset pricing model; see Meese (1989) or Hodrick (1987) for description and references to the literature.

time t of the spot exchange rate at $t+1$, the UIP hypothesis can be expressed as

$$E_t S_{t+1}(1 + r_t^*) = S_t(1 + r_t).$$ (5.3)

This is approximately the same as

$$E_t s_{t+1} - s_t \approx r_t - r_t^*.$$ (5.4)

Note that, in combination, the CIP and UIP hypotheses imply

$$E_t s_{t+1} \approx f_t.$$ (5.5)

Note also that CIP and UIP can be written for any duration of the time period between t and $t+1$. Thus, if both hypotheses and, accordingly, (5.5) were valid at all horizons, the observed term structure of forward exchange rates – or, from (5.2), the spot exchange rate and the observed term structures of domestic and foreign interest rates – could be used to infer the entire expected future time path of the spot exchange rate.[8]

From a policy perspective, interest in the validity of UIP derives partly from the debate over the effectiveness of official intervention in exchange markets – that is, actions by national authorities to push exchange rates up or down by buying and selling currencies themselves. To the extent that UIP is valid, official intervention cannot successfully change the prevailing spot exchange rate relative to the expected future spot rate unless the authorities allow interest rates to change. Thus, according to views that were widely held during the 1970s, if UIP was valid, exchange market intervention – insofar as its effects on the monetary base (or interest rates) were sterilized – would not provide the authorities with an effective policy instrument in addition to the monetary base (or interest rates). Consequently, the case for sterilized intervention was thought to depend on whether the UIP hypothesis could be rejected.[9] More recently, it has become recognized that, even if UIP was valid, sterilized intervention could be effective if it signaled new information about the intentions of policymakers to adjust interest rates or other policy instruments, as necessary, in order to achieve their exchange rate objectives.[10] The effectiveness of sterilized intervention is discussed in chapters 8 and 9.

A central assumption of the CIP hypothesis, and hence also of UIP, is the premise that the relevant currency A-denominated investments and currency B-denominated investments are equivalent in all respects other than

[8] Porter (1971).
[9] See Henderson and Sampson (1983) for a summary of various studies prepared as background material for an influential Report issued by the Working Group on Exchange Market Intervention, which was established in June 1982 at the Versailles Summit of leaders of the Group of Seven countries.
[10] Mussa (1981), Obstfeld (1990), Edison (1993).

their currency denominations and interest rates. Keynes, in fact, did not suggest this premise and, indeed, viewed CIP as, at best, a reasonable approximation, owing to the different credit risks associated with holding deposit balances in different countries.

If questions of credit did not enter in, the factor of the rate of interest on short loans would be the dominating one. Indeed, as between London and New York, it probably is so under existing conditions. Between London and Paris it is still important. But elsewhere the various uncertainties of financial and political risk, which the war has left behind, introduce a further element which sometimes quite transcends the factor of relative interest. The possibility of financial trouble or political disturbance, and the quite appreciable probability of a moratorium in the event of any difficulties arising, or of the sudden introduction of exchange regulations which would interfere with the movement of balances out of the country, and even sometimes the contingency of a drastic demonetisation, – all these factors deter bankers, even when the exchange risk proper is eliminated, from maintaining large floating balances at certain foreign centres. Such risks prevent the business from being based, as it should be, on a mathematical calculation of interest rate ... [parity].[11]

The views expressed by Keynes reflected the perspectives of the 1920s. Subsequently, extensive changes in international financial markets have made CIP a much more respectable hypothesis. In particular, the assets available to investors nowadays include many pairs of financial instruments that do indeed differ only with respect to their currencies of denomination and interest rates – such as dollar deposits and sterling deposits located at the same branch of the same bank. Such investment alternatives are subject to identical credit risks, capital controls, and explicit taxes; and for these cases the evidence suggests that the CIP hypothesis is almost always valid, with occasional exceptions during periods of exchange market turbulence.

2   Empirical evidence on covered interest parity

The empirical evidence on CIP comes from two sources: interviews with marketmakers, and studies of recorded data on exchange rates and interest rates. The interview findings reveal that CIP is actually used as a formula for determining the exchange rates and interest rates at which trading is conducted.[12] In particular, foreign exchange traders at marketmaking banks use interest rates on bank deposits denominated in different currencies to determine the forward exchange premiums or discounts that they

---

[11] Keynes (1923, pp. 126–7).
[12] Herring and Marston (1976), Marston (1976), Levich (1985).

quote to customers. At the same time, decisionmakers in other parts of the banks use the spreads between forward and spot exchange rates to set the interest rates they offer on foreign currency deposits relative to those on domestic currency deposits.

The second source of empirical evidence on CIP – studies of recorded data on exchange rates and interest rates – has not always generated the same impression as the interview findings. Initially, such studies tended to rely on interest rate data associated with claims on different countries and found that deviations from CIP appeared to be quite prevalent. Accordingly, various attempts were made to rationalize such deviations in terms of political risk,[13] capital controls,[14] or transactions costs.[15] As noted earlier, it is generally accepted that CIP is not a valid hypothesis when the interest rates are not associated with claims that are essentially identical in all respects other than their currency denominations and interest rates.[16]

The results of the initial studies stimulated subsequent investigators to select their data very carefully. In particular, some of the subsequent studies not only refrained from using interest rates associated with different sources of credit, but also devoted considerable effort to avoiding the data distortions that can arise when tests for CIP are based on exchange rate and interest rate observations that were recorded at slightly different points of time.

Among the most noteworthy efforts of this sort are those of Taylor (1987, 1989),[17] who constructed a data base of the bid and offer rates quoted contemporaneously for exchange rates and interest rates by foreign exchange and money market brokers, as recorded on the "pad" of the chief dealer at the Bank of England. Taylor's methodology for testing CIP was to calculate whether it was ever profitable for a trader to conduct covered arbitrage either from sterling to dollars – that is, to borrow sterling, convert spot into dollars, lend dollars, and arrange forward to reconvert the dollar proceeds back into sterling – or from dollars to sterling.[18] The data set employed by Taylor (1989) consisted of two or three observations per day for one-, two-, three-, six-, and twelve-month maturities during six historical episodes of up to three weeks each. The six episodes were chosen to include five periods of exchange market turbulence spaced over two

---

[13] Aliber (1973).   [14] Dooley and Isard (1980).

[15] Branson (1969), Frenkel and Levich (1975, 1977).

[16] Marston (1993) contrasts covered interest differentials during periods with and without capital controls, also pointing to evidence of significant covered interest disparities on assets subject to different default risks during periods without capital controls.

[17] See also McCormick (1979) and Clinton (1988).

[18] Slightly different formulas are appropriate in calculating the profitability of covered arbitrage in the two different directions; in particular, where arbitrage in one direction involves bid rates, arbitrage in the other direction involves offer rates, and vice versa.

decades, along with a control period during which "no significant news occurred."[19]

Taylor's study reached three broad conclusions. First, it confirmed his earlier finding that there was no evidence of unexploited profit opportunities during relatively calm periods in foreign exchange and money markets, while also indicating that

potentially exploitable profitable arbitrage opportunities do occasionally occur during periods of turbulence.[20]

Second, it noted that "fewer and smaller profit opportunities" seemed to arise during the later periods of turbulence than during the earlier periods, suggesting that market efficiency had increased over time. Third, it found that

the frequency, size, and persistence of profitable arbitrage opportunities appear to be positive functions of the length of maturity examined.[21]

The third finding suggests that the first set of evidence needs to be interpreted carefully. Discrepancies from CIP during times of market turbulence may partly reflect the limited ability of market participants to process information quickly, but it seems there is more to the story than this. In particular, the evidence that the extent of such discrepancies is related to maturity calls for an explanation of why foreign exchange traders tend to be more reluctant to exploit profit opportunities at longer than they are at shorter maturities. The apparent explanation is that bank managers, for prudential reasons, generally place limits on the total liabilities that the bank may have outstanding to each other bank or nonbank customer at any point in time, and the prospect of small arbitrage profits may not compensate for the opportunity cost of keeping these credit limits "full" for a lengthy period.[22]

3   Interest differentials as predictors of exchange rate changes

Unlike CIP, the UIP hypothesis involves the expected value of the future spot exchange rate – a variable on which available data are limited in scope

---

[19] The five episodes of turbulence were periods that surrounded the devaluation of sterling in November 1967, the flotation of sterling in June 1972, the inception of the European Monetary System in March 1979, the UK general election of May 1979, and the UK general election of June 1987. The control period surrounded the US presidential election of November 1984, in which "a Republican victory was widely anticipated."

[20] Taylor (1989, p. 389).

[21] Taylor (1989, p. 386). This third finding is supported by anecdotal evidence reported by Group of Ten Deputies (1993).

[22] Taylor (1989, pp. 388–9). See also Hilley, Beidleman, and Greenleaf (1981).

and of questionable quality, as discussed further below. The absence of reliable data on exchange rate expectations makes it difficult to reach definitive conclusions about the validity of UIP.

The UIP hypothesis, however, is inherently not very interesting by itself. It becomes much more interesting when combined with the notion that the expected future spot rate, even if unobservable, can be regarded as a predictor of the actual future spot rate – that is,

$$s_{t+1} = E_t s_{t+1} + u_{t+1} \tag{5.6}$$

where u_{t+1} denotes the prediction error. Together with (5.4) and (5.5), (5.6) implies that the change in the spot rate can be predicted by the interest differential

$$s_{t+1} - s_t = r_t - r_t^* + u_{t+1} \tag{5.7}$$

or that the level of the spot rate can be predicted by the forward rate

$$s_{t+1} = f_t + u_{t+1}. \tag{5.8}$$

In evaluating the interest differential as a predictor of the change in the spot exchange rate, or the forward rate as a predictor of the level of the spot rate, one naturally wants to assess the general magnitude of the prediction errors. A second issue is whether the predictions have been systematically biased. Both issues have major relevance in considering the appropriateness of different conceptual and empirical models of exchange rate behavior.

With regard to the size of prediction errors, it has become widely acknowledged that interest differentials explain only a small proportion of subsequent changes in exchange rates.[23] This can be seen in table 5.1, which provides data on bilateral exchange rates between the three key currencies and three selected European currencies. Column (1) shows average absolute values of the actual quarter-to-quarter percentage changes in exchange rates, while column (2) shows the average absolute values of the percentage changes predicted *ex ante* by the corresponding 3-month Eurocurrency interest differentials. Not only were the predicted changes much smaller on average than the actual changes, but for three of the four exchange rates shown the "unpredicted changes" – that is, the actual changes minus the predicted changes – exceeded the actual changes in average absolute value. Roughly speaking, for these three exchange rates, the sum of the absolute values of those predicted changes that were not even in the same direction as the changes that actually occurred outweighed the corresponding sum for predicted changes that proved correct in direction.[24]

---

[23] Isard (1978), Mussa (1979), Frenkel (1981).

[24] This explanation would be precise if the actual changes always exceeded the predicted changes in absolute value.

Table 5.1. *Predicted and unpredicted components of exchange rate changes, 1980–94*

	Average absolute value of		
	Actual change[a] (1)	Predicted change[b] (2)	Unpredicted change[c] (3)
Japanese yen per US dollar	5.15	0.26	5.12
Deutsche marks per US dollar	5.75	0.29	5.84
French francs per Deutsche mark	1.12	0.45	1.18
Austrian schillings per Deutsche mark[d]	0.40	0.08	0.43

Notes:
[a] Percentage change from end of previous quarter to end of current quarter.
[b] 3-month Eurocurrency interest differential at end of previous quarter, in percent per quarter.
[c] Actual change minus predicted change.
[c] Based on data for 1987–94.
Sources: Exchange rates from International Monetary Fund, *International Financial Statistics*; Eurocurrency interest rates from Data Resources Inc. and Reuters.

The widespread evidence that interest differentials tend to predict only a small component of the changes in exchange rates that actually occur (and often mispredict the direction of change) has been generally interpreted as implying that the predominant part of observed changes in exchange rates is triggered by unexpected information – or "news" – about economic statistics, policies, or other relevant developments. A related empirical observation is that the variances of contemporaneous spot and forward exchange rates are essentially the same over any data sample during the period since 1973,[25] consistent with CIP and the fact that the interest differential or forward premium represents a small proportion of the variation in the spot rate.

The second issue – whether predictions have been systematically biased – is often referred to as a question of whether the foreign exchange market is "efficient."[26] In turn, the efficient market hypothesis has sometimes been viewed as an implication of the hypothesis that market participants are risk neutral and form their expectations rationally, given whatever relevant information is available.

[25] Mussa (1979). See also Poole (1967).
[26] See the discussion in Baillie and McMahon (1989).

In testing the efficient market hypothesis, extensive regression analysis has been conducted on the specification forms[27]

$$s_{t+1} = a_0 + a_1 f_t + u_{t+1} \qquad (5.9)$$

and

$$s_{t+1} - s_t = b_0 + b_1 (r_t - r_t^*) + u_{t+1}. \qquad (5.10)$$

Under the assumption that exchange rate expectations are formed rationally, conditional on whatever relevant information is available, the expectational errors u_{t+1} are taken to be serially uncorrelated with zero means, and the unbiasedness hypothesis is then $a_1 = 1$ or $b_1 = 1$. Some studies have also tested for $a_0 = 0$ or $b_0 = 0$. The tests have generally focused on data for which CIP is valid.

Notably, the hypothesis that the slope coefficient is unity receives strong support from studies based on (5.9), but is soundly rejected by studies based on (5.10). The apparent conflict between the two sets of regression evidence, however, has been resolved in favor of the latter finding. In particular, it is now accepted that (5.9) is not a legitimate regression equation,[28] and accordingly, that the hypothesis of unbiasedness is very strongly rejected by the data.[29] Indeed, there is a large body of regression evidence in which estimates of b_1 not only are significantly different than one, but in many cases are negative.[30]

4   Possible explanations of prediction bias

Economists have not yet resolved how to interpret the strong rejection of the unbiasedness hypothesis. Several alternative explanations have been suggested. The different explanations lead to different views on the appropriate way to analyze the behavior of exchange rates.

The different possible interpretations can be divided into several categories. One category rejects the UIP hypothesis but not the rational expectations assumption, providing explanations based on risk premiums. A second category consists of conjectures that do not require the rejection of either the UIP hypothesis or the rational expectations assumption, including explanations based on the "peso problem," simultaneity bias, incom-

---

[27] See Meese (1989) for further discussion of the conceptual basis for these specification forms, including the terms a_0 and b_0.

[28] Meese (1989, p. 164). The explanation is based on the fact that the sample variances of the spot rate and the forward rate are essentially equal.

[29] Hodrick (1987, p. 4), Meese (1989, p. 165).

[30] Froot and Thaler (1990). Hansen and Hodrick (1980) and Bilson (1981) were among the first to draw attention to such findings.

plete information with rational learning, and self-fulfilling prophecies or rational "bubbles." A third category abandons the assumption that all market participants are fully rational.

The conjecture that the prediction bias reflects the existence of risk premiums, and consequently, that the UIP hypothesis should be abandoned, has argued in favor of the portfolio-balance approach to exchange rate analysis. This approach, as discussed in subsequent chapters, has directed attention at building conceptual models of the risk premium (ξ), generally defined as the deviation from UIP

$$\xi_t = f_t - E_t s_{t+1}. \tag{5.11}$$

Substitution from (5.2) yields

$$\xi_t = s_t + r_t - r_t^* - E_t s_{t+1} \tag{5.12}$$

which combines with (5.6) to imply

$$s_{t+1} - s_t = r_t - r_t^* - \xi_t + u_{t+1}. \tag{5.13}$$

This suggests, by comparison with (5.7), that the prediction bias may be the result of an omitted variable problem which can be addressed by extending the right-hand side of (5.10) to include a behavioral model of ξ_t.

A second possible explanation, known as the "peso problem," was suggested by Rogoff (1980) and Krasker (1980), taking its name after an episode in which the Mexican peso sold at a forward discount for a prolonged period prior to its widely-anticipated devaluation in 1976.[31] Although market expectations eventually proved correct and may well have been rational *ex ante*, the fact that the devaluation did not materialize immediately after it first became anticipated made the forward rate a biased predictor over finite data samples that included the predevaluation period. The general point is that, even if expectations are formed rationally, within finite data samples the forward rate can be biased as a predictor of the future spot rate whenever market participants repeatedly expect the spot rate to change in response to a policy action or some other event that fails to materialize over a relatively long sequence of observations. As a related point, the peso problem can explain the negative estimates of b_1 in (5.10).[32]

A third possible explanation of the regression evidence, emphasized by McCallum (1994), is that the estimates of b_1 may be biased by the failure to estimate (5.10) simultaneously with a second relationship between the

---

[31] See Lewis (1992). Lizondo (1983) helped define the phenomenon further by postulating how traders with rational expectations formed their forecasts. Salant and Henderson (1978) presented the first theoretical analysis of a peso-type problem in modeling the price of gold.

[32] Lewis (1988), Obstfeld (1989). Obstfeld notes that peso problems can also rationalize the finding of seemingly predictable and conditionally heteroskedastic forward forecast errors.

interest differential and the change in the exchange rate.[33] The existence of a second relationship is suggested by the fact that the monetary authorities in most industrial countries rely on short-term interest rates as policy instruments that they are prepared to adjust in response, *inter alia*, to undesired exchange rate movements.[34] Some indirect support for this view is provided by an empirical finding analogous to the negative estimates of b_1 – namely, the finding that single-equation regressions of changes in exchange rates on the level of exchange market intervention have also generated statistically significant coefficients with the wrong sign and, thus, also suggest a problem of simultaneity bias.[35]

A fourth possible explanation of prediction bias, suggested by Lewis (1988, 1989), is that market participants do not have complete information and have been engaged in a process of rational learning about changes in the monetary policy regime or other structural shifts that affect the behavior of exchange rates. This suggestion is analogous to the peso problem insofar as it provides an interpretation in which market participants are viewed as fully rational but prone to making repeated mistakes.

A fifth conjecture – that the prediction bias might result from self-fulfilling prophecies of rational market participants, often referred to as rational "bubbles" – has received attention as a logical possibility; but few economists, if any, consider it to have much plausibility as an empirical phenomenon. The theoretical scope for rational bubbles reflects the fact that many rational expectations models have indeterminacies.[36] Such indeterminacies arise, for example, in the class of exchange rate models that have the reduced form

$$s_t = x_t + bE_t s_{t+1} \qquad \text{with } 0 < b < 1 \tag{5.14}$$

where x_t depends on some relevant set of economic variables and b is a

---

[33] McCallum (1994) does not defend the UIP condition defined by (5.4); however, he departs from traditional semantics in referring to (5.12) – which he does defend – as the UIP hypothesis. Semantics aside, McCallum argues that (5.12) is more realistic than (5.4), particularly in a world in which different market participants have different expectations, since it allows for time-varying aggregation "errors" and other measurement errors, as well as for exchange-risk premia. He also notes (p. 109) that (5.12) appears as

a key behavioral relationship in virtually all the prominent current-day models of exchange rate determination . . . [including] multicountry econometric models.

[34] As noted by Isard (1988), even if the authorities did not react directly to exchange rate movements, central bank behavior that tends to hold short-term interest rates relatively constant, and hence to suppress the variability of the interest differential relative to the variability of factors influencing ξ_t in (5.13), can potentially explain the fact that estimates of (5.10) have typically yielded negative values of b_1; see also Boyer and Adams (1988).

[35] Domínguez and Frankel (1993a).

[36] Blanchard (1979) and Flood and Hodrick (1990), who cite early contributions on the topic by Brock (1974), Taylor (1977), and Shiller (1978).

constant parameter.[37] Through forward iteration of (5.14), it can be shown that the expectation at time t of the value of the exchange rate at time $t + k$ is

$$E_t s_{t+k} = E_t z_{t+k} + B_k \tag{5.15}$$

for

$$z_{t+k} = \sum_{j=0}^{\infty} b^j x_{t+k+j} \tag{5.16}$$

and

$$B_k = c(1/b)^k \tag{5.17}$$

where c is an arbitrary number.[38] Accordingly, in the absence of exogenous disturbances, and with expectations formed rationally and exhibiting perfect foresight, the model has an infinite number of solutions for the timepath of the exchange rate, each corresponding to a different value of c. B corresponds to a rational speculative bubble that grows exponentially over time (since $0 < b < 1$) when c is not equal to zero. The fact that such bubbles, once started, live a life of their own that cannot be deflated by changes in policies or other economic fundamentals, has led some economists to rule out nonzero values of c as absurd solutions.[39] More generally, the theoretical case for ruling out rational bubbles is strong,[40] and the fact that the observed variance of forward forecast errors does not explode over time also suggests that rational bubbles are an unlikely explanation of the forward rate prediction bias.[41]

These five possible explanations of forward rate bias – each consistent with the rational expectations hypothesis – have been investigated in a number of empirical studies.[42] Although the prevailing opinion today is that none of the five interpretations by itself provides a sufficiently convincing explanation,[43] in combination several of them deserve further attention. In this connection, chapter 9 presents a framework for characterizing the risk premium when the source of risk is the type of policy action on

---

[37] As discussed in chapters 7 and 8, such a model has been developed by Mussa (1976), Bilson (1978a), and Frenkel and Mussa (1980, 1985), in which $b = \lambda/(1 + \lambda)$, where λ can be interpreted as the absolute value of the interest rate semi-elasticity of the demand for money.

[38] Mussa (1990).   [39] Mussa (1990).   [40] Obstfeld and Rogoff (1986).

[41] Obstfeld (1989), who also points to the Flood and Garber (1980) argument that bubbles are observationally equivalent to changes in the process generating the exogenous variables. Accordingly, Obstfeld suggests that econometric results purporting to show the existence of bubbles are more likely to be the result of misspecifying agents' information sets.

[42] For example, Meese (1986), Borensztein (1987), Froot and Frankel (1989), Evans and Lewis (1992a, 1992b), Kaminsky (1993), and Edison (1993).

[43] Froot and Thaler (1990), Krugman (1993b).

which the peso-problem literature has focused. Chapter 10 discusses the possibility that exchange rate expectations may not be fully rational; it also returns to the conjecture that market participants may be rational but endowed with limited information and therefore engaged in a continuing process of drawing inferences from information generated by the market trading process.

5 Inferences from survey data

Analysis of the various possible explanations for the rejection of the unbiasedness hypothesis has focused attention, *inter alia*, on the data that are available from surveys of exchange rate expectations. Such data have been collected by several different sources since the early 1980s.[44] The surveys reveal that exchange rate expectations, measured by the average forecasts of sample respondents, have deviated considerably from prevailing forward exchange rates. To the extent that such survey measures are meaningful and expectations are formed rationally, the apparent discrepancy between exchange rate expectations and forward rates is inconsistent with the UIP assumption, suggesting that the rejection of the unbiasedness hypothesis is attributable, at least in part, to the existence of a risk premium. However, when the change in the spot exchange rate expected by survey respondents is regressed on the interest rate differential, the slope coefficient does not differ significantly from one. The average survey responses thus provide no support for the view that rejection of the unbiasedness hypothesis can be attributed to a risk premium that varies over time.[45]

Analysis of panel data from one of the surveys, focusing on time series observations of the exchange rate expectations of each individual respondent, has been much more informative.[46] Such analysis reveals that market participants have heterogeneous expectations, calling into question the appropriateness of the traditional assumption that aggregate behavior can be inferred from the optimizing decisions of a single representative agent. It also indicates, however, that individual respondents tend to have biased forecasts of future spot exchange rates, implying that the observed bias in consensus or average forecasts cannot be simply attributed to the fact that heterogeneous agents base their individual forecasts on different "private information sets."

Another finding from the survey data – both at the micro level and in the

---

[44] Frankel and Froot (1987, 1990), Takagi (1991).

[45] Frankel and Froot (1990, p. 4). See also Liu and Maddala (1992).

[46] Ito (1990). See also Bryant (1995a), who finds little merit in the conventional use of regression analysis to test for, or try to explain, the risk premium.

consensus forecasts – is that expectations for relatively short horizons tend to extrapolate recent observed changes in exchange rates, while expectations for longer horizons tend to forecast a reversal of recent observed changes.[47] Some studies have emphasized the difficulty of formulating internally consistent hypotheses about expectations formation that can explain this "twist" in the survey data, but these studies have also noted that this difficulty may be a reflection of peso problems.[48] The issue of how to interpret the twist in the data is discussed further in chapter 10.

6   Concluding perspectives

In academic circles during the past two decades, discussions of the relationship between exchange rates and interest rates have focused to a large extent on the two main forms of the interest rate parity hypothesis, as well as on the finding that interest rate differentials are biased predictors of changes in exchange rates. There is strong evidence that, except during rare episodes of financial market turbulence, the covered interest parity hypothesis is valid when the interest rates are associated with claims that differ only in their currencies of denomination and interest rates, and when the data on interest rates and exchange rates can indeed be regarded as simultaneous observations. Covered interest parity is not generally observed, however, when the interest rates are associated with claims on different creditors – in particular, claims on the governments or private residents of different countries.

To the extent that expectations about future exchange rates are unobservable, or that survey data on exchange rate expectations are suspect, the uncovered interest parity hypothesis cannot be reliably tested on its own. It is possible, however, to test jointly the uncovered interest parity hypothesis and the hypothesis that the expected level of the future spot rate is an unbiased predictor of the actual future spot rate. In particular, the two propositions are jointly equivalent to the hypothesis that the observable interest differential or forward exchange premium is an unbiased predictor of the change in the spot exchange rate.

Extensive testing has soundly rejected this joint hypothesis, leaving economists to try to rationalize the evidence against unbiasedness. The choice between different conceptual models of exchange rate behavior hinges on how this evidence is interpreted. Several possible interpretations – including risk premiums, peso problems, simultaneity bias, incomplete information with rational learning, and rational speculative bubbles – are

---

[47] Frankel and Froot (1988, 1990), Ito (1990, 1994).
[48] Froot and Ito (1989), Ito (1990, 1994).

consistent with the assumption that exchange rate expectations are formed rationally. Although none of these interpretations by itself is widely regarded as a convincing explanation of the empirical evidence, several are plausible as partial explanations and are discussed further in chapters 9 and 10. As an alternative to models in which expectations are rational and uniform among market participants, a number of economists have begun to develop models in which one group of market participants acts rationally on the basis of expectations about future fundamentals, while another group bases its expectations on "technical analysis" of the recent behavior of exchange rates. This direction for model building is also discussed in chapter 10.

In policy circles, interest in the relationship between exchange rates and interest rates arises primarily from the challenge of controlling the behavior of exchange rates through the adjustment of interest rates. Central bankers frequently observe changes in exchange rates in response to interest rate adjustments, and tend to sharply contest the suggestion that changes in interest rates do not have significant effects on exchange rates, other things being equal. At the same time, however, they acknowledge that exchange rates are influenced strongly – perhaps predominantly in many cases – by factors that are exogenous to monetary policy.

In macroeconometric forecasting models, which national authorities have come to rely upon as one of their useful sources of guidance when formulating economic policies, changes in exchange rates generally have important effects on many nominal and real variables, beginning within a year or a few quarters. In recent vintages of these models, expectational variables – including exchange rate expectations – have a major influence on macroeconomic behavior, with the hypothesized relationship between actual and expected exchange rates having an important influence on the predicted behavior of many nominal and real variables. As chapter 8 describes, in most macroeconometric forecasting models today the relationship between current and expected future exchange rates is specified as the uncovered interest parity condition or its extension to include a time-varying premium.

6 Exchange rates and the balance of payments

In addition to recognizing the close links between the behavior of exchange rates and the behavior of national price levels and interest rates, economists have long emphasized the interdependence between exchange rates and the balance of payments. A rudimentary awareness that exchange rates adjust to international payments imbalances can be traced back at least as far as the fourteenth century, when secondary markets had emerged for the bills of exchange issued by different European banking centers.[1] By the early seventeenth century, moreover, the influence of exchange rates and the balance of payments on domestic economic conditions was recognized in British and Italian policy circles, where domestic economic hardships associated with the outflow of specie had raised strong concerns.[2] Since the middle of the twentieth century, major developments in both macroeconomic analysis and the evolution of the world economy – most notably, the Keynesian revolution and the rapid expansion of international capital transactions relative to the growth of international trade – have altered perceptions of the behavioral linkages between exchange rates and the balance of payments. At the same time, analysis of the exchange rate adjustment process has become firmly embedded in conceptual models that focus on the simultaneous pursuit of policy objectives for the balance of external payments and the strength of internal economic activity.

This chapter summarizes several important stages of economic thought on both the relationship of the balance of payments to the exchange rate and the interplay of external and internal pressures for exchange rate adjustment. The first section focuses on early models of the current account – specifically, the elasticities approach and its integration with national income analysis in a static Keynesian framework. The second section focuses on early models of stabilization policy for the open economy – in particular, the early Mundell–Fleming framework, which analyzed the conditions for external and internal balance on the basis of a flow model of

[1] Einzig (1970). Recall also the discussion in chapter 2 (p. 12).
[2] Einzig (1970, pp. 142–3).

the capital account. The third section turns to asset equilibrium models of the balance of payments under fixed exchange rates, with separate attention to the monetary approach and the portfolio balance approach. These asset equilibrium models largely replaced the flow model of the capital account after the mid-1960s and became the basis for modeling the behavior of flexible exchange rates following the collapse of the Bretton Woods system in the early 1970s. The fourth section provides concluding perspectives.

1   Early models of the current account

Macroeconomic modeling during the 1940s and 1950s predominantly reflected the revolution in thinking catalyzed by Keynes (1936). Notably, *The General Theory* had presented a model of a closed or insular economy, with no attempt to incorporate international transactions or exchange rate developments.[3] One of the challenges for economic theorists was thus to add appropriate international dimensions to the Keynesian model of national income determination.

The manner in which the closed economy model was opened reflected two prevailing features of the world economy.[4] First, exchange rates were pegged and infrequently adjusted under the Bretton Woods system. The architects of the system, harboring memories of the poor functioning of both freely floating and fixed-but-uncoordinated exchange rate arrangements during the interwar period, had not only been unwilling to trust markets to set exchange rates, but had also been concerned not to allow countries the autonomy to engage in competitive devaluations.[5] Accordingly, the Articles of Agreement of the International Monetary Fund required countries to notify and obtain the consent of the IMF before changing their par values. Such consent was incumbent upon the emergence of a "fundamental disequilibrium" in a country's balance of payments, as distinct from a temporary deficit that could be financed either by spending reserves or with credit extended by the IMF.[6] Second, throughout the 1950s and into the 1960s, international capital flows remained small relative to the value of merchandise trade.

In this environment, most models of exchange rates and the balance of payments during the 1940s and 1950s treated the current account – and usually simply the trade balance – as the only endogenous component of the overall balance of payments. At the same time, the exchange rate was regarded as either exogenously given or a choice parameter to be fixed by policymakers. Those were also the days before it was common to pay much

[3] McKinnon (1981).   [4] Kenen (1985), Krueger (1983).   [5] Kenen (1985).
[6] Both the concept and the empirical assessment of fundamental disequilibrium were based on the current account balance.

attention to the role of expectations in modeling the behavior of economic variables. Despite these limitations, however, some of the main features of the early current account models continue to be featured in modern forward-looking models of flexible exchange rates. In many of the modern models, as discussed in chapters 7 and 10, expectations about the future path of the exchange rate are constrained to be consistent with a sustainable path for the current account.

The earliest models relating the current account to the exchange rate followed an "elasticities approach" in the Marshallian tradition of treating the exchange rate as a relative price that cleared a market with well-defined flow demand and supply curves. In efforts to address the deficiencies of the early models, subsequent contributions to the literature sought to integrate the elasticities approach with an analysis of the national income accounts in the Keynesian tradition. These latter contributions emphasized that an exchange rate change could only affect the current account balance if it induced a change in domestic absorption relative to domestic production.

Among the most widely cited contributions to the early development of the elasticities approach are Bickerdike (1920), Marshall (1923), Lerner (1944), Robinson (1947), and Metzler (1949). The standard model analyzes the effect of an exchange rate change on the current account in terms of separate markets for home-produced and foreign tradable goods, typically abstracting from the existence of any nontradable goods.

The following streamlined exposition of the model draws heavily on Dornbusch (1975).[7] Export supplies and import demands depend only on nominal prices measured in the home-currency units of exporters and importers, and cross-price effects between markets are ignored. The basic equations are:

$$M(P_M) = X^*(P_M^*) \tag{6.1}$$

$$X(P_X) = M^*(P_X^*) \tag{6.2}$$

$$T = P_X X - P_M M \tag{6.3}$$

$$P_M = SP_M^* \tag{6.4}$$

$$P_X = SP_X^* \tag{6.5}$$

where M (M^*) denotes the quantity of imports that the home (foreign) country demands, X (X^*) denotes the quantity of exports that the home (foreign) country desires to supply, P_M and P_X (P_M^* and P_X^*) are the home-currency (foreign-currency) prices of the home country's import and

---

[7] More extensive discussions can be found in Kenen (1985, section 3), and Krueger (1983, chapter 3).

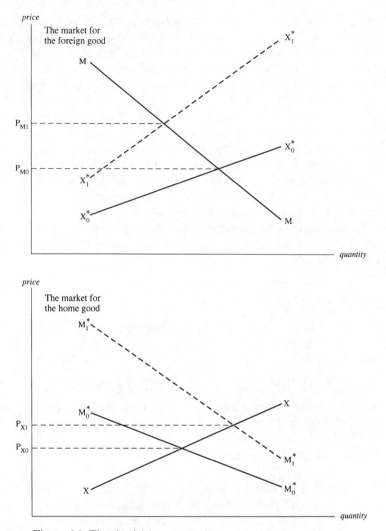

Figure 6.1 The elasticities approach

export goods, S is the nominal exchange rate measured in home currency per unit of foreign currency, and T is the home country's trade (and current account) balance measured in home-currency units. (6.1) and (6.2) describe the market-clearing conditions for the two goods, (6.3) defines the trade balance, while (6.4) and (6.5) assume that the "law of one price" prevails for each good.

In figure 6.1, the solid demand curves (MM, $M_0^* M_0^*$) and supply curves

$(XX, X_0^*X_0^*)$ are drawn for an initial exchange rate S_0 at which the trade balance is in equilibrium, defined as $T=0$. The initial market-clearing prices of the two goods, in home-currency units, are P_{M0} and P_{X0}. The dashed curves $(M_1^*M_1^*, X_1^*X_1^*)$ indicate the new positions of the foreign country's demand and supply curves (as functions of home-currency price) following a devaluation of the home currency; both curves are shifted upward, relative to their solid counterparts, such that prices in home currency increase by the same proportion as the devaluation. The devaluation raises the market-clearing home-currency price of each good, increasing the volume of trade in the home good and reducing the volume of trade in the foreign good. Thus, the home-currency value of the home country's exports increases, while that of its imports may rise or fall, implying that the net effect on the trade balance is ambiguous.

A sufficient condition for the trade balance to improve can be stated in terms of the various demand and supply elasticities. In particular, let the elasticities η, η^*, ε, and ε^* be defined by

$$\hat{M} = -\eta \hat{P}_M \qquad \hat{X} = \varepsilon \hat{P}_X$$
$$\hat{M}^* = -\eta^* \hat{P}_M^* \qquad \hat{X}^* = \varepsilon^* \hat{P}_X^* \tag{6.6}$$

where the $\hat{}$ denotes a proportionate change in a variable. In terms of this notation, (6.1), (6.2), (6.4), and (6.5) imply that the changes in the market-clearing home-currency prices following a change in the exchange rate are[8]

$$\hat{P}_M = [\varepsilon^*/(\varepsilon^* + \eta)]\hat{S} \quad \text{and} \quad \hat{P}_X = [\eta^*/(\varepsilon + \eta^*)]\hat{S}. \tag{6.7}$$

Accordingly, by differentiating (6.3) and using (6.6) and (6.7), it can be shown that when $T=0$ initially,

$$dT/dS > 0 \text{ if and only if } \frac{\eta\eta^*(1 + \varepsilon + \varepsilon^*) - \varepsilon\varepsilon^*(1 - \eta - \eta^*)}{(\varepsilon + \eta^*)(\varepsilon^* + \eta)} > 0. \tag{6.8}$$

This condition is often referred to as the Bickerdike–Robinson–Metzler condition, derived by Bickerdike (1920) and exposited by Robinson (1947) and Metzler (1949).[9] For the special case in which export supplies are infinitely elastic $(\varepsilon = \varepsilon^* = \infty)$, the expression in (6.8) reduces to $(1 - \eta - \eta^*) < 0$; in this case a devaluation of the home-currency unit (that is, an increase in S) improves the trade balance if and only if the sum of the two import demand elasticities is greater than one. The latter inequality is often referred to as the Marshall–Lerner condition.

As described by (6.1)–(6.8), the elasticities approach has a number of limitations. First, the import demand functions and export supply func-

---

[8] To derive (6.7), differentiate (6.1) using (6.4) and substituting from (6.6), and differentiate (6.2) using (6.5) and substituting from (6.6).   [9] Kemp (1992).

tions depend only on the nominal prices of the goods in question, rather than on relative prices and appropriate scale variables such as real income and productive capacity. Second, the very concept of a trade imbalance implies that goods are paid for with an asset that has not been explicitly included in the analysis. Third, changes in the trade balance correspond identically in the national income accounts to changes in the difference between domestic production and domestic absorption, neither of which enters the model explicitly. (6.1)–(6.8) thus provide only a partial equilibrium framework for analyzing the balance-of-payments effects of exchange rate changes.

The early expositors of the elasticities approach recognized its limitations.[10] By the beginning of the 1950s, the effects of a devaluation on national income and/or employment had been modeled formally by Robinson (1947), Harberger (1950), Meade (1951), and Alexander (1952), among others. This new body of analysis – sometimes referred to as the "absorption approach" – was properly perceived not as a rejection of the Marshallian focus on price elasticities, but rather as an attempt to integrate the elasticities approach with the Keynesian focus on national income. The integrated approach emphasized that a devaluation of the home currency, by lowering the relative price of the home good and thereby inducing a shift in the composition of demand, would lead to an increase in home output (unless the economy was initially producing at full capacity) and a decline in foreign output. It was also recognized that the effects on home output and income would have feedback effects on trade flows, and accordingly, that a devaluation that improved the trade balance would do so by less than the amount suggested by a simple elasticities approach in which these feedback effects were ignored.[11] As viewed today, the main limitation of the integrated elasticities–absorption model is that it is based on a static approach to national income analysis rather than an intertemporal optimization approach; this is discussed further in chapter 10.

The static elasticities–absorption model of the current account received a new burst of attention in the early 1970s. The exchange rate changes that followed the collapse of the Bretton Woods system, including in particular the depreciation of the US dollar, renewed interest in the time profiles of the responses of traded-good prices and quantities to changes in the exchange rate. The vocabulary of international economists soon included frequent references to the concept of the "J-curve" – a term meant to convey that a country's current account balance, measured in home-currency units, could be expected initially to deteriorate following a devaluation of the home currency, and only subsequently to improve. The underlying premise was

---

[10] Kenen (1985, p. 646).   [11] Kenen (1985, p. 647).

that, in the short run, import prices in home-currency terms would rise more rapidly than export prices, whereas trade volumes would only respond with a lag. Perceptions about the likely response pattern clouded, however, after economists began to focus more carefully on the currency denominations of trade contracts and the lags involved in passing through prices and adjusting quantities. The more sophisticated analysis suggested that the set of feasible time profiles of the current account following a devaluation resembled "alphabet soup."[12]

2   Early models of stabilization policy for the open economy

In addition to underscoring a need to integrate the elasticities approach with national income analysis in modeling the current account, the extension of Keynesian macroeconomics to the open economy stimulated new perspectives and questions about the conduct of stabilization policy. The pathbreaking contribution came from Meade (1951), who revived the simultaneous analysis of internal and external balance. Following Meade, it soon became common practice – when analyzing the relationship of the balance of payments to exchange rates and other variables – to focus simultaneously on the relationship that determined the level of domestic output or employment.

Another important contribution to the literature during the 1950s was a paper delivered in 1955 but not published until eight years later. Stimulated by the debate over full employment in Australia, Swan (1963) posed the central issue as follows:

Since Keynes published *The General Theory* in 1936, it has been widely accepted that the two fundamental propositions of a full employment policy are (a) that incomes and employment depend on the level of spending; and (b) that there is no automatic mechanism to keep spending near its full employment level, without conscious action by economic and financial authorities. But the balance of payments equally depends on the level of spending. Must it be only a happy chance if the "internal balance" and "external balance" levels of spending coincide? Is there an automatic mechanism to ensure this, or what kind of conscious action by the authorities is required?[13]

To analyze the issue, Swan introduced a diagram that soon became famous; see figure 6.2. The starting point of the analysis was to recognize that internal balance and external balance – defined, respectively, as full employment and balance-of-payments equilibrium – could each be achieved under various combinations of the level of aggregate domestic real expenditure (absorption) and the cost (or price) of foreign goods relative to

---

[12] Magee (1973).   [13] Swan (1963, p. 384).

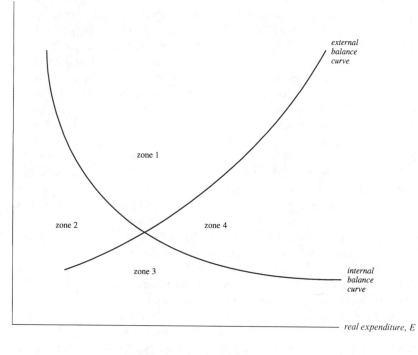

cost ratio, R

external
balance
curve

zone 1

zone 2

zone 4

zone 3

internal
balance
curve

real expenditure, E

zone 1: over full employment and balance of payments surplus
zone 2: under full employment and balance of payments surplus
zone 3: under full employment and balance of payments deficit
zone 4: over full employment and balance of payments deficit

Figure 6.2 The Swan diagram

that of home goods. As the basis for the diagram, the level of home-country employment was positively related to domestic real expenditure (E) and also positively related to the relative cost of foreign goods (R), so the internal balance (or full employment) curve was drawn with a negative slope: E and R had to change in opposite directions to preserve full employment, other things being equal. The balance of trade tended to deteriorate with an increase in domestic real expenditure and to improve with a rise in the relative cost of foreign goods, so the external balance curve was drawn with a positive slope.[14] Swan emphasized that changes in the

[14] In treating the balance of trade as a function of both the relative cost of foreign goods and the aggregate level of domestic absorption, the Swan diagram illustrates that mainstream economic analysis had moved beyond the early partial equilibrium version of the elasticities approach.

economy would shift the two curves over time, and that short-run disruptions could push the economy away from internal and/or external equilibrium. The challenge confronting the authorities was to devise policies for
influencing R and E in a manner that would keep the economy as close as
possible to the intersection of the curves, where internal and external
balance were simultaneously achieved. As the literature on open economy
macroeconomics expanded, it became common practice to distinguish
between "expenditure-changing policies" – that is, policies for reducing or
increasing E – and "expenditure-switching policies" – that is, policies for
changing R to induce a shift in the composition of expenditure between
home and foreign goods.[15]

By the start of the 1960s, the evolution of the world economy had
stimulated interest in formulating models in which the balance of payments
included endogenous private capital flows in addition to merchandise
transactions. This gave rise to a series of important contributions by
Mundell (1960, 1961a, 1961c, 1962, 1963) and Fleming (1962), exploring
the policy implications of international capital mobility.

The Mundell–Fleming framework combined a simple Keynesian model
of the goods and money markets for an open economy with the assumption
that net international capital flows into the economy depended positively
on the home rate of interest. The analysis took foreign prices and interest
rates as exogenous, focusing on either the home interest rate or the home
money supply as the instrument of monetary policy, and often on the
budget balance as the instrument of fiscal policy.

As presented by Mundell (1961a), the analysis extended the standard
diagrammatic model of the closed economy into the form shown in the top
panel of figure 6.3. The Mundell diagram differed from the Swan diagram in
several related respects. One difference was that Mundell drew three curves:
the XX and LL curves represented the loci of goods market and money
market equilibria, similar to those in the standard IS-LM diagram that
Hicks (1937) had introduced for the closed economy. The FF curve
represented the locus of balance of payments equilibria, analogous to
Swan's external balance curve. In addition, the variables placed on the axes
in Mundell's diagram were different than those in the Swan diagram, again
reflecting the IS-LM approach. Thus, in conformity with the standard
model of the closed economy, Mundell chose to analyze equilibrium in
terms of the levels of home-money income (Y) and the home interest rate
(r), rather than home real expenditure and the relative price (cost) of foreign
and home goods.

---

[15] Johnson (1961). In addition to models in which each country was treated as essentially
producing a single traded good, the literature considered models in which each country
produced a nontraded good as well as a traded good; for example, Salter (1959).

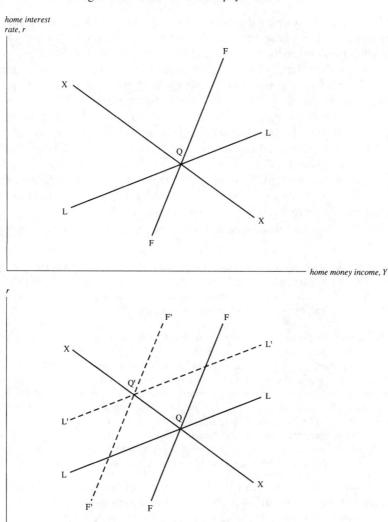

Figure 6.3 The Mundell diagram

The two different ways of characterizing equilibrium were associated, *inter alia*, with two different models of the balance of payments. In Mundell's analysis, the trade balance depended on home income, while the overall balance of payments also reflected the relationship of the capital account balance to the home interest rate. The *FF* curve, along which the overall balance of payments was zero, was thus positively sloped (except in the limiting cases in which capital was either perfectly mobile or perfectly immobile, which gave rise, respectively, to horizontal or vertical FF curves). The XX curve, along which the excess of home investment over home saving was equal to the balance of trade deficit, and the LL curve, along which the demand for money was equal to the given supply, were respectively drawn with the same slopes as the traditional IS and LM curves. Notably, the influence of the exchange rate on the balance of payments did not enter the picture explicitly, although the relative price of foreign and home goods could be regarded as a parameter affecting the positions of the FF and XX curves. A devaluation of the home currency unit would shift both the FF and XX curves to the right. That is to say, with an improved trade balance at any level of Y, a lower r would be required for balance of payments equilibrium and a higher r for goods market equilibrium.

Mundell's analysis of stabilization policy was motivated by the following perspectives:

The fundamental proposition of classical international trade theory, that there is an automatic mechanism ensuring balance-of-payments equilibrium, ... is now outdated: the history of international economic relations in the past thirty years has not been characterized by a persistent tendency toward balance-of-payments equilibrium ...

The decline of automaticity dates from the first attempts of central banks to adjust the domestic supply of notes to accord with the needs of trade (the banking principle) instead of the requirements of external equilibrium (the bullionist principle); and while these attempts have their origin far back in history, the abandonment of the bullionist principle became widespread ... especially after legal or de facto recognition in post-war years of full employment as a primary goal of public policy ... The basic instrument of the adjustment process (monetary policy) has now been diverted away from its original function toward the new requirement of internal stability, and no new weapon has been developed to cope with the balance of payments ... There is, therefore, a policy vacuum ...[16]

These perspectives are illustrated in the lower panel of figure 6.3. Suppose that the economy was initially in an equilibrium position at which there was full employment; this corresponds to point Q. Consider the effects of a disturbance that shifted the FF curve leftward to $F'F'$, such as an increase in the foreign interest rate that reduced the desired net capital inflow, other things being equal. Following the shock, the economy at Q would move into balance of payments deficit. Under the automatic adjustment mechanism envisioned by Hume (1752), this would lead to an outflow of specie and a reduction in the home money supply, thereby shifting the LL curve leftward until a new equilibrium was reached at Q'. In a Keynesian world of downward price and wage rigidity, however, the latter position of the economy would entail lower levels of output and employment than the

[16] Mundell (1961a, p. 153).

initial point Q. For this reason, the monetary authorities, in their dedication to full employment as a primary goal of public policy, would not passively allow the automatic adjustment process to operate, but rather would actively attempt to neutralize the effects of the balance of payments deficit on the money supply, preventing the shift in LL and keeping the economy at Q.

As Mundell recognized, however, this characterization of "the international disequilibrium system" – with a continuing balance of payment deficit – was incomplete. In particular, an unbalanced international payments position could be difficult to sustain over the long run:

To maintain this situation requires a substantial level of foreign exchange reserves in deficit countries, and a willingness to make unrequited capital exports in surplus countries. If this disequilibrium policy evens out – so to speak – over the business cycle no long-run difficulty exists if international liquidity is sufficient. But any secular change in the competitive situation, or a persistent tendency in some countries to inflate at faster rates than other countries, must eventually bring the day of reckoning, and either an abandonment of income stabilization, or further policy steps ...[17]

The implication was that monetary policy alone would not generally be sufficient to preserve full employment on a sustainable basis. Sustainability required balance of payments equilibrium along with full employment, and by a principle made famous by Tinbergen (1952), the attainment of any given number of independent policy targets generally required at least an equal number of policy instruments.

Against this background, the ensuing literature on how to achieve internal and external balance simultaneously was cast for the most part in terms of monetary and fiscal policy as the two instruments available to the stabilization authorities. The analysis initially proceeded on the premise that the assignment of policy instruments should be simple: one of the two policy instruments should be adjusted only in response to departures from internal balance without any regard to the external position, while the other should be adjusted only in response to external imbalances without any sensitivity to the internal position. This premise led to the principle of effective market classification:

a system works best if ... [policy instruments] respond to the ... [imbalances] on which they exert the most direct influence.[18]

---

[17] Mundell (1961a, p. 166).
[18] Mundell (1960, p. 250). Subsequently, Mundell (1969) and others adopted a more general definition of the assignment problem: specifically, as the task of establishing rules or guidelines indicating, as a general simultaneous equation system, how each particular policy instrument should be adjusted to insure that the dynamic system converged to a position of simultaneous internal and external equilibrium.

One of the major inferences from the Mundell–Fleming model was that the relative effectiveness of monetary and fiscal policies depended on both the nature of exchange rate arrangements and the degree of capital mobility.[19] Mundell (1963) considered the case of perfect capital mobility in which the elasticity of the capital account with respect to the home interest rate was infinite. With perfect capital mobility and fixed exchange rates, a change in the money supply through open market operations would give rise to an equal change in the level of foreign exchange reserves, with no impact on home output or employment, while an expansionary fiscal policy would stimulate home output and have a negative effect on the balance of trade. With perfect capital mobility and flexible exchange rates, a change in the fiscal balance would give rise to an equal change in the trade balance with no impact on home output or employment, while monetary expansion, despite having no effect on the home rate of interest, would depreciate the exchange rate, have a positive effect on the trade balance, and stimulate home output and employment.

The literature on stabilization policies for open economies was enriched in many ways during the 1960s and 1970s.[20] Moreover, alongside the analysis of the appropriate use of monetary and fiscal policies under each type of exchange rate arrangement, a second body of literature began to focus on the characteristics that made it optimal for countries to choose fixed or flexible rates. This "optimum currency area" literature is discussed in chapter 11.

3   Asset equilibrium models of the balance of payments

By the second half of the 1960s, the analysis of exchange rates and the balance of payments was entering a new stage. Critics of the Mundell–Fleming model had argued that the capital account balance should be conceptualized not as an ongoing flow, but rather as a reflection of efforts to adjust asset stocks to the levels that economic participants desired.

This new conceptualization of the capital account was reflected in two different classes of asset equilibrium models: the monetary approach to the balance of payments, and the portfolio-balance approach. The former approach, which extends back to contributions by Hume in the eighteenth century, was resurrected by Polak (1957) and Hahn (1959), and was subsequently pushed into the limelight by Johnson (1972), among others.[21]

---

[19] Rhomberg (1964) provided empirical perspectives on some of the issues based on an econometric model of the Canadian economy under fixed and flexible exchange rates.
[20] Marston (1985) and Frenkel and Razin (1987) provide extensive surveys.
[21] Kenen (1985, pp. 669–71). See Frenkel and Johnson (1976) for a collection of theoretical and empirical contributions.

The second class of models, which descended from Metzler (1951) in its treatment of savings and wealth, was formulated along the lines of the theory of portfolio selection developed by Markowitz (1959) and Tobin (1967).[22]

The monetary approach

The monetary approach to the balance of payments represented a major intellectual advance insofar as it shifted attention to stock-adjustment models of the capital account. It also reflected a controversial philosophy of how the balance of payments should be analyzed.

The formulation of the monetary approach emphasized that the balance sheet identity of the central bank, in first-differenced form, could be substituted into the balance-of-payments identity to eliminate the change in official international reserve assets, thereby linking the nonsettlement items in the balance of payments to the change in the stock of base money.[23] The combined identity also included any changes in other items on the central bank's balance sheet. This approach provided a framework in which the balance of payments could be analyzed as

a monetary phenomenon ... with the tools of monetary theory and not barter or "real" trade theory[24]

that is, in terms of relationships linking balance of payments behavior to the change in the stock of base money. Changes in the stock of base money were in turn viewed as responses to excess demands or supplies in the money market. This implied that,

as a fundamental proposition, balance-of-payments deficits and surpluses ... are monetary symptoms of monetary disequilibria that will cure themselves in time without any inherent need for a governmental balance-of-payments policy.[25]

The following illustration of the monetary approach draws heavily on Frenkel and Mussa (1985). Consider the case of a small open economy with no international capital mobility. Private home residents hold asset portfolios consisting of home money, M, and home interest bearing securities or bonds, B, which are denominated in units of home money. Thus, the nominal value of privately held assets, W, is simply

$$W = M + B. \tag{6.9}$$

---

[22] Allen and Kenen (1980, p. 4).
[23] Base money corresponds to the liabilities of the central bank, namely currency plus the reserve deposits of commercial banks.
[24] Johnson (1977, p. 251).   [25] Johnson (1977, p. 265).

Output consists of a single composite tradable good with home currency price, P, and exogenously given foreign price, P^*, such that

$$P = SP^* \tag{6.10}$$

where the exchange rate, S, is measured as the home-currency value of one unit of foreign exchange. The trade balance, T, is identically equal to the difference between home income (output), Y, and home expenditure, E,

$$T = Y - E. \tag{6.11}$$

For present purposes, T, Y, and E are each measured in real terms – that is, in units of the composite good. Real income (output) is taken to be constant at the full employment level, arrived at through adjustment of the home price level.

The home money supply, which is assumed to consist only of base money, can be described in terms of the central bank's balance sheet identity

$$M = B_c + SX + N \tag{6.12}$$

where B_c denotes the central bank's holdings of home securities, X denotes its international reserve holdings in units of foreign currency, and the residual, N, represents its net worth.[26] In the assumed absence of private international capital movements,[27] the balance-of-payments identity implies that the increase in official reserve holdings must equal the foreign currency value of the trade balance, or

$$\Delta X = P^* T. \tag{6.13}$$

Accordingly, from (6.12) and (6.10), if B_c and N are held constant and the exchange rate is fixed

$$\Delta M = PT. \tag{6.14}$$

(6.14) is analogous to one of the central components in the automatic adjustment mechanism envisaged by Hume: trade deficits lead to outflows of money (gold); trade surpluses to inflows. To extend this into a behavioral model of the balance of payments requires a description of private-sector behavior.

For present purposes, private-sector behavior is summarized by a money demand function and an aggregate expenditure function. The former is embedded in the condition for money market equilibrium, expressed as

---

[26] Among other things, N is sensitive to the effects of any exchange rate changes on the home-currency value of foreign exchange reserves.

[27] That is, when private residents restrict their asset holdings to claims on their own countries.

$$M/P = L(r, Y, W/P) \quad \text{with } \partial L/\partial r < 0, \ \partial L/\partial Y > 0, \ 0 < \partial L/\partial (W/P) < 1.$$
$$(6.15)$$

The demand for real money balances, L, depends negatively on the home nominal interest rate, r, and positively on both real income and the real value of private asset holdings. To keep the model simple, it is assumed that the home price level consistent with full employment is expected to remain constant, so that r represents both the nominal and the real rate of interest.

The condition for money market equilibrium implicitly determines the home interest rate

$$r = r(M/P, B/P, Y) \quad \text{with } \partial r/\partial (M/P) < 0, \ \partial r/\partial (B/P) > 0, \ \partial r/\partial Y > 0.$$
$$(6.16)$$

The market-clearing interest rate depends negatively on the real stock of money and positively on both private real bond holdings and real income.

Real expenditure is assumed to depend negatively on the real interest rate and positively on both real income and the real value of private asset holdings

$$E = E(Y, r, W/P) \quad \text{with } \partial E/\partial Y > 0, \ \partial E/\partial r < 0, \ \partial E/\partial (W/P) > 0.$$
$$(6.17)$$

Together, (6.16), (6.17), and (6.9) are taken to imply

$$E = E(M/P, B/P, Y) \quad \text{with } \partial E/\partial (M/P) > 0, \ 0 < \partial E/\partial Y < 1. \quad (6.18)$$

An increase in the real stock of money increases real expenditure both by reducing the interest rate and by raising private asset holdings. An increase in private real bond holdings pushes up both the interest rate and total private asset holdings; it thus has an ambiguous net effect on real expenditure. An increase in real income can be presumed to stimulate real expenditure provided that the direct effect outweighs the indirect effect operating through the interest rate; moreover, the sum of the direct plus indirect marginal propensities to spend out of income can be presumed to be less than one. Thus, from (6.11) and (6.18)

$$T = T(M/P, B/P, Y) \quad \text{with } \partial T/\partial (M/P) < 0, \ \partial T/\partial Y > 0. \quad (6.19)$$

An increase in the real money stock raises expenditure and deteriorates the trade balance, while an increase in real income (output) raises expenditure by less than output, thereby improving the trade balance.

The equilibrating process emphasized by the monetary approach is apparent from (6.14) and (6.19). A trade imbalance gives rise to monetary flows, and the feedback effects of the change in home money balances act to reduce the trade imbalance.[28]

The monetary approach to balance of payments analysis can be applied in models that are not as restrictive as the framework just presented. In this connection, it is worth noting two important directions in which the analysis can be extended.[29]

One direction aims to enrich the analysis of income determination and expectations formation. In the model just presented, income (output) is constant at the full employment level, the home-price level consistent with full employment is expected to remain constant, and for a given foreign-price level, the exchange rate is also expected to remain constant. The possibilities for modifying the treatment of income determination are not discussed here, but the general topic of expectations formation receives considerable attention in the remainder of the book, beginning in chapter 7.

A second direction for extending the analysis relaxes the assumption of no private international capital mobility and also recognizes that the monetary authorities may be led to sterilize or partially sterilize the effects of international reserve flows on the home-money supply. This requires expanding the balance-of-payments accounts to include net sales of privately-held nonmonetary assets by home residents to foreign residents, while also recognizing that the central bank's holdings of home securities may change .

The monetary approach has been extended in the second direction under the assumption that home securities are perfect substitutes for foreign securities.[30] This assumption implies that the home-interest rate, r, is equal to the exogenous foreign-interest rate, $r*$.[31] For the case of a fixed exchange rate, it also implies that the central bank has no independent policy instrument for influencing the demand for money, and hence no autonomy over the home-money supply.[32] If the change in the central bank's holdings

---

[28] The speed of convergence to balance of trade equilibrium depends on $\partial T/\partial(M/P)$, which can be expressed as:

$$\frac{\partial T}{\partial(M/P)} = -\frac{\partial E}{\partial(W/P)} - \frac{\partial E}{\partial r}\left[\frac{1 - \partial L/\partial(W/P)}{\partial L/\partial r}\right].$$

Convergence speed thus depends positively on the sensitivity of real expenditure to both the real value of private asset holdings and the interest rate, and negatively on the responsiveness of money demand to the same variables. Note that the equilibrating process would operate even in the absence of a real balance effect on expenditure.

[29] See Frenkel and Mussa (1985) for a discussion of additional directions, including the extension of the analysis to models with nontradable goods.

[30] Frenkel and Mussa (1985, pp. 709–14).

[31] Recall that price levels are expected to remain constant, which implies that the exchange rate is also expected to remain constant.

[32] This implication gave rise to a body of literature that tested the validity of the perfect substitutes assumption by estimating the extent to which, under fixed exchange rates, the

of foreign exchange reserves, as determined by the balance of payments, differs from the change in the demand for (base) money, the difference will be reflected in the change in the central bank's holdings of home securities.[33]

The portfolio-balance approach

The second class of models of asset stock equilibrium has been named the portfolio-balance approach. Like the monetary approach, the portfolio-balance approach focuses on the links between balance-of-payments flows and adjustments in asset stocks, emphasizing that models of the capital account should be rooted in behavioral models of the supplies of and demands for portfolio stocks. The main difference between the portfolio-balance and monetary approaches is that the monetary approach regards home-currency securities (which represent assets other than money) as perfect substitutes for foreign-currency securities, while the portfolio-balance approach regards them as imperfect substitutes.[34] Among other things, in the absence of perfect substitutability the larger set of distinct assets under the portfolio-balance approach implies that the equilibrium condition for at least one of the securities markets must be modeled explicitly. That is to say, since the uncovered interest parity condition does not prevail when the two securities are imperfect substitutes, the interest rate on home securities cannot simply be equated to the foreign interest rate plus the expected rate of change in the exchange rate.

The portfolio-balance approach emerged during the late 1960s but did not mature until the late 1970s, after the Bretton Woods system had collapsed. In its early development, the approach received nourishment from econometric efforts to explain the empirically-observed behavior of capital flows.[35] Branson (1968) was one of the first to put stock-adjustment terms into capital flow equations. McKinnon and Oates (1966) and McKinnon (1969) were early contributors to the conceptual framework, although their model included only one financial asset other than money

---

effect of home-credit expansion on the home-money supply was offset through central bank foreign reserve losses. See Porter (1972), Argy and Kouri (1974), and Kouri and Porter (1974) for early contributions, and Obstfeld (1982b) for an overview.

[33] This assumes that the net worth of the central bank remains constant.

[34] Both the monetary approach and the portfolio balance approach generally assume that each country's money balances are held entirely by the residents of that country. The literature of asset equilibrium models also includes a variety of "currency substitution models" – resembling in some cases the monetary approach and in other cases the portfolio balance approach – in which the menus of financial assets typically consist only of the money stocks or "currencies" of the two countries, which may be held by nonresidents as well as by residents; see Giovannini and Turtelboom (1994). For early contributions to the currency-substitution literature see Calvo and Rodríguez (1977) and Girton and Roper (1981).

[35] For references see Kenen (1985, pp. 671–2) and Allen and Kenen (1980, pp. 9–10).

and, by not treating the case of imperfect capital mobility, did not move as far as subsequent contributions in breaking away from the monetary approach. Argy and Porter (1972) were among the first to focus explicitly on how the nature of exchange rate expectations influenced the effects of changes in monetary and fiscal policies and various other internal and external shocks. Girton and Henderson (1973, 1976) extensively explored the effects of central bank policies on financial capital movements in a two-country model. The specification of portfolio-balance models was reviewed by Branson and Henderson (1985), who distinguish between models in which asset demand functions are postulated and models in which asset demand functions are derived from microeconomic foundations.[36]

The basic features of the portfolio-balance approach can be illustrated by considering the case of a two-country, two-currency world in which there are two composite private sectors with different sets of asset preferences; the following discussion of this case is based on Dooley and Isard (1983). The net portfolio holdings of the two private sectors combined correspond to the liabilities of the official sectors of the two countries, net of the liabilities of official agencies to each other.

To keep things simple, the menu of financial assets is limited to four entries: $\bar{M}$ and $\bar{M}^*$ respectively denote the stocks of noninterest bearing claims on the home and foreign governments, corresponding to the monetary bases; $\bar{B}$ and $\bar{F}$ respectively denote the privately-held stocks of interest bearing claims on the home and foreign governments, referred to as bonds or securities. It is assumed that $\bar{M}$ and $\bar{B}$ are denominated in the home-currency unit while $\bar{M}^*$ and $\bar{F}$ are denominated in foreign currency. The net portfolio holdings of home private residents, which are assumed to include the entire stock of home base money, are denoted by M, B, and F; those of foreign private residents, by M^*, B^*, and F^*. Thus

$$M = \bar{M} \tag{6.20}$$

$$M^* = \bar{M}^* \tag{6.21}$$

$$B + B^* = \bar{B} \tag{6.22}$$

$$F + F^* = \bar{F} \tag{6.23}$$

$$W = M + B + SF \tag{6.24}$$

$$W^* = M^* + B^*/S + F^* \tag{6.25}$$

---

[36] See also Allen and Kenen (1980), who develop and extensively analyze a portfolio balance model of an open economy in which the markets for three financial assets (money, domestic bonds, and foreign bonds) are fully integrated with markets for labor, traded goods, and nontraded goods.

where (6.20)–(6.23) are the relevant market-clearing conditions and (6.24) and (6.25) define the nominal portfolio wealths (W and W^*) of the two private sectors, with S representing the home-currency value of one unit of foreign exchange.

The stocks of the four financial assets are determined by the interactions of monetary policies, budget deficits, and official interventions in the foreign exchange market. $\bar{B}$ can be written as the cumulative government budget deficit of the home country ($\int DEF$), minus cumulative open market purchases of home-currency bonds in exchange for base money issued by the monetary authority of the home country ($\bar{M}$), minus cumulative purchases of home-currency bonds through the combined official foreign exchange market interventions of the national authorities of the two countries ($\int INT$):

$$\bar{B} = \int DEF - \bar{M} - \int INT. \tag{6.26}$$

Similarly

$$\bar{F} = \int DEF^* - \bar{M}^* + \int INT^* \tag{6.27}$$

where DEF^* is the foreign budget deficit and INT^* is the quantity of foreign bonds that are sold to purchase INT units of home bonds

$$INT^* = INT/S. \tag{6.28}$$

Note here the underlying presumption that each government finances its budget deficit entirely by issuing debt denominated in its own currency unit. Capital gains and losses on bonds are limited to those associated with exchange rate changes by assuming that $\bar{B}$ and $\bar{F}$ have one-period maturities; stocks of government debt are viewed to be refinanced at the beginning of each period. Moreover, the analysis follows the tradition of abstracting from the intertemporal budget constraints of the two governments.[37]

The desired composition of private portfolios in each country is assumed to depend on the own-currency rates of return on domestic and foreign bonds, together with a vector of other relevant variables, which conventionally includes a variable indicating the scale of monetary transactions within the country. The rates of return reflect the own rates of interest on home and foreign bonds, respectively denoted by r and r^*, along with the expected rate of appreciation of the home currency unit, denoted by π. Q

---

[37] As demonstrated rigorously by Obstfeld (1982a) and Stockman (1979), and emphasized by Rogoff (1984), it would not be valid to regard government bonds as outside assets in a pure Ricardian setting where homogeneous agents with infinite lifespans had rational expectations about their future tax liabilities, or where rational agents with finite lives left bequests to their infinitely-living family units. Accordingly, the specification of traditional portfolio-balance models would not be meaningful in a pure Ricardian setting.

and Q^* respectively denote the vectors of other variables that are relevant to home and foreign residents. No distinctions are drawn between the desired and actual compositions of financial portfolios. Thus

$$M/W = m(r, r^* - \pi, Q) \tag{6.29}$$

$$B/W = b(r, r^* - \pi, Q) \tag{6.30}$$

$$SF/W = f(r, r^* - \pi, Q) \tag{6.31}$$

$$M^*/W^* = m^*(r^*, r + \pi, Q^*) \tag{6.32}$$

$$(B^*/S)/W^* = b^*(r^*, r + \pi, Q^*) \tag{6.33}$$

$$F^*/W^* = f^*(r^*, r + \pi, Q^*) \tag{6.34}$$

where, by definition, the portfolio shares must add to unity

$$m + b + f = 1 \tag{6.35}$$

$$m^* + b^* + f^* = 1. \tag{6.36}$$

Private portfolio holders are assumed to be risk averse and, accordingly, to view home and foreign bonds as imperfect substitutes. For the present illustrative purpose, moreover, the magnitudes of the risks that portfolio holders perceive are assumed to remain constant.

In analyzing the model, it is convenient to focus on the case in which the asset stocks are determined exogenously by the policy authorities while interest rates and exchange rates (current and expected future) are the endogenous variables that adjust to clear markets. Although the model could be enriched considerably by endogenizing the behavior of the policy authorities, this is not pursued here.[38]

Portfolio equilibrium can be described by substituting the behavioral conditions (6.29)–(6.34) into the four market-clearing conditions (6.20)–(6.23). By constraints (6.35) and (6.36), only three of the four market-clearing conditions are independent. This means that the system can be solved for only three of the four variables S, π, r, and r^*. Thus, for example, if the solution variables include the two interest rates, the system of asset market equilibrium conditions, as it stands, cannot also determine both the current level and the expected rate of change of the exchange rate. To determine all four of the variables, an additional condition must be imposed on the asset equilibrium system, as is discussed further in subsequent chapters.

In describing the characteristics of asset equilibrium, the portfolio-

---

[38] Chapter 9 extends the portfolio-balance framework to a case with endogenous policy behavior in the home country, where the policy instruments include the exchange rate and the stock of foreign exchange reserves.

balance model has focused particular attention on the behavior of the differential between the expected own-currency rates of return on home and foreign bonds. This differential, ϕ, is identical for both home residents and foreign residents. When time subscripts are added,

$$\phi_t = r_t - (r_t^* - \pi_t) = (r_t + \pi_t) - r_t^* = r_t - r_t^* - (E_t s_{t+1} - s_t) \qquad (6.37)$$

which bears a close resemblance to condition (5.12) from chapter 5.[39] An important difference, however, is that in (5.12), r and r^* refer to interest rates on claims that are identical in all respects except their currencies of denomination and interest rates, whereas in (6.37), r and r^* refer to interest rates on claims against the governments of different countries. In the former case, the only source of *ex ante* uncertainty about the *ex post* yield differential is uncertainty about the *ex post* level of the exchange rate. Thus, on the presumption that exchange market participants behave rationally, ξ can be regarded as a premium or expected yield differential required for simply bearing exchange risk. By contrast, in the latter case the two types of assets represent different credit risks, and ϕ represents a premium for bearing a composite of exchange risk and the difference in credit risks. This distinction receives further attention in chapter 8, which reviews the empirical evidence on the portfolio-balance approach. It appears that almost all empirical tests of portfolio-balance models have used forward premiums or Eurocurrency data as measures of the interest rate differential, which is not the conceptually appropriate measure for portfolio-balance analysis.

In seeking to characterize the behavior of ϕ, one approach is to specify and solve the utility maximization problems of representative portfolio holders in each country, imposing restrictions that generate well-behaved portfolio-demand functions.[40] A common alternative approach is simply to postulate a system of portfolio-demand functions.

Here we postulate the following simplified structure of the portfolio-demand system (6.29)–(6.34):

$$M/W = m(r, Q) \quad \text{with } 0 \leq m \leq 1 \qquad (6.29a)$$

$$B/W = b(\phi)[1 - m(r, Q)] \quad \text{with } 0 \leq b \leq 1 \text{ and } \partial b/\partial \phi > 0 \quad (6.30a)$$

$$SF/W = [1 - b(\phi)][1 - m(r, Q)] \qquad (6.31a)$$

$$M^*/W^* = m^*(r^*, Q^*) \quad \text{with } 0 \leq m^* \leq 1 \qquad (6.32a)$$

$$(B^*/S)/W^* = b^*(\phi)[1 - m^*(r^*, Q^*)] \text{ with } 0 \leq b^* \leq 1 \text{ and } \partial b^*/\partial \phi > 0$$
$$(6.33a)$$

[39] The expected rate of appreciation of the home currency has been approximated as $\pi_t = -(E_t s_{t+1} - s_t)$, where $s = \log S$.
[40] See the survey by Branson and Henderson (1985).

$$F^*/W^* = [1 - b^*(\phi)][1 - m^*(r^*, Q^*)]. \tag{6.34a}$$

Money holdings depend on own-currency interest rates, transactions demand variables, and the levels of nominal wealths; while the shares of wealths that are not held as money are divided between home and foreign bonds as functions of the expected differential yield ϕ.

Proceeding further, substitute (6.29a)–(6.34a) into (6.22) – the market-clearing condition for bonds denominated in home currency – using (6.20) and (6.21). This yields

$$b(\phi)[W - \bar{M}] + b^*(\phi)[W^* - \bar{M}^*] = \bar{B}. \tag{6.38}$$

Next take the total differential of (6.38) and rearrange terms to obtain an expression that describes how the market-clearing level of ϕ is affected by changes in asset stocks and wealth variables:

$$d\phi = \frac{d\bar{B} - b(dW - d\bar{M}) - b^*(dW^* - d\bar{M}^*)}{(W - M)\partial b/\partial \phi + (W^* - M^*)\partial b^*/\partial \phi}. \tag{6.39}$$

Note from (6.30a) and (6.33a) that the denominator in (6.39) is positive.

The message of (6.39) is illustrated by figure 6.4, in which the home bond market clears at ϕ_0. The demand curves B and B^* are upward sloping functions of ϕ, other things being equal, as specified in (6.30a) and (6.33a). Note that, for given levels of private wealths, an increase in the stock of public debt denominated in home-currency units (issued in exchange for foreign bonds) would shift the vertical supply curve to the right, raising the premium necessary to induce home and foreign portfolio managers to increase their combined demand for home bonds by the increment in supply. Similarly, given the supply of home bonds, an increase in $W - \bar{M}$ or $W^* - \bar{M}^*$ through new public debt issues of foreign currency bonds would shift the combined demand curve $(B + B^*)$ to the right, leading to a reduction in ϕ.

To gain further insights, ϕ can be linked more directly to policy choice variables and balance-of-payments flows by transforming (6.39) as follows. Note that definitions (6.24) and (6.25) can be differentiated, using (6.22) and (6.23), to yield

$$dW - d\bar{M} = d\bar{B} - dB^* + SdF + FdS \tag{6.40}$$

$$dW^* - d\bar{M}^* = d\bar{F} - dF + (1/S)dB^* + B^*d(1/S). \tag{6.41}$$

Note also that these expressions contain the current account surplus of the home country measured in home-currency units

$$CAS = SdF - dB^*. \tag{6.42}$$

Thus, in combination, (6.39)–(6.42) imply

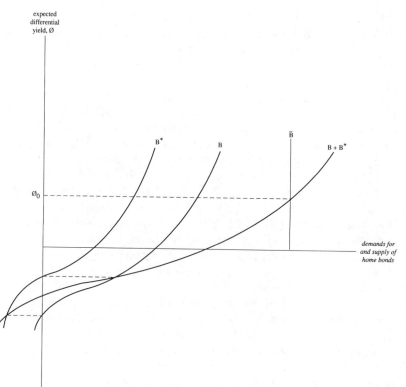

Figure 6.4 The portfolio-balance framework

$$d\phi = \frac{(1-b)d\bar{B} - b^*d\bar{F} - (b - b^*/S)CAS - [bSF - b^*(B^*/S)](dS/S)}{(W - \bar{M})\partial b/\partial\phi + (W^* - \bar{M}^*)\partial b^*/\partial\phi} \tag{6.43}$$

where (6.26) and (6.27) can be differentiated to yield

$$d\bar{B} = DEF - d\bar{M} - INT \tag{6.44}$$

$$d\bar{F} = DEF^* - d\bar{M}^* + INT/S. \tag{6.45}$$

The interpretation of these conditions is straightforward. Note first that, from (6.30a) and (6.33a), the parameters b, b^*, and $(1 - b)$ are all positive, as is the denominator of (6.43). Thus an increase in the stock of home-currency-denominated debt that is pushed into private portfolios ($d\bar{B} > 0$) raises the market-clearing level of the expected differential yield on home-currency-denominated debt, whereas an increase in the stock of foreign-currency debt that the private sector must be induced to hold ($d\bar{F} > 0$)

reduces ϕ. Accordingly – on the assumption that governments denominate their debts entirely in their own currency units, and that open market operations by monetary authorities involve exchanges of base money for interest bearing securities denominated in own-currency units – a home-country fiscal deficit ($DEF > 0$) or open market sale of securities ($d\bar{M} < 0$) leads to an increase in ϕ, other things being equal, while a foreign-country fiscal deficit or open market sale of securities tends to reduce ϕ. In addition, an intervention purchase of home-currency securities ($INT > 0$), when sterilized to avoid any changes in the home or foreign monetary bases, leads to a reduction in ϕ, while a transfer of wealth to home residents from foreigners through a home current account surplus ($CAS > 0$) reduces ϕ if and only if the net of the home and foreign wealth effects on the demand for home-currency bonds ($b - b^*/S$) is positive. Finally, a depreciation of the home-currency unit ($dS/S > 0$) leads to a reduction in ϕ if and only if the increase in the demand for foreign-currency bonds arising from the positive effect on the nominal wealth of home residents outweighs the decrease in demand for home-currency bonds arising from the negative effect on the nominal wealth of foreign residents.

(6.43) describes the behavior of the risk premium ϕ in a particularly simple portfolio-balance framework. Empirical applications are discussed in chapter 8. As already noted, the framework can be modified by allowing governments to issue debts denominated in the currencies of other countries, and the analysis can be enriched by endogenizing the behavior of the policy authorities. Extensions to cases with more than two countries can also be pursued. In general, however, the essence of the portfolio-balance framework boils down to a few key points.

First and foremost, the portfolio-balance framework reflects the premise that the financial portfolios held by private sectors contain assets that are distinguishable in terms of valuation risks, and that private portfolio holders are not risk neutral. Note, for example, that in the particular model described above, if either home residents or foreign residents were risk neutral, then either $\partial b/\partial \phi$ or $\partial b^*/\phi$ would be infinite, and (6.43) would in that case imply that the behavior of ϕ was completely independent of developments influencing the composition of private-sector portfolios.

Second, the portfolio-balance framework emphasizes that the magnitudes of the risk premiums that are required to clear financial markets depend on the relative stocks of the different types of net claims on governments (outside assets). Moreover, when the private residents of different countries have different portfolio preferences, risk premiums will generally change over time in response to international shifts through current account imbalances in the net financial wealths of the private sectors of different countries.

Third, the portfolio-balance model by itself – or more specifically, the set of conditions for market clearing during the current period – is not capable of determining the current equilibrium values of all of the market-clearing financial variables. For example, the model described above provides only three independent market-clearing conditions on four variables; thus, the two interest rates, the current exchange rate, and the expected change in (or future level of) the exchange rate cannot be determined without imposing an additional restriction on the analysis. In this connection, as discussed in chapter 7, it can be argued that the appropriate extension of the analysis requires an additional relationship between exchange rates and the balance of payments.[41] Thus, while the portfolio-balance model emphasizes that international payments imbalances may influence exchange rates through their effects on the market-clearing levels of risk premiums, the risk premium may not be the most important channel of influence.

4   Concluding perspectives

This chapter has provided an overview of: (i) early models of the current account of the balance of payments, with emphasis on the elasticities approach to determining the equilibrium level of the exchange rate; (ii) early models of stabilization policy for the open economy, with emphasis on the Mundell–Fleming model of an economy open to international transactions in both goods and financial assets; and (iii) models in which the balance of payments under fixed exchange rates is analyzed from the perspective of asset stock equilibrium. Chapters 7–10 continue to focus on asset equilibrium models, primarily in the context of flexible exchange rates.

The basic hypothesis of the elasticities approach – that the volumes of imports and exports are sensitive to real exchange rates – integrated with the recognition that the scale of a country's international trade is strongly linked to the scale of its national income and output, remain at the center of modern-day economic analysis of current account imbalances and their relationship to exchange rates. Over the past several decades, however, the best-practice empirical models of the current account have advanced considerably from the integrated elasticities–absorption models of the 1950s, owing partly to the revolution in data-processing technology and partly to the fact that accuracy in forecasting gross national product and

---

[41] To preview that discussion, in some models of flexible exchange rates the additional restriction takes the form of a constraint on the expected build-up of international net indebtedness, which constrains the expected path of the current account. In forward-looking models in which exchange rate expectations are taken to be model-consistent, the constraint on the expected path of the current account in turn places a constraint on the expected path of the real exchange rate.

other national income aggregates hinges critically on accuracy in forecasting the current account. It has thus become accepted practice to disaggregate imports and exports into several categories of merchandise trade, along with several categories of international transactions in services, and to specify behavioral equations for the prices as well as the volumes of the merchandise trade categories.[42] At the same time, economists have continued to focus on new directions for improving these models. As discussed in chapter 10, conceptual models of the current account now emphasize the importance of formulating the integrated elasticities–absorption approach in a dynamic framework that captures the intertemporal aspects of aggregate savings and investment decisions.

Just as the elasticities model with relevant modifications has remained central to current account analysis, the Mundell–Fleming model remains the "workhorse" in academic discussions of stabilization policy for the open economy. The Mundell–Fleming model has also been modified and extended in a number of ways over the years.[43] The most important theoretical advance in the evolution of open-economy macroeconomics based on the Mundell–Fleming framework has been the recognition that international capital movements and the behavior of exchange rates should be analyzed from the perspective of asset stock equilibrium.

Models of asset stock equilibrium are generally classified according to whether financial assets other than money are all regarded as perfect substitutes (the monetary approach) or are assumed to include items that are imperfect substitutes (the portfolio balance approach). The analysis of these models focuses on the insights that emerge from imposing the conditions that must simultaneously be satisfied for asset markets to clear at a single point (or during a single period) in time. For the two-country, two-currency case, the discussion of the portfolio balance model has emphasized that the conditions necessary for markets to clear at a point (or period) in time are insufficient to determine the market-clearing values of the two interest rates, the current exchange rate, and the expected future exchange rate. A similar indeterminacy arises under the monetary approach, as clarified in chapter 7. Thus, for example, the two interest rates and the current exchange rate can be determined when the expected future exchange rate is given, but an additional restriction must be imposed on the analysis to pin down the level of the expected future exchange rate.

---

[42] See, for example, Helkie and Hooper (1988).
[43] Frenkel and Razin (1987), Krugman and Obstfeld (1991), Argy (1994).

7 News, revisions in expectations, and exchange rate dynamics

Following the collapse of the Bretton Woods system in the early 1970s, international economists refashioned their asset equilibrium models of the balance of payments into models of flexible exchange rates.[1] The usual practice, at first, was to simplify the exchange rate models by assuming that exchange rate expectations were based on the current or past values of relevant economic variables. It was common to assume, for example, that exchange rate expectations were static, meaning that the expected future spot rate was the same as the current spot rate. An alternative was to equate the expected future spot rate with the prevailing forward rate.

After a few years of renewed experience with a flexible exchange rate system, it was widely realized that regardless of how well expectations about future exchange rates could be summarized *ex ante* by prevailing spot or forward exchange rates, each of the latter provided very poor predictions of the exchange rates that were actually observed *ex post*. In turn, recognition that the observed variation in exchange rates far exceeded the variation predicted *ex ante* by prevailing forward premiums or interest rate differentials[2] suggested the importance of designing models in which exchange rate expectations were related to expectations about other variables in a forward-looking manner. Much of the observed *ex post* variation in spot and forward rates could then be attributed to revisions in exchange rate expectations in response to "news" about relevant economic or political developments.[3]

A simple first step that had already been taken in moving toward forward-looking models was to assume that the realized *ex post* values of spot exchange rates provided unbiased measures of *ex ante* exchange rate expectations.[4] In some cases it was even assumed that exchange rate expectations exhibited perfect foresight. This early concept of "rational

---

[1] Girton and Roper (1977) formulated a model of exchange market pressure, based on the monetary approach, that could be used to explain either exchange rate movements or changes in official reserve holdings.

[2] Mussa (1979). Recall table 5.1 (p. 82).

[3] Mussa (1979), Dornbusch (1980), Frenkel (1981), Isard (1980, 1983).

[4] For example, Black (1973), in the spirit of Muth (1961).

expectations," however, was just as unsatisfactory as using the *ex ante* values of spot or forward rates to represent exchange rate expectations, since if foresight was either perfect or unbiased, one would not be likely to find empirical evidence that forward exchange rates were highly inaccurate and apparently biased predictors of future spot rates.

Subsequent work on forward-looking models has moved away from the perfect foresight assumption. In particular, with continuing conceptual and methodological advances in incorporating the criterion of rational expectations into macroeconomic models, it was natural for exchange rate models to gravitate toward formulations in which expectations about future exchange rates were explicitly related to expectations about the exogenous variables in the models, with the relationships constrained to be consistent with the hypothesized structures of the models.

The use of models with consistent expectations to analyze the dynamic adjustment of exchange rates in response to new information led to important insights about the variability of observed exchange rates relative to the variability of long-run equilibrium exchange rates. A pathbreaking theoretical contribution by Dornbusch (1976) emphasized that sluggish adjustment of national price levels could help explain the phenomenon of exchange rate "overshooting" – that is, a tendency for the exchange rate to jump in one direction in response to news and subsequently to retreat at least part of the way back to its initial position. It also divided subsequent efforts to model exchange rate behavior into "flexible-price" and "sticky-price" approaches.

The first section describes the sticky-price monetary model of exchange rate dynamics, illustrating in a continuous-time framework how the exchange rate responds to news about the money supply. A general discrete-time framework for analyzing exchange rate dynamics, with emphasis on the role of news, is described in the second section. Both frameworks require some form of long-run equilibrium condition to pin down the expected long-run level of the exchange rate. In this connection, the third section briefly addresses the concept of long-run equilibrium and the role of the current account in imposing a constraint on the expected long-run level of the real exchange rate. The fourth section turns to a third class of models of exchange rate dynamics, describing the target zone framework that has emerged since the late 1980s for analyzing the behavior of exchange rates in a system of adjustable exchange rate bands.

1   A continuous-time monetary model with sticky prices

Until the breakdown of the Bretton Woods system, many international economists clung to purchasing power parity (PPP) as a reasonable assumption when analyzing macroeconomic behavior in the open economy. As discussed in chapter 4, however, it did not take long for the experience with flexible exchange rates to discredit PPP as a description of the short-run relationship between exchange rates and ratios of national price levels.

One of the most influential contributions to exchange rate analysis during the 1970s resulted from abandoning the short-run PPP hypothesis in favor of a model in which the exchange rate was free to jump instantaneously in response to new information, while national price levels were constrained to be nonjumping slowly-adjusting variables. In developing such a model, Dornbusch (1976) retained the long-run PPP hypothesis and adopted the assumption of uncovered interest parity, following the monetary approach.

The basic equations of the Dornbusch model can be written as

$$r = r^* + \dot{s}^e \tag{7.1}$$

$$\dot{s}^e = -\theta(s - \bar{s}) \tag{7.2}$$

$$m - p = \phi y - \lambda r \tag{7.3}$$

$$y = u + \delta(p^* + s - p) + \gamma y - \sigma r \tag{7.4a}$$

and

$$\dot{p} = \pi(y - \bar{y}) \tag{7.5}$$

where r and r^* are the domestic and foreign interest rates; s is the logarithm of the spot exchange rate measured in domestic currency per unit of foreign currency; $\bar{s}$ is the long-run equilibrium level of s; $\dot{s}^e$ is the expected rate of change in s; m is the logarithm of the domestic money supply; p and p^* are the logarithms of the domestic and foreign price levels; $\dot{p}$ is the rate of change in p; y is the level of domestic real income (output); ϕ, λ, u, δ, γ, σ, and π are constant parameters; and θ is a model-consistent function of the other parameters, as described below. (7.1) represents the uncovered interest parity assumption; (7.2) expresses the expected rate of depreciation of domestic currency in terms of both the gap between the current and equilibrium exchange rates and the model-consistent parameter θ; (7.3) is the money market-clearing condition, in which the demand for real money balances is assumed to depend positively on the level of domestic real income (output) and negatively on the domestic interest rate; (7.4a) is the goods market-clearing condition, in which the demand for domestic output is positively related to both domestic real income and the relative price of foreign output ($p^* + s - p$), and negatively related to the domestic interest rate; and (7.5) is an assumption about the process of price adjustment.[5] It is convenient to rewrite (7.4a) as

$$y = \mu[u + \delta(p^* + s - p) - \sigma r] \quad \text{where } \mu = 1/(1 - \gamma) \tag{7.4b}$$

and to combine (7.1) and (7.2) into

$$r = r^* - \theta(s - \bar{s}). \tag{7.6}$$

(7.3)–(7.6) can be used to describe the relationships between the price level, output, and the exchange rate, both in the steady state and along the path of convergence to the steady state. Noting that $r = r^*$ in the steady state, and letting $\bar{p}$ denote the steady state level of p, the market-clearing conditions (7.3) and (7.4b) imply the following two steady state relationships:

$$\bar{p} = m - \phi\bar{y} + \lambda r^* \tag{7.7}$$

$$\bar{y} = \mu[u + \delta(p^* + \bar{s} - \bar{p}) - \sigma r^*]. \tag{7.8}$$

In addition, the relationships between prices, output, and the exchange rate during the adjustment to the steady state can be described by subtracting these two relationships from (7.3) and (7.4b), respectively, using (7.6). Thus

$$(p - \bar{p}) = -\phi(y - \bar{y}) - \lambda\theta(s - \bar{s}) \tag{7.9}$$

$$(y - \bar{y}) = \mu(\delta + \sigma\theta)(s - \bar{s}) - \mu\delta(p - \bar{p}). \tag{7.10}$$

These two conditions, in turn, can be solved simultaneously to yield

$$(y - \bar{y}) = -w(p - \bar{p}) \tag{7.11}$$

$$(s - \bar{s}) = -[(1 - \phi\mu\delta)/\Delta](p - \bar{p}) \tag{7.12}$$

where

$$\Delta = \phi\mu(\delta + \theta\sigma) + \theta\lambda \tag{7.13}$$

$$w = [\mu(\delta + \theta\sigma) + \mu\delta\theta\lambda]/\Delta. \tag{7.14}$$

Furthermore, substitution of (7.11) into (7.5) yields

$$\dot{p} = -\pi w(p - \bar{p}). \tag{7.15}$$

It may be noted from (7.11)–(7.15) that the convergence paths for p, y, and s depend on the parameter θ, which describes the expected rate of change of the exchange rate. The next step, in the spirit of rational

---

[5] This formulation corresponds to the case described in the appendix of Dornbusch (1976). The steady state rates of monetary growth and inflation are assumed to be zero; in the more general case, the steady state inflation rate (or differential) would be added to the right-hand side of (7.5), and the equilibrium nominal exchange rate would display a steady trend.

expectations macroeconomics, is to identify the model-consistent value of θ. This allows the Dornbusch model to be evaluated on the basis of the behavior it predicts when market participants are assumed to know the model and to form their expectations in a manner consistent with the model.

Before solving for the consistent value of θ, it is important to emphasize that the Dornbusch model abstracts completely from the possibility – indeed, the likelihood – that expectations will prove inaccurate. Generally speaking, the model-consistent expected path of the exchange rate cannot be defined precisely from knowledge of the model alone, since exchange rate expectations are formed simultaneously with, and depend upon, expectations about other variables, including variables that are exogenous to the model. In the exchange rate literature, as elsewhere, economists have often ignored the scope for rational market participants to form inaccurate expectations about exogenous variables, which can be a source of imprecision and inaccuracy in their model-consistent expectations about endogenous variables. In particular, many exchange rate models, including the Dornbusch model, have abstracted completely from the possibility of peso problems (recall chapter 5) or other sources of inaccuracy in rationally-formed expectations by assuming (directly or indirectly) that the model-consistent expected path of the exchange rate corresponds to the perfect foresight path.

In the Dornbusch model, such a correspondence is achieved by abstracting from any distinctions between the expected values and the actual realizations of the exogenous variables (r^*, p^*, $\bar{y}$, m). Because behavior is assumed to depend on the realized values of these variables rather than the values expected *ex ante* (recall (7.3)–(7.6)), the model-consistent expected path of the exchange rate depends entirely on the actual paths of the exogenous variables in the model. The internal logic of the model thus implies that the model-consistent expected path of the exchange rate is unique and corresponds to the perfect foresight path.

To solve for the expected path of the exchange rate that is consistent with the model, the observed state of the economy at initial time 0, and the implicit assumption that the exogenous variables will remain constant forever, note from (7.2) that the expected value at time 0 of the time-t exchange rate can be expressed as

$$s^e(t) = \bar{s} + [s(0) - \bar{s}]e^{-\theta t}. \tag{7.16}$$

Similarly, from (7.15), the price level at time t can be written as

$$p(t) = \bar{p} + [p(0) - \bar{p}]e^{-\pi w t}. \tag{7.17}$$

Substitution of (7.17) into (7.12) gives the actual path of the exchange rate when all the exogenous variables remain constant

$$s(t) = \bar{s} - [(1 - \phi\mu\delta)/\Delta][p(0) - \bar{p}]e^{-\pi wt} \qquad (7.18)$$

and, hence,

$$s(t) = \bar{s} + [s(0) - \bar{s}]e^{-\pi wt}. \qquad (7.19)$$

Accordingly, from (7.16), (7.19), (7.13), and (7.14), the model-consistent expected path of the exchange rate is given by the solution to the equation

$$\theta = \pi w = \pi[\mu(\delta + \theta\sigma) + \mu\delta\theta\lambda]/[\phi\mu(\delta + \theta\sigma) + \theta\lambda]. \qquad (7.20)$$

The basic motivation for the Dornbusch model was

to develop a theory that is suggestive of the observed large fluctuations in exchange rates while at the same time establishing that such exchange rate movements are consistent with rational expectations formation.[6]

To illustrate that his model was capable of generating large fluctuations in exchange rates in response to unexpected shocks ("news"), Dornbusch analyzed the process of adjustment to an unanticipated change in the money supply, demonstrating that the initial jump in the exchange rate exceeded the adjustment in the long-run equilibrium exchange rate. This predicted pattern of "overshooting" is the most celebrated implication of sticky-price models of exchange rate dynamics.

The overshooting response of the exchange rate to a monetary shock is illustrated by figure 7.1. The negatively-sloped QQ line, which corresponds to (7.12), describes the set of combinations of p and s that clear the money and goods markets simultaneously. Prior to the monetary shock, the economy is in a position of steady state equilibrium at (s_0, p_0). The authorities then announce a permanent increase in the money supply. From (7.8) it can be seen that – with $\bar{y}$, p^*, and r^* unchanged – the new steady state values of s and p must lie along a positively-sloped 45 degree line through (s_0, p_0); and from (7.7), the steady state value of p must increase by the same amount as the (logarithm of the) money supply. Accordingly, the QQ curve shifts upward to $Q'Q'$, leading to a new steady state equilibrium at (s_2, p_2). The impact effect of the shock, however, is to shift the economy to (s_1, p_0) since the price level is a nonjumping variable that can only adjust over time. The jump depreciation of the domestic currency (from s_0 to s_1) coincides with a decline in the domestic interest rate, which is necessary to clear the money market according to (7.3). The positive differential that emerges between the foreign and domestic interest rates in turn gives rise, according to (7.1), to expectations that the initial jump depreciation of the domestic

---

[6] Dornbusch (1976, p. 1161).

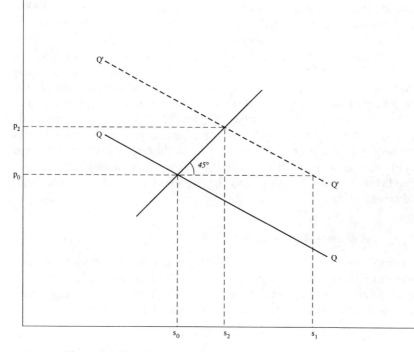

Figure 7.1 The Dornbusch model of "overshooting"

currency will be followed by a period of appreciation. This is the overshooting result. It may be noted, from (7.4b), that the initial jumps in the exchange rate and the domestic interest rate act to stimulate domestic output, thereby setting in motion the price adjustment process described by (7.5).

The example just considered focuses on the behavior of the exchange rate following an unexpected current and permanent shift in the money supply. The literature on exchange rate dynamics has not been limited to the model provided by Dornbusch or to the analysis of monetary shocks.[7] Moreover, the analysis of various types of shocks includes studies of the responses to current announcements of future changes in policy variables[8] as well as analysis of the effects of transitory shocks.[9]

---

[7] Mussa (1977, 1982) made important contributions to the development of dynamic flexible-price monetary models; Kouri (1976), to dynamic portfolio-balance models. See Obstfeld and Stockman (1985) for a survey of exchange rate dynamics in a variety of continuous-time rational-expectations models.

[8] See, for example, Wilson (1979) and Buiter and Miller (1982).

[9] For example, Henderson (1984).

Nevertheless, the Dornbusch model has played a dominant role in shaping the literature on exchange rate dynamics through the early 1990s. Its prominence has reflected both the analytic elegance of the model and empirical evidence that strongly rejects models based on the classical assumption of perfectly flexible prices. At the same time, two handicaps of the Dornbusch model – in particular, its ad hoc specification of the price determination process and its failure to provide an explicit role for the current account in exchange rate determination – may have contributed to its poor empirical performance (see chapter 8),[10] and have greatly limited its relevance in policy-oriented discussions of exchange rate dynamics. In this connection, recent models based on an intertemporal optimization approach (see chapter 10) have made progress in overcoming the two major handicaps[11] and may ultimately be regarded as a major conceptual advance.

2   A discrete-time framework

Attempts to explain the behavior of exchange rates empirically normally rely on discrete-time models. A general framework for discrete-time analysis can be developed from the condition linking the observed spot rate at time t to the expected value at t of the spot rate at $t+1$[12]

$$s_t = z_t + E_t s_{t+1} \qquad (7.21)$$

where, from (6.37), z_t corresponds to the risk-adjusted interest differential – that is, the interest differential net of any risk premium

$$z_t = r_t - r_t^* - \phi_t. \qquad (7.22)$$

Recall that when the two interest rates are associated with claims on different countries – which is the appropriate choice in portfolio-balance models – ϕ_t is a premium for bearing a composite of exchange risk and credit risk.

Through forward iteration, (7.21) can be used to derive an expression relating observed changes in the exchange rate to various combinations of realized variables and revisions in expectations. Such an accounting framework, of course, does not represent a behavioral model of exchange rates until it is supplemented with a set of behavioral hypotheses about the relationships between expectational variables and observable exogenous

[10] See Engel and Flood (1985) for an extension of the conceptual model to incorporate current account dynamics.
[11] See Obstfeld and Rogoff (1994), who explore exchange rate dynamics in an intertemporal optimizing model with monopolistic competition.
[12] Such an "accounting framework" received early emphasis in Isard (1983).

variables, so that revisions in expectations can be linked to new information about the observable exogenous variables.

From (7.21), by forward iteration,

$$s_t = \sum_{k=t}^{T-1} E_t z_k + E_t s_T \tag{7.23}$$

where T denotes a distant point in time.[13] Thus, for two points in time denoted by a and b (with $b > a$)

$$s_b - s_a = -\sum_{k=a}^{b-1} E_a z_k + \sum_{k=b}^{T-1} (E_b z_k - E_a z_k) + (E_b s_T - E_a s_T). \tag{7.24}$$

Note that

$$\sum_{k=a}^{b-1} E_a z_k = \sum_{k=a}^{b-1} z_k - \sum_{k=a}^{b-1} (z_k - E_a z_k) \tag{7.25}$$

and that $E_b z_b = z_b$. Accordingly,

$$s_b - s_a = -\sum_{k=a}^{b-1} z_k + \sum_{k=a}^{b} (z_k - E_a z_k) + \sum_{k=b+1}^{T-1} (E_b z_k - E_a z_k) + (E_b s_T - E_a s_T). \tag{7.26}$$

(7.26) decomposes the observed change in the spot exchange rate between times a and b into four components: the change warranted by the sequence of risk-adjusted interest differentials realized between times a and $b-1$; the change associated with errors in time-a expectations about the sequence of risk-adjusted interest differentials realized through time b; the change associated with revisions in expectations between times a and b about the sequence of risk-adjusted interest differentials to be realized between times $b+1$ and $T-1$; and the revision in expectations between times a and b about the long-run exchange rate s_T.

For the case in which the two types of claims are perfect substitutes, the z_k terms correspond to observable interest differentials. Moreover, under a flexible exchange rate regime, the interest rates can be regarded as the settings of foreign and domestic monetary policy instruments. Thus, (7.26) in this case relates the observed change in the nominal exchange rate between times a and b to the realized path of the nominal interest differential, errors in expectations about the monetary policy settings

---

[13] The bubble component of the rational-expectations solution has been suppressed as empirically irrelevant, for reasons discussed in chapter 5. T will later be interpreted as a point in time at which the economy can be expected to have settled into a steady state equilibrium.

realized through time b, revisions in expectations about future settings of monetary policy instruments, and revisions in expectations about the long-run nominal exchange rate. When the two types of claims are not perfect substitutes, various terms involving risk premiums also enter the relationship.

An approximate accounting identity analogous to (7.26) can be derived for describing changes in the real exchange rate, q_t, in terms of realizations and revisions in expectations about real interest differentials, x_k. In particular, define the real exchange rate and the real risk-adjusted interest differential as

$$q_t = s_t + p_t^* - p_t \tag{7.27}$$

$$x_t = z_t - E_t[(p_{t+1} - p_t) - (p_{t+1}^* - p_t^*)] \tag{7.28}$$

and note that (7.21) then implies

$$q_t = x_t + E_t q_{t+1}. \tag{7.29}$$

Accordingly, just as (7.21) leads to (7.26), so (7.29) implies

$$q_b - q_a = -\sum_{k=a}^{b-1} x_k + \sum_{k=a}^{b} (x_k - E_a x_k) + \sum_{k=b+1}^{T-1} (E_b x_k - E_a x_k) + (E_b q_T - E_a q_T). \tag{7.30}$$

The approximate identities (7.26) and (7.30) should be regarded as constraints or consistency requirements that it may be useful to impose on behavioral exchange rate models. To move from either of these accounting identities to a behavioral model requires hypotheses that link the behavior of interest rates (perhaps viewed as policy instruments) and price levels to various exogenous variables. Such hypotheses also serve to link, in a model-consistent manner, the expected future values of interest rates and price levels to the expected future values of exogenous variables. Note, however, that the approximate accounting identities also include terms in the expected long-run nominal or real exchange rate. A complete behavioral model of the exchange rate built upon the identity (7.30) thus requires a behavioral hypothesis linking the expected long-run level of the real exchange rate to the observed and expected values of exogenous variables.

As an alternative to building an accounting framework from (7.21), a number of studies[14] have focused on an exchange rate pricing formula built from the reduced form

$$s_t = \chi_t + \lambda(E_t s_{t+1} - s_t) \quad \text{with } \lambda > 0 \tag{7.31}$$

[14] Mussa (1976), Bilson (1978a), Frenkel and Mussa (1980, 1985).

where χ_t represents "the basic economic conditions that affect the foreign exchange market in period t."[15] The reduced form can be derived from a flexible-price monetary model (see chapter 8, p. 134) in which the parameter λ corresponds to the interest rate semi-elasticity of the demand for money and χ is a function of money supplies and income levels. Since (7.31) implies

$$s_t = \frac{1}{1+\lambda} \chi_t + \frac{\lambda}{1+\lambda} E_t s_{t+1} \tag{7.32}$$

with $0 < \lambda/(1+\lambda) < 1$, repeated forward iteration leads to a relationship describing the spot exchange rate in terms of the expected time paths of money supplies and income levels over an infinite horizon:

$$s_t = \frac{1}{1+\lambda} \sum_{j=0}^{\infty} \left(\frac{\lambda}{1+\lambda}\right)^j E_t \chi_{t+j}. \tag{7.33}$$

An apparent advantage of (7.33) over (7.26) or (7.30) is that the former does not require an explicit boundary condition on the long-run level of the nominal or real exchange rate. As discussed in chapter 4, however, the flexible-price assumptions of the monetary model embedded in (7.33) are strongly disputed by the empirical evidence. And on a related point, most large-scale macroeconometric forecasting models with consistent expectations have specified their exchange rate equations in ways that require boundary conditions.[16]

3   The concept of long-run equilibrium and the role of the current account

The conceptual literature provides two approaches to modeling long-run equilibrium. One approach argues that purchasing power parity holds in the very long run, as discussed in chapter 4, so that the long-run real exchange rate can be assumed to be time-invariant. The second approach rests on the belief that the current account balance – which affects a country's stock of net claims on, or indebtedness to, the rest of the world – has an important constraining influence on exchange rates over the long run. Under the latter approach, the boundary condition that pins down the expected long-run level of the real exchange rate is derived from the hypothesis that the current account – or the stock of net indebtedness to the rest of the world – is expected to be in equilibrium in the long run.[17]

[15] Frenkel and Mussa (1985, p. 726).
[16] These models employ iterative solution procedures that involve finite numbers of forward substitutions; see Taylor (1988).
[17] Kouri (1976), Dornbusch and Fischer (1980), Isard (1980), Rodríguez (1980), Hooper and Morton (1982), Mussa (1984), Engel and Flood (1985), Krugman (1990).

The belief that current account developments impose a constraint on the exchange rate in the long run rests on the notion that large and persistent current account imbalances are unsustainable,[18] together with the perception that current account adjustment can be achieved through changes in real exchange rates, all else being equal. Thus, given the time paths of other variables that influence the current account, the real exchange rate cannot be sustained at a level that would generate large and persistent current account imbalances. Obversely, exogenous developments that permanently shift the current account, other things being equal, redefine the equilibrium level of the real exchange rate. In this context, the definition of exchange rate equilibrium is conditional, for example, on a definition of the equilibrium path of employment or economic activity; see chapter 10, which discusses different methodologies that have been used to construct measures of equilibrium exchange rates.

As just noted, the proposition that current account developments influence the prevailing nominal exchange rate through their influence on the expected long-run level of the real exchange rate has implications for how exchange rates should respond to permanent shifts in the supply of output or other developments that have permanent effects on the current account, other things being equal. It says little, however, about the likely responses of exchange rates to temporary supply or demand shocks or other developments that have transitory effects on the current account. The time profiles of the responses of the exchange rate and the current account to transitory shocks, as predicted by an intertemporal optimization approach to modeling the current account, are also discussed in chapter 10.

4   The target zone framework

The models described in the first and second sections were developed in the 1970s and early 1980s for the purposes of analyzing the dynamic behavior of flexible exchange rates. By the mid-1980s, the policymaking community was actively discussing proposals for replacing the system of flexible exchange rates among major currencies with a system of target zones,[19] and by the end of the decade, economists were actively developing models of exchange rate dynamics within a target zone framework. To the Deputies of the Group of Ten, a "target zone" implied an arrangement with "wide margins around an adjustable set of exchange rates,"[20] as distinct from the relatively narrow margins that prevailed under the Bretton Woods system and within the Exchange Rate Mechanism of the European Monetary

---

[18] Dooley and Isard (1982b, 1987), Krugman (1985, 1988b).
[19] Williamson (1983), Goldstein (1984), Crockett and Goldstein (1987).
[20] Group of Ten Deputies (1985, paragraph 31).

System. A similar definition of target zones was provided by Frenkel and Goldstein:

Perhaps the easiest way to think of them is as a hybrid exchange rate system that combines some of the attributes and characteristics of both pegged and flexible exchange rate systems.[21]

This section provides perspectives on the target zone literature. It summarizes the key assumptions, predictions, and deficiencies of the early models of exchange rate dynamics within a target zone, but without writing down a formal model. It also devotes a few paragraphs to historical perspectives and empirical applications, which does not fit the logic of a chapter on exchange rate dynamics, but which permits an integrated summary of the different aspects of the target zone literature.

The attention that target zone systems began to receive around the mid-1980s was stimulated by the behavior of US dollar exchange rates. During the first half of the decade, the US Treasury Department, which had higher authority than the Federal Reserve in determining exchange market intervention policy, had essentially taken the position that it

would be wrong in principle for them to second-guess the markets' views and futile in practice to pit their own resources against the vast amounts of private capital that might be bet against them.[22]

Thus, during the first four-year term of President Reagan, the US authorities did little to resist the dramatic appreciation of the US dollar.[23] In early 1985, however, following a change of leadership at the Treasury Department, the US policy of "benign neglect" was replaced by a new activism in exchange markets, motivated by sentiment that the markets were prone to unstable behavior in the absence of policy commitments to limit exchange rate variation. In words written by Paul Volcker before he became Federal Reserve Chairman:

If ... markets come to believe exchange rate stability is not itself a significant policy objective, we should not be surprised that snowballing cumulative movements can develop that appear widely out of keeping with current balance-of-payments prospects or domestic price movements.[24]

The development of conceptual models of exchange rate dynamics within a target zone system began with an important contribution by

---

[21] Frenkel and Goldstein (1986, p. 635). Issues that arise in designing a system of target zones include: how wide the zones should be; whether they should be "loud" (that is, announced to the public) or "quiet;" and whether the system should involve "hard" or "soft" commitments to take policy actions whenever exchange rates approach or hit the edges of the zones.   [22] Kenen (1988, p. 2).   [23] Pauls (1990).

[24] Volcker (1978, p. 7).

Krugman (1991), which was circulated in 1988.[25] Notably, Krugman's analysis was based on the strong assumption that the target zone was perfectly credible, in the sense that market participants expected the exchange rate to remain within the zone forever. It also assumed that the policy authorities did not act to resist exchange rate movements unless the exchange rate reached one of the boundaries of the zone.

Initially, the target zone literature focused on exploring the implications of Krugman's analysis. One implication is that the frequency distribution of the exchange rate within the target zone should be U-shaped, with the exchange rate spending most of the time near the edges of the zone. A second prediction, when the uncovered interest parity condition is also assumed, is that the correlation between the interest rate differential and the exchange rate should be strongly negative. Both implications, however, have been strongly rejected in empirical tests.[26] Moreover, in connection with the European experience with fixed exchange rate zones over the past decade, there is clear evidence that the target zones have not been perfectly credible, and that policy authorities have frequently intervened to resist exchange rate movements while exchange rates were within their fluctuation margins.

In light of such evidence, it did not take long for the target zone literature to move away from analysis based on the perfect credibility assumption. The second generation of target zone models thus decomposed the expected change in the exchange rate into two parts: an expected change in the central parity, and an expected change in the deviation of the exchange rate from the central parity. Let

$$s_t = c_t + e_t \tag{7.34}$$

where c_t is the (logarithm of the) central parity at time t and e_t is the deviation of the observed exchange rate from the central parity, such that

$$(E_t s_{t+1} - s_t) = (E_t c_{t+1} - c_t) + (E_t e_{t+1} - e_t). \tag{7.35}$$

Using this decomposition, the literature has employed regression techniques to derive estimates of the expected exchange rate movement within the target zone;[27] has used these estimates, together with the uncovered interest rate parity assumption and observed data on exchange rates and interest rate differentials, to construct implied estimates of the expected realignment of central parities; and has analyzed the empirical behavior of

---

[25] The discussion here draws heavily on Svensson (1992b), who provides references to the literature. See also Flood and Garber (1991).

[26] Bertola and Caballero (1992), Svensson (1991), Flood, Rose, and Mathieson (1991), Lindberg and Söderlind (1994).

[27] See the discussion in Svensson (1993, pp. 773–6).

the latter estimates in various attempts to shed light on the causes of realignment expectations.[28]

Interest in understanding the nature of the relationship between realignment expectations and macroeconomic developments has intensified following the summer 1992 crisis in European currency markets,[29] and it is now recognized that such relationships are appropriately analyzed in the context of an explicit policy objective function. This new direction in analyzing the behavior of exchange rates within a target zone system is discussed at length in chapter 9.

Notably, most of the formal target zone literature assumes that market participants are rational and completely informed about macroeconomic fundamentals. As such, the formal literature has largely ignored the central point of the original, policy case for target zones – namely, to cope with the perceived speculative inefficiency of foreign exchange markets.[30] Recognition of this point has been reflected in new efforts to construct exchange rate models in which market participants are either not fully rational or have limited information, as discussed in chapter 10.

---

[28] For example, Caramazza (1993), Rose and Svensson (1994). See also Chen and Giovannini (1993), who use a one-step methodology.

[29] The summer 1992 events are discussed in chapter 11.

[30] Krugman and Miller (1993).

8   Empirical estimates of structural exchange rate models

The period from the mid-1970s to the early 1980s has been characterized as "a 'heroic age' of exchange rate theory."[1] During that time, international economists focused attention on three major structural approaches to modeling the empirical behavior of exchange rates and engaged in continuing efforts at theoretical extension in a spirited competition to explain the observed evidence. The three structural approaches have become known as flexible-price monetary models, sticky-price monetary models, and portfolio-balance models. For the most part, the various specification hypotheses that were entered in the empirical horse race were single-equation (or small-scale) reduced-form models. The heroic age ended when statistical tests revealed the sobering fact that none of the specification hypotheses could significantly outperform a naive random walk model in predicting the out-of-sample behavior of the exchange rate.

This chapter focuses on the empirical performance of structural exchange rate models, along with some implications for policies and macroeconomic model design.[2] The first section describes the specifications of the small-scale reduced-form models associated with the three theoretical approaches. Although proponents of the different specifications initially assessed their models in terms of in-sample goodness-of-fit statistics, by late 1981 the criterion of out-of-sample prediction accuracy had become widely regarded as a more appropriate basis for model comparisons. The second section discusses the out-of-sample performance of the single-equation reduced-form empirical models. Because the out-of-sample tests have not adequately covered the range of portfolio-balance models, the third section reviews the in-sample evidence from the different approaches that have been taken in estimating such models, and also discusses the implications of the statistical evidence for evaluating the

---

[1] Krugman (1993b, p. 6).
[2] Several other major facets of empirical research on exchange rates have been discussed in chapters 4 and 5. See MacDonald and Taylor (1992), Taylor (1995a, 1995b), and Frankel and Rose (1995) for recent surveys with more extensive references. See Frankel (1984), Boughton (1988), and Isard (1988) for earlier perspectives on the empirical literature.

effectiveness of exchange market intervention policy. The fourth section then addresses the approaches that have been taken in describing and projecting the behavior of exchange rates in fully-specified large-scale macroeconometric models.

1   Reduced-form specifications

This section characterizes the three different classes of structural exchange rate models that have been tested empirically. The notation is the same as in previous chapters: m, p, and y (m^*, p^*, and y^*) denote logarithms of the domestic (foreign) money supply, price level, and real income level; s is the logarithm of the domestic currency price of one unit of foreign exchange; and r (r^*) is the domestic (foreign) nominal interest rate.

Although the structural models generally do not include expectations terms among the variables that explicitly appear in their reduced-form estimation equations, virtually all models provide scope for exchange rates to jump when market participants revise their expectations in response to news. In particular, virtually all models include the short-term nominal interest differential among their sets of explanatory variables, so that, when transformed by replacing the interest differential with the expected change in the exchange rate (plus any risk premium), the models can be rewritten in the reduced form

$$s_t = \chi_t + \lambda(E_t s_{t+1} - s_t) \tag{8.1}$$

where χ_t is a function of relevant explanatory variables (and reflects any risk premium). Thus, using the identity $s_{t+1} - s_t = (E_t s_{t+1} - s_t) + (s_{t+1} - E_t s_{t+1})$ and substituting expressions for s_{t+1} and $E_t s_{t+1}$ based on (8.1), the observed change in the exchange rate can be regarded as the change expected *ex ante* $(E_t s_{t+1} - s_t)$, plus a change associated with any errors in expectations about the explanatory variables $(\chi_{t+1} - E_t \chi_{t+1})$,[3] plus a change associated with revisions in expectations about the exchange rate at a future horizon $(E_{t+1} s_{t+2} - E_t s_{t+2})$

$$s_{t+1} - s_t = (E_t s_{t+1} - s_t) + \frac{1}{1+\lambda}(\chi_{t+1} - E_t \chi_{t+1})$$
$$+ \frac{\lambda}{1+\lambda}(E_{t+1} s_{t+2} - E_t s_{t+2}). \tag{8.2}$$

---

[3] A number of studies have explored whether statistical innovations (from ARIMA processes) in macroeconomic variables, or deviations of *ex post* realizations from published *ex ante* forecasts, are statistically significant in explaining observed changes in exchange rates; see the discussion in Frankel and Rose (1995).

Flexible-price monetary models

A central assumption of flexible-price monetary models is that purchasing power parity holds continuously, such that

$$s_t = p_t - p_t^*. \tag{8.3}$$

The second key characteristic is the assumption that price levels must be consistent with money market equilibrium conditions. The latter conditions are usually written in the form[4]

$$m_t = p_t + \phi y_t - \lambda r_t \text{ and } m_t^* = p_t^* + \phi^* y_t^* - \lambda^* r_t^* \tag{8.4}$$

where the parameters ϕ and ϕ^* are the income elasticities of the demands for real money balances while λ and λ^* are the interest rate semi-elasticities. Together, (8.3) and (8.4), with the addition of a disturbance term (u), imply

$$s_t = m_t - m_t^* - \phi y_t + \phi^* y_t^* + \lambda r_t - \lambda^* r_t^* + u_t. \tag{8.5}$$

Moreover, when the two money demand functions are assumed to be identical

$$s_t = (m_t - m_t^*) - \phi(y_t - y_t^*) + \lambda(r_t - r_t^*) + u_t. \tag{8.6}$$

Specifications (8.5) and (8.6) provided the basis for some of the earliest attempts to fit exchange rate models to data from the 1970s.[5] The out-of-sample prediction accuracy of these models, which many economists regard as more relevant than in-sample goodness-of-fit, is described in the second section below.

Sticky-price monetary models

As discussed in chapter 7, one of the central assumptions of flexible-price monetary models – continuous purchasing power parity – was abandoned by Dornbusch (1976) in an influential paper that spawned a new class of monetary models with sluggish price adjustment. The first attempts to fit the sticky-price monetary model to empirical data were based on a specification form introduced by Frankel (1979):

$$s_t = (m_t - m_t^*) - \phi(y_t - y_t^*) - \alpha(r_t - r_t^*) + \beta(\rho_t - \rho_t^*) + u_t \tag{8.7}$$

where ρ_t and ρ_t^* denote expectations held at time t about the long-run rates of inflation in the two countries.

---

[4] By contrast, in studying exchange rate behavior during periods of hyperinflation, Frenkel (1976) assumed that the demand for real money balances depended simply on the expected rate of inflation, and that the expected inflation differential could be measured by the forward exchange premium.

[5] For example, Bilson (1978a, 1978b), Hodrick (1978).

In deriving (8.7), Frankel argued that the basic assumptions of the original Dornbusch model, as described by (7.1)–(7.5), should be modified to allow for differences in secular rates of inflation. More specifically, Frankel chose to replace (7.2) with

$$\dot{s}^e = -\theta(s-\bar{s})+(\rho-\rho^*) \tag{8.8}$$

where $\bar{s}$ was interpreted as an equilibrium value of s conditional on maintaining m, m^*, y, and y^* at their current values. Together, (8.8) and (7.1) imply that the gap between the current exchange rate and its equilibrium level is proportionate to a real interest differential

$$s-\bar{s} = -(1/\theta)[(r-r^*)-(\rho-\rho^*)]. \tag{8.9}$$

In addition, (7.3), together with the long-run PPP assumption and the conditional interpretation of $\bar{s}$, implies

$$\bar{s} = \bar{p}-\bar{p}^* = (m-m^*)-\phi(y-y^*)+\lambda(\bar{r}-\bar{r}^*). \tag{8.10}$$

(8.7) then follows directly from (8.9), (8.10), and the long-run equilibrium condition $\bar{r}-\bar{r}^* = \rho-\rho^*$, where $\alpha = 1/\theta$ and $\beta = \lambda+(1/\theta)$.

In empirical estimation of (8.7), long-term interest rates have generally been used as proxy variables for expected long-run inflation rates. For purposes of judging whether the regression evidence favors the sticky-price monetary model over the flexible-price monetary model, attention has focused both on the sign of the estimated coefficient attached to the short-term interest differential – which is positive in (8.6) and negative in (8.7) – and on the significance of the estimated coefficient attached to the long-term interest differential.

Portfolio-balance models

As discussed in chapter 6, the portfolio-balance approach assumes that financial portfolios include nonmonetary claims on different countries that cannot be regarded as perfect substitutes. Thus, unlike in the flexible-price and sticky-price monetary approaches, the uncovered interest parity condition does not prevail.

Until the early 1980s, attempts to explain the behavior of exchange rates with portfolio-balance models,[6] while breaking important new ground, were generally based on ad hoc assumptions about exchange rate expectations. The early empirical applications of portfolio-balance models were often based also on the heroic assumption that the currency composition of financial portfolios could be measured simply by cumulating current

---

[6] Examples include Kouri and Porter (1974), Artus (1976), Branson, Halttunen, and Masson (1977, 1979), Haas and Alexander (1979). Tryon (1983) provides a survey.

account flows. The first attempt to construct more accurate data on the currency composition of the financial portfolios of the residents of different countries was made by Dooley and Isard (1982a), who also introduced the use of an iterative procedure to estimate an exchange rate equation in which data on the expected future exchange rate were generated in a model-consistent manner.

Empirical tests of portfolio-balance models, which are summarized in the third section below, took two directions in the early 1980s. One set of tests was developed under the premise that the difference between the change in the exchange rate expected *ex ante* (that is, the interest differential minus the risk premium) and the change observed *ex post* was a serially uncorrelated random error term. These tests looked for statistically significant evidence that the risk premium varied over time in the manner predicted by the portfolio-balance model,[7] or alternatively, that the composition of bond portfolios was sensitive to the risk premium.[8] A second type of test, following Hooper and Morton (1982), adapted the sticky-price monetary model to formulate an estimable exchange rate equation that allowed, *inter alia*, for the existence of a risk premium. An adaptation that became widely employed in the latter type of test, particularly after early drafts of Meese and Rogoff (1983a, 1983b) were circulated, was the specification form

$$s_t = a_0 + a_1(m_t - m_t^*) + a_2(y_t - y_t^*) + a_3(r_t - r_t^*)$$
$$+ a_4(\rho_t - \rho_t^*) + a_5 \int TB + a_6 \int TB^* + u_t \qquad (8.11)$$

where $\int TB$ and $\int TB^*$ represent the cumulative trade balances of the two countries. It should be noted that the cumulative trade balance terms were introduced as proxy variables for cumulative current account balances in empirical tests based on monthly time series data.[9]

The classification of (8.11) as a portfolio balance model can be misleading. In the model originally derived by Hooper and Morton (1982), the cumulative current account (adjusted for cumulative official intervention flows) appears as a risk premium term, while changes in the expected long-run real exchange rate are captured by including among the explanatory variables a measure of the nontransitory unexpected change in the current account. By contrast, in adopting the specification form (8.11), Meese and Rogoff (1983a, 1983b) interpreted the cumulative trade balance or current account terms as variables that allowed for changes in the long-run real exchange rate, rather than variables that allowed for the existence of a risk premium. Such an interpretation is supported by the view that cumulative current account imbalances redistribute wealth internationally, with effects

[7] Dooley and Isard (1983), Rogoff (1984), Danker *et al.* (1987).
[8] Frankel (1982b), Danker *et al.* (1987).
[9] Current account data are available only on a quarterly basis.

– other things being equal – on subsequent levels of each country's expenditures, incomes, and current account imbalances, and accordingly, with implications for the level of the real exchange rate that is consistent with long-run current account balance.[10] For this reason, it seems preferable to refer to (8.11) as a sticky-price hybrid model.[11]

2 Out-of-sample prediction accuracy

By the end of 1981, the economics profession had been forced to confront the initial drafts of Meese and Rogoff (1983a, 1983b), which reported the results of an extensive set of thoughtfully formulated tests in which existing empirical models failed to significantly outperform a random walk model in predicting the behavior of exchange rates out of sample – even when the predictions from the empirical models were assumed to reflect perfect accuracy in predicting the exogenous variables. The tests focused on exchange rates for the US dollar against the German mark, the Japanese yen, and the British pound, as well as on a trade-weighted average exchange rate for the US dollar.

The reduced-form structural models that Meese and Rogoff estimated – corresponding to a flexible-price monetary model, a sticky-price monetary model, and a sticky-price hybrid model – can be described as three constrained versions of the specification form (8.11). All three cases were constrained by setting $a_1 = 1$, reflecting the assumption that the exchange rate exhibits first-degree homogeneity in relative money supplies. In addition, the flexible-price monetary model was constrained by imposing $a_4 = a_5 = a_6 = 0$; and the sticky-price monetary model, by $a_5 = a_6 = 0$. The models were estimated using monthly data series extending from March 1973, the beginning of the floating rate period, through June 1981.

The procedure that Meese and Rogoff employed to construct out-of-sample forecasts had become accepted methodology for comparing the forecasting performances of different macroeconomic models.[12] Each model was estimated initially for the period through November 1976, providing a set of estimated parameters that were used – along with actual

---

[10] Dornbusch and Fischer (1980). Frankel (1982a) developed a monetary model with a specification form somewhat analogous to (8.11) by adding wealth to the money demand functions (8.2) and (8.3); specifically, the cumulative trade balance terms are replaced by wealth terms that incorporate cumulative current account balances. As noted, however, by Dornbusch (1980, p. 164), the absence of an empirically significant wealth effect on money demand reduces the plausibility of this interpretation of (8.11).

[11] Evidence suggesting the importance of wealth effects operating through the long-run equilibrium level of the real exchange rate has been provided by Hacche and Townend (1981), who found that observed exchange rates for the British pound responded significantly to unexpected changes in the price of oil during 1972–80.

[12] See the references listed in Meese and Rogoff (1983a, pp. 10–11).

realized values of the explanatory variables – to generate forecasts at horizons of 1, 3, 6, and 12 months, corresponding to the maturities of the forward exchange rates for which data were available. Then the sample was extended through an additional month (December 1976), the model was re-estimated using rolling regressions, and new forecasts were generated at the same horizons. And so forth. By basing the forecasts from the structural models on the actual future values of the explanatory variables, Meese and Rogoff eliminated the possibility that the structural models could be outperformed by other forecasting models for reasons that simply reflected inaccuracies in projecting the explanatory variables, as distinct from deficiencies in the structural models *per se*.[13]

Using several alternative but similar measures of out-of-sample forecasting accuracy,[14] Meese and Rogoff (1983a) compared the forecasting performances of the reduced-form structural models with those of a random walk model, with the various maturities of forward exchange rates, and with both univariate and vector autoregression models. The random walk model, in which the current spot rate was used as a predictor of all future spot rates, almost invariably outperformed the other models over all forecast horizons and across all exchange rates. In short, neither the behavioral relationships suggested by theory, nor the information obtained through autoregression, provided a model that could forecast significantly better than a random walk. And furthermore, while the random walk model performed at least as well as the other models, it predicted very poorly.

Meese and Rogoff contemplated several possible reasons for the poor out-of-sample fits of the reduced-form structural models. Since the structural model forecasts had been purged of any errors associated with inaccurate predictions of explanatory variables, their disappointing performance was regarded as

most likely ... attributable to simultaneous equation bias, sampling error, stochastic movements in the true underlying parameters, or misspecification. ... [including] possible nonlinearities in the underlying models.[15]

As an initial set of explorations to address these possibilities, Meese and Rogoff tried (i) testing the models on exchange rates between currency pairs that excluded the US dollar, (ii) estimating the models in first-differenced form, (iii) relaxing the constraint of identical values for the

[13] As Meese and Rogoff (1983a, p. 10) noted, however, when the explanatory variables are endogenous, they will generally be correlated with the error term in the model, and information about the correlations could be used to construct better model forecasts.

[14] Root mean squared error, mean absolute error, and mean error. See Ericsson (1992b) for a general discussion of model evaluation criteria.

[15] Meese and Rogoff (1983a, p. 17).

parameters of the domestic and foreign money demand functions, (iv) modifying the choice of monetary aggregates, (v) substituting price levels for money supply variables, and (vi) replacing long-term interest rates with other proxies for expected inflation rates. None of these explorations changed the general qualitative results of the out-of-sample comparisons.

Meese and Rogoff also investigated the possibility that the forecasting performance of the structural models could be improved by taking steps to eliminate any simultaneous equation bias. After instrumental variables techniques and estimating a vector autoregression failed to shed more favorable light on the structural model forecasts, they explored the forecasting performance of a range of constrained coefficient models, searching over a grid of coefficient values based on the existing theoretical and empirical literature. As reported in Meese and Rogoff (1983b), these experiments simply reinforced the evidence that the structural models could not outperform the random walk model in forecasting out-of-sample at horizons of up to 12 months.[16]

The Meese–Rogoff findings gave rise to various studies investigating the forecasting performance of (i) models in which money demand functions were specified in partial-adjustment form,[17] (ii) alternative specifications of portfolio-balance models,[18] (iii) models with time-varying parameters,[19] and (iv) models with nonlinearities.[20] Some of these studies found that modified structural models could outperform the random walk model – but not very impressively.[21] Other lines of investigation explored whether explanatory power could be gained by examining the simultaneous behavior of several different exchange rates[22] or making careful attempts to capture the release dates for new information about relevant economic variables.[23]

In a third paper, Meese and Rogoff (1988) respecified the structural models as relationships between real exchange rates and real interest

---

[16] As suggestive corroborating evidence, Meese (1990) notes that sample moments (means and standard deviations) of the levels and first differences of nominal exchange rates have very low coefficients of correlation with corresponding moments of the levels and first differences of the explanatory variables that enter monetary models – namely, nominal interest rate differentials, relative national price levels, relative money supplies, and relative real output levels.   [17] Woo (1985), Finn (1986).

[18] Backus (1984), Boughton (1984).   [19] Wolff (1987), Schinasi and Swamy (1989).

[20] Diebold and Nason (1990), Meese and Rose (1991).

[21] As characterized by Frankel and Rose (1995), some structural models with a lagged endogenous variable have tended to predict somewhat better than the lagged endogenous variable by itself (that is, the random walk model); and in general, the predictive power of structural models relative to the random walk has tended to be better at relatively long horizons than at short horizons.   [22] Edwards (1982).

[23] Hoffman and Schlagenhauf (1985). See Frankel and Rose (1995) for a discussion of approaches that have been taken for quantifying the "news" about macroeconomic variables.

differentials, focusing on a data period that extended through March 1986, nearly five years beyond that of their two earlier studies. In some cases, the structural models outperformed the random walk model in out-of-sample forecasting – but only slightly.

In concluding their third paper, Meese and Rogoff conjectured:[24]

one possible explanation of why monetary models perform so poorly ... is that the disturbances impinging on exchange markets are predominantly real. Thus, models that focus primarily on monetary disturbances should not be expected to explain very much.[25]

Furthermore, in drawing inferences from cointegration tests, they noted:

Real interest differentials and real exchange rates are linked by international parity conditions, so our findings of no cointegration suggest that a variable omitted from relation [sic], possibly the expected value of some future real exchange rate, must have large variance as well. Alternatively, the set of shocks inducing near nonstationarity in real exchange rates cannot be the same as the set of shocks impinging on real interest rate differentials.[26]

Such views have generally been supported by other econometric studies, as discussed further in chapter 10. At the same time, as may be recalled from chapter 4, since the mid-1980s numerous studies of the long-run relationships between nominal exchange rates and national price levels – or of changes in real exchange rates over the long run – have provided clear evidence that structural models of nominal exchange rates can outpredict the random walk at long horizons.

3   Empirical evidence on portfolio-balance models and the effectiveness of sterilized intervention

The search for empirical evidence that risk premiums vary over time – and in the systematic manner suggested by portfolio-balance models – has been stimulated to a large extent by interest in evaluating the effectiveness of official intervention in foreign exchange markets. The relevant policy issue is whether sterilized intervention – defined as intervention that leaves unchanged the monetary liabilities of the official sector of each country[27] – can have a significant effect on the exchange rate.

Since a sterilized intervention operation is analytically equivalent to a particular type of change in the composition of the nonmonetary financial assets held in private-sector portfolios, the effectiveness of sterilized

---

[24] See also the reflections in Meese (1990).   [25] Meese and Rogoff (1988, p. 943).
[26] Meese and Rogoff (1988, p. 942).
[27] See Adams and Henderson (1983) for a discussion of the definition and measurement of exchange market intervention.

intervention depends on whether or not the private sector in the aggregate is indifferent to such changes in its financial portfolio. If the aggregate private sector regards the new assets in its portfolio as perfect substitutes for the assets relinquished, the sterilized intervention operation will have no portfolio-balance effect on market-clearing interest rates or exchange rates. If the assets are not regarded as perfect substitutes, however, market pressures will generate an adjustment in their relative expected yields – involving a change in the spot exchange rate relative to interest rates and the expected future spot rate – in order to induce the private sector to alter its aggregate portfolio in the manner dictated by the intervention operation.

The out-of-sample tests conducted by Meese and Rogoff (1983a, 1983b, 1988) did not provide an adequate empirical assessment of the portfolio-balance approach. In particular, the last two terms of (8.11) bear only a limited resemblance to the risk premium specifications suggested by the conceptual literature; recall, for example, condition (6.43). Indeed, as noted on p. 136 above, Meese and Rogoff interpreted the cumulative trade balances in (8.11) as terms that extended the sticky-price monetary model "to allow for changes in the long-run real exchange rate,"[28] rather than terms introduced to capture the risk premium.

Comprehensive discussions of the empirical evidence on portfolio-balance models and the effectiveness of sterilized intervention have recently been provided by Obstfeld (1990) and Edison (1993).[29] Several empirical approaches can be distinguished. Two of the approaches are based on postulated systems of asset demand functions and abstract completely from any changes over time in either the perceived riskiness of assets or the risk aversion of portfolio holders. One of these approaches estimates the asset demand equations directly, with asset stocks as dependent variables; the other inverts the asset demand equations and treats the risk premium as the dependent variable.[30] A third approach, pioneered by Frankel (1982c), is based on asset demand functions derived from maximizing a function of the mean and variance of one-period-ahead financial wealth,[31] with empirical applications postulating explicit variation over time in the covariance matrix of unexpected asset returns. A fourth approach derives the risk premium as the solution to a consumption-based optimization problem rather than adopting the more traditional portfolio-balance focus on financial wealth.[32] Although most empirical studies are based on monthly

---

[28] Meese and Rogoff (1983a, p. 5).   [29] See also the earlier survey by Tryon (1983).

[30] In several studies these approaches have been incorporated into small macroeconomic models that include policy reaction functions among the set of simultaneously estimated equations; see the discussion in Edison (1993).

[31] See Dornbusch (1983b) for development of the conceptual framework.

[32] See Obstfeld (1990).

or quarterly data, efforts have been made to improve on the treatment of time aggregation by focusing on weekly or daily data.[33]

For the most part, the empirical literature finds weak support, at best, for the hypothesis that risk premiums vary over time in the manner suggested by portfolio-balance models.[34] This failure, however, can be viewed from several perspectives. As a number of economists have argued, the lack of empirical evidence that portfolio-balance effects on exchange rates are important would be much more damaging to the portfolio-balance approach if there was significant evidence that other effects on exchange rates could be predicted with statistical confidence.[35] More fundamentally, given that changes in exchange rates appear to be largely unexpected, and that the forward rate unbiasedness hypothesis is strongly rejected empirically for reasons that economists do not yet adequately understand, there is a strong presumption that the econometric search for a time-varying risk premium has been based on inappropriate specification hypotheses. For example, as discussed in chapter 9, in an environment in which the incentives of the policy authorities generate peso problems, the expected change in the exchange rate and the magnitude of perceived exchange rate risk may be strongly correlated, which would present econometric difficulties in attempting to capture the behavior of the risk premium. Thus, as Obstfeld has emphasized:

The role of risk aversion cannot be assessed adequately until more refined procedures for purging the data have been developed.[36]

On a more straightforward econometric issue, it appears that, in almost all empirical tests of the portfolio-balance model,[37] data on forward exchange premiums have been used to measure the interest differential, which is equivalent, by virtue of covered interest parity, to using differentials between Eurocurrency interest rates. Although the use of such data is appropriate when attempting to explain the rejection of the unbiasedness hypothesis, which rests on the uncovered interest parity condition, it neglects an important element of the portfolio-balance channel and may bias the inferences that are drawn about the effectiveness of sterilized intervention.

---

[33] Rogoff (1984) and Loopesko (1984) are early examples.

[34] Recent exceptions are Domínguez and Frankel (1993b) and Ghosh (1992). Cumby (1988) and Obstfeld (1990) find weak support for the consumption-based model of the risk premium.

[35] Edison (1993, p. 5), who notes, however, that the search for portfolio-balance effects has focused almost entirely on in-sample evidence, and that the poor out-of-sample predictive accuracy of other exchange rate models may not be a valid standard of comparison for the in-sample fits of portfolio balance terms.   [36] Obstfeld (1989, p. 193).

[37] This includes my own efforts in Dooley and Isard (1982a, 1983).

The choice of interest rates on claims against different countries (for example, rates on short-term government securities) would be more appropriate for testing the portfolio-balance model and analyzing the effectiveness of intervention. This is because the nonmonetary "outside assets" that are distinguished in the portfolio-balance framework represent claims on the official sectors of different countries, as well as claims denominated in different currencies; recall the model described in chapter 6, pp. 108–13. As a similar point, a sterilized official intervention operation not only changes the currency composition of the aggregate financial portfolio of the private sector, but also changes its relative stocks of net claims on the official sectors of different countries. For example, when the Federal Reserve System intervenes to purchase dollars from a marketmaking bank in New York using Deutsche marks drawn from Fed's reserve deposits at the Bundesbank, settlement takes place through the delivery of Deutsche mark deposits to the New York bank against a reduction in the bank's dollar deposits with the Federal Reserve. In response, both central banks act automatically to sterilize the effects of the foreign exchange transaction on the stocks of base money in private circulation: the Federal Reserve, by adding liquidity to the money market; the Bundesbank, by withdrawing liquidity. This generally involves money market operations in which the Federal Reserve purchases US Treasury securities from the private sector while the Bundesbank sells the private sector claims on the German government or some other resident of Germany. The private sector in the aggregate thus winds up with unchanged holdings of US and German base moneys, reduced holdings of dollar-denominated claims on the US government, and increased holdings of mark-denominated net claims on the German public sector.

The fact that existing tests of portfolio-balance models have been based on inappropriate interest rate data provides a modicum of hope that future empirical studies will find stronger evidence that risk premiums vary systematically in the manner predicted by portfolio-balance considerations. Without conceptual advances in modeling the risk premium, however, it seems unlikely that data refinements alone will change the prevailing consensus that the portfolio-balance effect of sterilized intervention on exchange rates is not quantitatively significant relative to the effect of the same amount of unsterilized intervention (that is, of intervention that changes the domestic and foreign monetary bases).

In addition to whatever effects it may have through the risk premium or portfolio-balance channel, sterilized intervention may have an influence on exchange rates through the expectations or signaling channel.[38] When it is

[38] Mussa (1981).

not kept secret from market participants, sterilized intervention provides a signal that the authorities want the exchange rate to change in a certain direction. If this signal leads market participants to revise their exchange rate expectations in that direction, the shift in expectations will pull the current spot exchange rate along with it, achieving the desired result.

In general, the strength of the signaling effect depends on how it affects market perceptions of what the authorities will do if the exchange rate fails to adjust in the desired direction, or if the exchange rate moves in the opposite direction. Notably, sterilized intervention, when it is not kept secret, tends to provide a more powerful signal about the authorities' exchange rate objectives than simply announcing those objectives publicly, since by selling or purchasing foreign exchange reserves the authorities "put their money where their mouth is" by exposing the government to financial losses should the exchange rate move in the undesired direction. More fundamentally, however, the magnitude of the signaling effect depends on the extent to which market participants have limited information *ex ante* about the motives of the authorities, as well as on the relative strength of the authorities' incentives to avoid intervention losses. These points are developed in chapter 9.

A number of empirical studies have found positive evidence of signaling effects.[39] In general, however, these studies have not treated the strength of the signal conveyed by a given amount of sterilized intervention as something that varies over time as changes in economic and political circumstances affect market perceptions of what the authorities will do if the exchange rate fails to respond to the intervention. This point is also developed in chapter 9. As argued by the Group of Ten Deputies (1993) in their analysis of the pressures on exchange rates among European currencies during the summer and autumn of 1992, the effectiveness of the signals conveyed through sterilized intervention appears to depend critically on whether the authorities' exchange rate objectives are consistent with "underlying economic fundamentals."

4   Large-scale macroeconometric models

The poor empirical performance of reduced-form single-equation exchange rate models has led some economists to argue that simultaneous equations frameworks would be preferable for capturing the comovements of exchange rates and other variables in response to different types of exogenous shocks.[40] Other economists, however, are skeptical of this view,

---

[39] See Domínguez and Frankel (1993a), Kaminsky and Lewis (1993), and references cited in Edison (1993).

[40] Isard (1988), Papell (1988) and, in a somewhat different context, McCallum (1994).

noting that a simultaneous equations approach has both advantages and disadvantages. While multi-equation estimation offers the potential for increased precision of parameter estimates, it also runs the risk that misspecification of any single equation can contaminate the estimated parameters in every equation.[41]

Notably, none of the large-scale multicountry macroeconometric forecasting models includes an exchange rate equation specified in one of the forms tested by Meese and Rogoff – namely, one of the constrained or unconstrained versions of (8.11). This reflects the fact that (8.11) represents a combination of several distinct behavioral equations that are not collapsed into a reduced-form specification in the large-scale models. It may be noted, also, that even the reduced forms of these models do not include (8.11) insofar as the money demand equations in the large-scale models are different from those embodied in (8.11).

Nevertheless, most large-scale macroeconometric models – like the models that lead to the reduced-form specification (8.11) – contain the uncovered interest parity (UIP) condition as a specific equation for the exchange rate, or else a modified UIP condition that includes either an exogenous residual or an endogenous risk premium.[42] The level of the exchange rate in any time period is thus linked to the short-term interest rate differential and the expected level of the next period's exchange rate.[43] Moreover, there has been a trend toward estimating and simulating these models using techniques that constrain exchange rate expectations to be consistent with the model solution for the exchange rate next period.[44] In some models, however, exchange rate expectations are not specified in a model-consistent manner. For example, the most recently published version of the Federal Reserve Board's Multicountry Model[45] assumes that the nominal exchange rate is expected to change by the full amount of the expected inflation differential plus a fraction (γ) of the gap between its prevailing long-run equilibrium value ($\bar{s}_t$) and its actual value

---

[41] Meese (1990).

[42] Some models may rely instead on the purchasing power parity condition as a specific equation for the exchange rate. In other models, the exchange rate is implicitly determined from the balance of payments identity; see Gandolfo, Padoan, and Paladino (1990).

[43] In some models this relationship reflects the influence of current account flows or external indebtedness positions. Although some of the first multicountry macroeconometric models included equations for different categories of international capital flows (see Stevens *et al.* [1984]), attempts to disaggregate the capital account have been largely abandoned, following the lead of Haas and Alexander (1979).

[44] Taylor (1988) discusses the techniques for imposing model consistency. For descriptions of selected models, see Masson, Symansky, and Meredith (1990), McKibbin and Sachs (1991), Richardson (1988), Taylor (1988), Edison, Márquez, and Tryon (1987), and other references cited in Bryant, Hooper, and Mann (1993, chapter 3). Bryant (1995a) discusses the need to reevaluate the treatment of exchange rate expectations in multicountry models.

[45] Edison, Márquez, and Tryon (1987).

$$E_t s_{t+1} - s_t = \gamma(\bar{s}_t - s_t) + E_t(p_{t+1} - p_t) - E_t(p_{t+1}^* - p_t^*) \qquad (8.12)$$

where the long-run equilibrium nominal exchange rate is defined as the long-run equilibrium real exchange rate (assumed constant) adjusted by the expected ratio of national price levels.

Fisher *et al.* (1990) provide an econometric evaluation of the exchange rate equations used in five different models of the UK economy. As a framework for comparative testing, a general equation is formulated within which various specific exchange rate equations can be nested. Comparative tests are then conducted, leading to a preferred equation of the form:

$$q_t = E_t q_{t+1} - i_t + i_t^* - \gamma(CAS/GDP)_t \qquad (8.13)$$

where q_t is the logarithm of the real exchange rate

$$q_t = s_t + p_t - p_t^* \qquad (8.14)$$

i_t and i_t^* are real one-period interest rates

$$i_t = r_t - (E_t p_{t+1} - p_t) \qquad (8.15)$$

$$i_t^* = r_t^* - (E_t p_{t+1}^* - p_t^*) \qquad (8.16)$$

and CAS/GDP is the current account balance expressed as a proportion of nominal gross domestic product. Note that substitution of (8.14)–(8.16) into (8.13) yields

$$s_t = E_t s_{t+1} - r_t + r_t^* - \gamma(CAS/GDP)_t. \qquad (8.17)$$

(8.13) and (8.17) are alternative forms of a modified UIP condition that includes an endogenous or time-varying risk-premium term. Through the latter term, an increase in the net claims of UK residents on the rest of the world – corresponding to a surplus in the UK current account – is estimated to lead, other things being equal, to an appreciation of the pound (i.e., a reduction in s and q). By contrast, the MULTIMOD model developed at the International Monetary Fund includes a modified nonlinear form of the UIP condition (recall equation (5.3)) with an exogenous residual[46]

$$1 + r_t = (1 + r_t^*)(E_t S_{t+1}/S_t) + v_t. \qquad (8.18)$$

Despite the introduction of computational techniques for insuring that exchange rate expectations are model-consistent, the large-scale econometric models – like existing small-scale analytic models – have several features that may seriously impair their ability to explain the observed behavior of exchange rates. Although a number of these models have modified the UIP condition in simple ways to allow for a risk premium,

---

[46] Masson, Symansky, and Meredith (1990, p. 41).

unless the models are also capable of identifying errors in expectations about explanatory variables, and of allowing for serial correlation in such errors, they may fail to capture the type of time-variation in the risk premium that can arise when the incentives of the policy authorities create peso problems; see chapter 9. In addition, the exchange rate behavior predicted by these models is likely to be influenced considerably by the boundary conditions that are imposed under the model-consistent solution techniques, which makes it important to ensure that such boundary conditions correspond to conceptually appealing models of expected long-run equilibrium exchange rates; see chapter 10.

9   New perspectives from optimizing models of realignments under fixed exchange rates

The sobering empirical findings of the early 1980s dampened enthusiasm for exchange rate modeling, effectively marking the end of "the heroic age of exchange rate theory." Yet the pervasive economic effects of exchange rate movements, and the continuing political attention they have consequently received, have kept research on exchange rates alive. This chapter discusses a relatively new approach to modeling macroeconomic behavior under fixed-but-adjustable exchange rate arrangements. Chapter 10 then turns to new directions for conceptual models of flexible exchange rates.

The new approach to modeling macroeconomic behavior under fixed exchange rates treats the timing and magnitude of exchange rate realignments as solutions to an explicit policy optimization problem. The analysis thus focuses on the implications of simultaneous optimizing behavior by policymakers and private market participants. This approach helps clarify how differences in policy objective functions under fixed and flexible exchange rate regimes may contribute – through differences in actual and expected policy behavior – to the regime-sensitivity of the short-term variability of real exchange rates. It also has the potential to improve our understanding of several other issues, including the relationship between realignment expectations (loosely synonymous with "exchange rate pressures") and macroeconomic variables, the associated behavior of interest rate differentials, the nature of the risk premium, and the effectiveness of sterilized intervention. The first section provides an overview of these issues, along with a brief discussion of the literature on speculative attacks. The second section presents a specific example of the new conceptual framework, focusing primarily on the nature of the policy optimization problem, and the third section then analyzes the example. The fourth section provides concluding perspectives.

1   Some relevant issues

The defining characteristic that distinguishes an adjustable peg system from a flexible exchange rate arrangement is the explicit statement of the policy authorities' intention to prevent the exchange rate from moving outside a fixed fluctuation band. This stated policy objective, when supported by impressions that monetary policy is indeed oriented toward stabilizing the exchange rate, provides an anchor for exchange rate expectations – particularly in the short run – that is not usually present in a flexible exchange rate system. Consistently, there is abundant empirical evidence that the short-term variability of both nominal and real exchange rates is substantially lower under adjustable peg regimes than under flexible rate systems.[1]

Needless to say, the credibility of announced policy intentions can easily be eroded, and nominal exchange rate pegs generally require adjustment from time to time in order to avoid undesirable macroeconomic outcomes. In practice, moreover, the process of adjusting exchange rate pegs over time has generally involved periodic episodes of financial market turbulence. Typically, decisions to realign exchange rates are not taken until some time after strong market pressures have emerged; thus, in most cases realignments follow efforts by the policy authorities to resist market pressures through sterilized intervention or interest rate adjustments.

Speculative attacks

The stylized sequence of developments leading to exchange rate adjustments – that is, the emergence of market pressures, the efforts to resist such pressures, and the eventual realignment – has stimulated conceptual analysis of the conditions that trigger exchange market pressures, often referred to as "speculative attacks." The literature on speculative attacks, emanating from a pathbreaking paper by Krugman (1979), was inspired by the literature on government price-fixing schemes in markets for exhaustible resources.[2] The Krugman model is based on the premise that countries have limited resources for defending their exchange rates and must abandon their currency pegs when foreign exchange reserves are exhausted.[3] One of the celebrated insights from the analysis is that rational private "speculators" in an environment with limited official reserves will inevitably attack a country's exchange rate peg before its foreign exchange reserves are fully depleted. Another insight is that, even when market participants project an eventual depletion of reserves under prevailing

---

[1] Recall chapter 4 (pp. 67–9).

[2] See, in particular, the analysis of gold prices by Salant and Henderson (1978).

[3] Obstfeld (1994) gives a concise and insightful description of the Krugman model. Flood and Garber (1984a, 1984b) and Obstfeld (1986a) made early contributions to the literature on speculative attacks. Agénor, Bhandari, and Flood (1992) and Blackburn and Sola (1993) provide surveys.

macroeconomic policies, they will not necessarily attack the exchange rate peg immediately. An exchange rate peg, in theory, can thus remain "inconsistent with macroeconomic fundamentals" for some time before the behavior of rational market participants will cause pressures on the exchange rate to surface.

These perspectives are helpful in reconciling the notion that exchange rate pressures reflect macroeconomic imbalances with the empirical observation that the emergence of exchange rate pressure has often not coincided closely in time with unexpected changes in macroeconomic prospects.[4] Yet, the need to strengthen the conceptual foundations of speculative attack models – and, in particular, to abandon the central premise of an exhaustible supply of official reserves – has also been emphasized in recent years.[5] For countries with access to world capital markets, it is difficult to defend the premise that the supply of reserves is exhaustible, and it therefore seems appropriate to model the decision to realign a currency as the outcome of the interactions between rational private market participants and a government pursuing well-defined policy objectives. This approach can also help clarify and reconcile the notions of speculative attacks associated with unsustainable macroeconomic imbalances and speculative attacks that are random and self-fulfilling.

Realignment expectations and the risk premium

As discussed in chapter 7, conceptual models of target zones have attracted considerable attention in recent years, and the associated analysis of realignment expectations has become an active area of empirically-oriented research. In this context, a model in which the government pursues well-defined policy objectives that are understood by market participants – and absorbed into the information sets used by market participants in forming their rational expectations – provides an appealing conceptual framework for specifying a testable hypothesis about the nature of the relationship between realignment expectations and the macroeconomic variables that enter the policy objective function.[6] It also provides a framework for

---

[4] For example, constructed measures of realignment expectations for European exchange rates did not begin to widen before the summer of 1992, despite the fact that the macroeconomic conditions then prevailing had existed for some time; see Rose and Svensson (1994), Chen and Giovannini (1993), Research Department, IMF (1993).

[5] Obstfeld (1994), Ozkan and Sutherland (1994).

[6] Although some recent empirical studies of international interest rate differentials (for example, Bartolini [1993], Caramazza [1993], Halikias [1994], Helpman et al. [1994], and Thomas [1994]) have made progress in relating constructed measures of realignment expectations to macroeconomic fundamentals, the policy optimization framework provides a less ad hoc approach to hypothesis specification.

analyzing the correlation between realignment expectations and the exchange risk premium.

In empirical studies of exchange rate fluctuations within target zones, and of the conditions that give rise to pressures for realignments, the techniques used to obtain measures of realignment expectations have generally been based on the assumption of uncovered interest parity (UIP).[7] Proponents of this methodology recognize that "it is crucial whether the foreign exchange risk premium can be neglected or not," and have made a serious effort to explore whether the UIP assumption can be justified. In particular, Svensson (1992a) extended the analysis of real and nominal risk premiums to the target zone framework and derived generous upper bounds on their empirical magnitudes, suggesting that they were "relatively small." Notably, this assessment was based on the assumption that the probability distribution of realignments is time-invariant and not state-contingent – in particular, not contingent on the macroeconomic state variables that tend to generate political pressures for realignments. To provide an alternative perspective, Svensson also calculated an upper bound on the risk premium associated with a depreciation that is anticipated with probability one, suggesting that even in the limiting case, the upper bound on the risk premium is only about one-eighth the size of the expected realignment.[8] The literature has thus continued to rely on the UIP assumption on the grounds that the empirical results are not significantly affected by a small time-varying risk premium "unless its movements coincide with changing realignment expectations for some mysterious reason."[9]

Some additional perspectives on this issue are provided by reformulating the analysis of realignment expectations in the context of a policy optimization problem. As illustrated in the third section below, to the extent that market participants are risk averse, such analysis establishes a strong and unmysterious possibility that the comovements of realignment expectations and the risk premium may indeed be highly correlated. This points to the possibility of bias in the existing methodology for constructing measures of realignment expectations, although it does not necessarily imply that the bias has been quantitatively large.

The effectiveness of sterilized intervention

The introduction of policy optimization into the conceptual framework is also useful for addressing issues relating to the effectiveness of sterilized

[7] See, for example, Bertola and Svensson (1993) and Lindberg, Söderlind, and Svensson (1993).

[8] Svensson (1992a, pp. 35–6). The calculation focuses on exchange rate jumps within the band but is also relevant to realignments anticipated with probability one.

[9] Rose and Svensson (1994, n. 1, p. 1188).

intervention. As discussed in chapter 8, it is common to distinguish the effects of sterilized intervention on the risk premium through the portfolio balance channel from the effects on exchange rate expectations through a signaling channel. The discussion of signaling effects, however, has suffered to some extent from the failure of many discussants to focus explicitly on how much market participants are assumed to know about the policy authorities' incentives. One of the issues to be clarified is whether sterilized intervention can have any effect on exchange rate expectations when market participants are fully rational and completely informed of the incentives of the policy authorities. A second issue concerns the possible correlation between the signaling effect on expectations and the portfolio balance effect on the risk premium.

Recent analysis of these issues has elucidated how signaling can be effective even when market participants are fully rational and completely informed of the authorities' incentives. In particular, it is now recognized that, in exposing themselves through sterilized intervention to the prospect of a greater valuation loss on foreign exchange reserves if the exchange rate is realigned, the authorities signal that their incentive to resist realignment has strengthened endogenously. This effect of sterilized intervention can be described analytically in a framework in which valuation gains and losses are explicitly included in the policy objective function,[10] or alternatively, in a framework that explicitly imposes a government budget constraint, such that prospects of valuation losses influence policy decisions indirectly through their prospective implications for taxes (or government spending).[11]

2   The conceptual framework: an example

Optimizing models of exchange rate realignments can be found in a number of recent contributions to the literature.[12] In the spirit of modern discussions of rules versus discretionary strategies for monetary policy,[13] the choice of an adjustable exchange rate peg – like any other simple rule for monetary policy that tends to be overridden or modified in extreme circumstances – can be regarded as a strategy for balancing the credibility that can be gained from committing to a rule with the flexibility that is desirable when macroeconomic developments make the social costs of

---

[10] Isard (1994).

[11] De Kock and Grilli (1993), Obstfeld (1994).

[12] For example, Obstfeld (1991, 1994), de Kock and Grilli (1993), Drazen and Masson (1994), Masson (1995), Cukierman, Kiguel, and Leiderman (1994), Ozkan and Sutherland (1994), and Isard (1994).

[13] Flood and Isard (1989), Lohmann (1992).

continuing to adhere to the rule very high.[14] Such strategies have become known as "rules with escape clauses."[15] As a proposition in positive economics, the prevalence of simple rules that can be overridden in extreme circumstances – such as money supply growth targets and exchange rate pegs[16] – reflects two things. First, the fact that fully state-contingent rules are not a relevant possibility for monetary policy when knowledge about the structure of the economy and the nature of disturbances is incomplete; and second, the fact that partially state-contingent rules and discretion cannot be unambiguously ranked. This being said, however, it is obviously important to establish "rules with escape clauses" in forms that limit the scope for the potential long-run gains from flexibility to be eroded by the credibility-undermining effects of using discretion inappropriately. As discussed below, success in committing the authorities to exercise the escape clause in extreme circumstances, and only in such circumstances, can depend importantly on the nature of the institutional mechanisms through which society holds its policymakers accountable for their discretionary decisions – whether decisions to exercise, or not to exercise, the discretion given to them.

The following example, taken from Isard (1994), illustrates the basic conceptual framework. To simplify, the model of policy optimization is cast in terms of a one-dimensional problem of output stabilization, home-country output is also modeled in one-dimensional terms as a function of its relative price, and in contrast to the target zone literature, the band around the adjustable peg is assumed to have zero width.[17] The timing and magnitudes of any adjustments in the exchange rate reflect the optimizing behavior of the policy authority in the home country. The home-country interest rate adjusts endogenously to clear markets, given a fixed foreign interest rate. Private market participants are assumed to be fully rational and risk averse, with complete information about the incentives of the policy authority. The relevant asset portfolios of private market partici-

---

[14] The gold standard crisis of 1847, as analyzed by Dornbusch and Frenkel (1984), provides an outstanding example of a case in which a large unanticipated shock in the form of a harvest failure led to the temporary suspension of a simple policy rule in order to avert a confidence crisis and restore economic stability.

[15] Persson and Tabellini (1993).

[16] The fact that fixed exchange rate regimes provide an avenue for "escape" through exchange rate adjustment has led Portes (1993) to remark that " 'Permanently fixed exchange rates' is an oxymoron." Notably, some fixed exchange rate regimes have given priority to other avenues of escape. Indeed, as Bordo (1993a) and Eichengreen (1993b) suggest, the longevity of the classical gold standard era may have been partly attributable to the fact that the core countries in the international gold standard regime, until World War I, had relied on temporary suspensions of convertibility (and manipulation of the gold points), rather than parity changes, as mechanisms for escape during times of war or other major disruptions.

[17] Cukierman, Kiguel, and Leiderman (1994) provide insights into the case of a band with nonzero width.

pants are allocated between home-currency-denominated interest bearing net claims on the home-country government and foreign-currency-denominated interest bearing net claims on the foreign government. In the tradition of much of the portfolio-balance literature, the analysis abstracts from the intertemporal budget constraints of the two governments.

The centerpiece of the analysis is the loss function that governs the behavior of the home-country policy authorities. Interesting perspectives can be derived by distinguishing between losses related to macroeconomic performance, valuation losses on foreign exchange reserves, and costs associated with exercising the option to realign the exchange rate. It is thus interesting to consider the case in which the policy objective at time t is to minimize the expected value of a loss function with three components

$$L_{t+1} = (y_{t+1})^2 - 2a\alpha(s_{t+1} - s_t + r_t^* - r_t)X_t + c_{t+1} \tag{9.1}$$

where: y_{t+1} is the deviation of the logarithm of output from its full employment level; X_t is the stock of foreign exchange reserves; s is the logarithm of the exchange rate in home currency per unit of foreign exchange; r_t and r_t^* are the one-period home- and foreign-currency interest rates at time t; $s_{t+1} - s_t + r_t^* - r_t$ represents the return on holdings of foreign securities relative to that on holdings of domestic securities; α is the elasticity of home-country output with respect to its relative price, as defined in (9.3) below; a is a parameter of the loss function, where $2a\alpha$ reflects the weight that society places on avoiding foreign exchange valuation losses relative to the objective of stabilizing output; and c_{t+1} is a fixed cost associated with realignment

$$c_{t+1} = \begin{cases} c^2 & \text{if } s_{t+1} \neq s_t \\ 0 & \text{if } s_{t+1} = s_t \end{cases} \tag{9.2}$$

It seems realistic, moreover, to assume that deviations of home-country output from its full employment level are persistent, but that they respond positively to a decline in the relative price of home-country output, here equivalent to a depreciation of the home currency[18]

$$y_{t+1} = y_t + \alpha(s_{t+1} - s_t) + u_{t+1} \tag{9.3}$$

where u_{t+1} is a serially uncorrelated disturbance. In this particularly simple case, home-country output changes only in response to changes in its relative price or to random shocks. The assumption that output depends only on the policy choice variable, and not on endogenous variables such as the interest rate, rules out the possibility of self-fulfilling speculative

---

[18] The home-currency price of home output and the foreign-currency price of foreign output are fixed and normalized to unity.

attacks.[19] An extension of the model with feedback from the interest rate to the level of output would provide an appealing framework for integrating the notion of self-justifying shifts in confidence with the view that balance-of-payments crises are linked to macroeconomic fundamentals.

Several additional points should be noted about this analytic framework. First and foremost is the assumption that the policy authorities optimize over a one-period horizon. As already mentioned, the fact that a fixed rate regime involves a commitment to stabilize the one-period ahead exchange rate helps justify this assumption. Moreover, the analysis of a one-period optimization problem is equivalent to the analysis of a multiperiod problem in the limiting case in which the policymakers' discount rate is infinite; and it can be argued that policymakers tend to have very high discount rates, focusing mainly on generating macroeconomic stability during the near term, and giving little weight to outcomes beyond a short horizon. Nevertheless, while the one-period horizon greatly simplifies the analysis and helps to achieve useful insights, the assumption should not be left unchallenged, particularly in a model in which changes in output have a persistent component. It may be noted here that, in considering new directions for modeling the behavior of flexible exchange rates, chapter 10 formulates the analysis in terms of a multiperiod horizon.

Turning to other aspects of the loss function specified in (9.1), the first component – the squared deviation of output from its full employment level – has a long tradition.[20] The fact that an inflation objective is not included, however, may limit the relevance of the example in some contexts.[21]

The second term in the loss function focuses on the one-period valuation gain on holdings of foreign exchange reserves, $(s_{t+1} - s_t + r_t^* - r_t)X_t$. The larger the volume of reserves accumulated (spent) to resist appreciation

---

[19] As discussed in Obstfeld (1994), if the ultimate target variables that enter the policy loss function depend on endogenous variables such as the interest rate, which in turn are driven by the market's realignment expectations, then arbitrary shifts in realignment expectations can become self-fulfilling by driving the target variables past the critical thresholds at which the authorities have an incentive to realign. Although the model abstracts from this possibility of multiple equilibria or self-fulfilling attacks, the issue has attracted serious discussion in analyzing the European exchange market crisis of 1992–93; see Eichengreen and Wyplosz (1993) and Eichengreen, Rose, and Wyplosz (1994b).

[20] Following applications by Gray (1976), Flood and Marion (1982), and others, Aizenman and Frenkel (1985) derived this component as the optimal specification of the objective function for a world with sticky nominal wages when social welfare depends positively on consumption and negatively on labor. See Aizenman (1994) for a recent reconsideration based on an argument that the expected level of full-employment output is sensitive to the nature of the exchange rate regime. Barro and Gordon (1983b) and others have added squared changes in the price level to the loss function, while noting the difficulty of justifying such an extension; see Fischer (1994), however, on the costs of inflation.

[21] Presumably this is not a significant issue for interpreting the pressures that were imposed on exchange rates between European currencies during 1992–93, when many European countries were not concerned about their inflation prospects in the short run.

(depreciation), the greater will be the valuation losses, or the smaller the valuation gains, associated with a subsequent decision to revalue upward (devalue) the home currency. This component of the loss function isolates a well-defined component of the costs of adjusting an exchange rate peg[22] and plays a central role in making sterilized intervention effective in influencing exchange rate expectations and the risk premium in a rational expectations environment. As argued below, the effectiveness of intervention also depends on whether the home-country authorities have the scope to issue unlimited amounts of foreign-currency-denominated debt if they desire to do so, contrary to the central premise of much of the literature on speculative attacks.

The third component of the loss function – which amounts to a fixed cost that is incurred whenever the escape clause is exercised – is intended to capture the social costs of exercising discretion in the context of time-consistency problems.[23] As indicated below, it also establishes an explicit frame of reference for relating the credibility of the fixed exchange rate – or the probability of a realignment – to both the weights in the policy objective function and prevailing macroeconomic conditions.[24]

The simple ad hoc specification of the third component of the loss function partly reflects an incomplete understanding of the costs that society wants the policymaker to weigh in contemplating decisions to exercise escape clauses. Indeed, a limited understanding or lack of consensus is reflected in the fact that the mechanisms through which society holds its policymakers accountable for their performances, and the associated penalty and reward structures, are generally not defined in a complete and explicit manner *ex ante*. Recent research on designing institutions for monetary stability, focusing primarily on cases in which society's welfare depends on both the rate of inflation and the unexpected component of inflation (with real economic activity sensitive to unexpected inflation), has provided examples in which it is possible to derive the optimal form, from a social welfare perspective, of an *ex ante* contract that links the rewards

---

[22] As already noted, an alternative approach is to include taxes (net of spending on public goods) in the loss function, and to impose a government budget constraint linking taxes to valuation losses; see de Kock and Grilli (1993) and Obstfeld (1994).

[23] This treatment follows Flood and Isard (1989). Although the present example, by not including inflation in the policy loss function, departs from the traditional way of illustrating the time-consistency problem for monetary policy (see, for example, Barro and Gordon [1983b] and Rogoff [1985b]), the model of real output determination introduces a temptation to override the announced exchange rate peg. This temptation is mitigated by the cost of exercising the escape clause.

[24] In contrast to the analysis here, much of the literature on the credibility of exchange rate pegs has been developed under the assumption that private market participants lack complete information about the objective function of the policymaker. See Cukierman, Kiguel, and Leiderman (1994), Drazen and Masson (1994), Masson (1995), and references cited therein.

received by (or penalties imposed on) the policy authorities to *ex post* outcomes for the economy.[25] In theory, explicit contracts with such reward/penalty structures can be used to motivate the authorities to maximize a weighted sum of society's welfare and the private rewards of the authorities,[26] analogous in (9.1) to minimizing the sum of the first two terms of the loss function (a social cost function) plus the third term (a penalty imposed on the policymaker whenever the exchange rate is realigned). If future research succeeds in extending these examples to the case in which the policy instrument is an exchange rate peg, a more appealing specification form may emerge for the third term in (9.1).

For now, condition (9.1) is justified by asserting that, under fixed exchange rate regimes, policymakers appear to behave as if they were minimizing the sum of a social cost function and a cost of exercising the option to realign. Indeed, unless one assumes that policy authorities do in fact perceive it to be costly to override announced policy rules, it is difficult to explain why exchange rates exhibit much lower short-term variability under fixed rate than under flexible rate regimes. And although countries do not normally design explicit contracts linking the rewards of policymakers to macroeconomic outcomes,[27] most countries do rely on regular accountability procedures to insure that policy authorities do not treat the exercise of discretion as costless.[28]

3   Analysis of the example

This section defines the example further, and then analyzes it to derive insights on the issues discussed in the first section. Readers with little interest in the formal solution may move on to the fourth section.

The description of optimal behavior and market-clearing conditions is assumed to reflect the following sequence of actions and events, starting just after the determination of s_t and continuing through the determination of s_{t+1}. First, the stock of foreign exchange reserves X_t is set (at an exogenous level in the first instance and an optimal level in a second case) and the private sector forms its expectations and chooses its asset portfolio, given information about X_t and the *ex ante* probability distribution of u_{t+1}. These actions generate the market-clearing levels of the unobserved risk premium

---

[25] See Persson and Tabellini (1993), who credit Walsh (1992) for providing substantial insights.

[26] This assumes, following Flood and Isard (1989) and Persson and Tabellini (1993), that the reward/penalty can be expressed in the same utility metric as social welfare, and that social welfare is not directly affected by the reward/penalty *per se*.

[27] An exception is New Zealand, where the central bank leadership is held explicitly accountable for keeping inflation within a target range; see Nicholl and Archer (1992).

[28] Fischer (1994) provides insights on some of these issues.

and the observed home-currency interest rate, given the fixed foreign-currency interest rate. Second, the realization of u_{t+1} occurs. Third, the authorities set s_{t+1} at the level that minimizes the policy loss L_{t+1}, conditional on u_{t+1}.

The private sector's portfolio choice problem involves allocating wealth between claims on the home government bearing the home-currency interest rate, and claims on the foreign government bearing the foreign-currency interest rate. The literature reflects several approaches to modeling this problem. One approach distinguishes between home and foreign goods and assumes that residents of the two countries have identical consumption preferences, often specified as Cobb–Douglas functions of the amounts of each of the two goods consumed.[29] Another approach assumes that home-country (foreign-country) residents have relatively strong preferences for the home (foreign) good, sometimes specifying each group's utility as a function of the mean and variance of its consumption.[30] In addition to requiring a decision on how to represent consumer preferences, model specification requires a choice between ignoring nonportfolio income or specifying a model of the income earned from goods production.

With regard to these various modeling choices, the approach taken here ignores nonportfolio income and assumes that residents of the two countries hold portfolios of both assets but have different consumption preferences, with each group consuming only the good produced in its own country. It also postulates a mean–variance utility function, such that market-clearing conditions depend in a simple approximate way on the perceived mean and variance of the one-period ahead exchange rate. The objective of home-country (foreign-country) residents at time t is to maximize a function of the mean and variance of their one-period ahead normalized wealth as valued in the home (foreign) currency after the realization of s_{t+1}.

As additional notation, let W describe the portfolio wealth of home-country residents and B and B^* their holdings of home and foreign bonds, with $\tilde{W}^*$, $\tilde{B}$, and $\tilde{B}^*$ describing analogously the aggregate portfolio of foreign residents. Variables superscripted (not superscripted) with $*$ are measured in foreign-currency (home-currency) units. Accordingly, for home-country residents at time t, the levels of initial wealth and one-period ahead wealth can be expressed as

$$W_t = B_t + S_t B_t^* \tag{9.4}$$

$$\begin{aligned} W_{t+1} &= B_t(1+r_t) + B_t^*(1+r_t^*)S_{t+1} \\ &= W_t(1+r_t) + S_t B_t^*[(1+r_t^*)(S_{t+1}/S_t) - (1+r_t)] \\ &\approx W_t(1+r_t) + S_t B_t^*[r_t^* + s_{t+1} - s_t - r_t] \end{aligned} \tag{9.5}$$

[29] For example, Svensson (1992a).   [30] For example, Dornbusch (1983b).

where S denotes the level (and s the logarithm) of the exchange rate. To economize on notation, let

$$\gamma_{t+1} = r_t - r_t^* - s_{t+1} + s_t \tag{9.6}$$

$$\phi_t = E_t \gamma_{t+1} \tag{9.7}$$

$$\sigma_t^2 = \text{var}_t \gamma_{t+1} = \text{var}_t s_{t+1} \tag{9.8}$$

$$b_t = S_t B_t^* / W_t \tag{9.9}$$

where E_t and var_t denote expected values and perceived variances at time t. Note that if the covered interest parity condition is approximately valid, even though the two assets represent claims against different countries, (9.6) and (9.7) can be re-expressed as

$$\gamma_{t+1} \approx f_t - s_{t+1} \tag{9.6a}$$

$$\phi_t \approx f_t - E_t s_{t+1} \tag{9.7a}$$

where $f_t \approx s_t + r_t - r_t^*$ is the logarithm of the forward exchange rate. The term, γ_{t+1}, represents the *ex post* measure of the forward-rate forecast error. The risk premium, ϕ_t, can be viewed as the expected excess yield on home-country securities that is required *ex ante* to compensate market participants for the risk of realignment. It also measures the forward-rate forecast bias, or more precisely, the expected value *ex ante* of the forward-rate forecast error.

Assume that the utility function to be maximized is

$$U = U[E_t(W_{t+1}/W_t), \text{var}_t(W_{t+1}/W_t)]. \tag{9.10}$$

Note that the arguments of U can be expressed as

$$E_t(W_{t+1}/W_t) = 1 + r_t - b_t \phi_t \tag{9.11}$$

$$\text{var}_t(W_{t+1}/W_t) = (b_t)^2 \sigma_t^2. \tag{9.12}$$

Thus, for home-country residents the optimal choice of the portfolio share b_t must satisfy the first-order condition

$$b_t = \frac{U_1 \phi_t}{2 U_2 \sigma_t^2} = -\phi_t / \theta \sigma_t^2 \tag{9.13}$$

where $U_1 > 0$ and $U_2 < 0$ are the first derivatives of U with respect to its two arguments and $\theta = -2 U_2 / U_1 > 0$ reflects the degree of risk aversion.

The portfolio choice problem for foreign-country residents can be specified and solved analogously. The analogs of (9.5), (9.9), (9.11), (9.12), and (9.13) are

$$\tilde{W}_{t+1}^* \approx \tilde{W}_t^*(1 + r_t^*) + (\tilde{B}_t / S_t)(r_t - r_t^* - s_{t+1} + s_t) \tag{9.5a}$$

$$\tilde{b}_t = (\tilde{B}_t/S_t)/\tilde{W}_t^* \tag{9.9a}$$

$$E_t(\tilde{W}_{t+1}^*/\tilde{W}_t^*) = 1 + r_t^* + \tilde{b}_t\phi_t \tag{9.11a}$$

$$\text{var}_t(\tilde{W}_{t+1}^*/\tilde{W}_t^*) = (\tilde{b}_t)^2\sigma_t^2 \tag{9.12a}$$

$$\tilde{b}_t = \phi_t/\theta\sigma_t^2. \tag{9.13a}$$

Accordingly, the market-clearing condition for claims on the foreign public sector can be written as

$$\bar{B}_t^* - X_t = b_t(W_t/S_t) + (1 - \tilde{b}_t)\bar{W}_t^* = \bar{W}_t^* - \bar{W}_t^*\phi_t/\theta\sigma_t^2 \tag{9.14}$$

where $\bar{B}^*$ is the stock of such claims that would be pushed into private portfolios in the absence of any official holdings of foreign exchange reserves by the home-country authorities and $\bar{W}_t^* = (W_t/S_t) + \tilde{W}_t^*$ is the initial level of aggregate private wealth valued in foreign currency. Note that the stock of noninterest bearing monetary assets does not enter the analysis explicitly and thus is implicitly assumed to remain constant in this example; hence, all official intervention is sterilized. The analysis concentrates on the case in which market participants have full knowledge of X_t at time t; intervention operations are not kept secret.

The next steps in solving the model are to derive the expected exchange rate and the market-clearing domestic interest rate and risk premium that would emerge at any level of X_t. Note that, whenever it is optimal to change the exchange rate peg, the optimal value at which to set the new peg, s_{t+1}^0 – after observing the realization of u_{t+1} – is determined by the first-order condition $\partial L_{t+1}/\partial s_{t+1} = 0$; in particular, from (9.1) and (9.3)

$$s_{t+1}^0 = s_t - \frac{y_t - aX_t + u_{t+1}}{\alpha}. \tag{9.15}$$

Whether or not a realignment to s_{t+1}^0 dominates a decision to maintain the peg at s_t depends on whether $L_{t+1}(s_{t+1}^0) < L_{t+1}(s_t)$. From (9.1) and (9.3) it is straightforward to demonstrate that maintaining the peg at s_t is optimal if and only if $-c \leq y_t - aX_t + u_{t+1} \leq c$. This condition provides the basis for characterizing the market-clearing conditions that would emerge under rational expectations prior to the realization of u_{t+1}, given information about y_t, X_t, a, c, and the *ex ante* probability distribution of u_{t+1}.[31]

To illustrate, suppose u_{t+1} is uniformly distributed on the interval $[-U, U]$. For this distribution, the set of possible combinations of initial conditions (in period t) and parameter values gives rise to four cases:

---

[31] In this simple example, the range of u_{t+1} over which it is optimal to maintain the peg at s_t is independent of the domestic interest rate, and hence of the expected rate of change in the exchange rate. As noted earlier, this would not be the case if (9.3) was modified to make y_{t+1} dependent on r_t, which would give rise to the possibility of multiple equilibria.

Case 1: $-c<y_t-aX_t-U<y_t-aX_t+U<c$
Case 2: $y_t-aX_t-U\leq-c\leq y_t-aX_t+U\leq c$
Case 3: $-c\leq y_t-aX_t-U\leq c\leq y_t-aX_t+U$
Case 4: $y_t-aX_t-U<-c<c<y_t-aX_t+U.$

(9.16)

In case 1 there is no incentive to realign under any feasible realization of the shock.[32] In case 4 there are incentives to depreciate the domestic currency under large positive realizations of u_{t+1} and to appreciate under large negative realizations. In cases 2 and 3 the incentives to realign are one-sided.

Consider case 3, in which a sufficiently large positive shock would overheat the home-country economy and provide an incentive to appreciate the home currency. In such a setting, market participants – with an understanding of this incentive and knowledge of the *ex ante* probability distribution of the shock – will rationally form expectations about s_{t+1} such that, from (9.15) and (9.16), using the notation $z=y_t-aX_t+u_{t+1}$[33]

$$E_t s_{t+1}=s_t-1/\alpha \int_c^{y_t-aX_t+U} (z/2U)dz$$

(9.17)

$$=s_t-\frac{1}{4\alpha U}[(y_t-aX_t+U)^2-c^2]<s_t.$$

Similarly, the probability of realignment can be expressed as

$$\text{prob}(s_{t+1}<s_t)=\int_c^{y_t-aX_t+U} (1/2U)dz=m/2U$$

(9.18)

where

$$m=y_t-aX_t+U-c.$$

(9.19)

Note that (9.17) gives a nonlinear (in this case, quadratic) expression for the magnitude of the expected realignment as a function of y_t+U, which can be seen from (9.3) to represent the maximum degree to which the economy could be left overheated (i.e., the upper bound on y_{t+1}) in the absence of realignment. The level of X_t does not affect the conditional probability distribution of y_{t+1} given the event of no realignment, but (when $a>0$) it does affect the authorities' incentives to realign and thereby influences the

---

[32] It is easily shown in this case that $\phi_t=0$ and $r_t=r_t^*$.
[33] Recall that maintaining the peg at s_t is optimal if $z<c$.

ex ante assessments of realignment probabilities and expectations by rational market participants.

From (9.6), (9.7), and (9.17), the risk premium – or equivalently, the expected error in using the forward rate as a predictor of the future spot rate – can be expressed as

$$\phi_t = r_t - r_t^* + \frac{1}{4\alpha U}[(y_t - aX_t + U)^2 - c^2] \tag{9.20}$$

whereas (9.14) implies

$$\phi_t = -\theta\sigma_t^2[(\bar{B}_t^* - X_t - \tilde{W}_t^*)/\bar{W}_t^*]. \tag{9.21}$$

Thus,

$$r_t = r_t^* - \frac{1}{4\alpha U}[(y_t - aX_t + U)^2 - c^2] - \theta\sigma_t^2[(\bar{B}_t^* - X_t - \tilde{W}_t^*)/\bar{W}_t^*]. \tag{9.22}$$

In general, as can be seen from (9.21), the sign of the risk premium depends on the sign of $(\bar{B}_t^* - X_t - \tilde{W}_t^*)$. If the foreign country is an international creditor and the home country has positive net holdings of foreign exchange reserves, $\bar{B}_t^* - X_t - \tilde{W}_t^* < 0$ and $\phi_t > 0$.

(9.21) indicates that time variation in the risk premium has two main sources: variation in portfolio stock variables and time variation in σ_t^2, which in this particular example has the nonlinear form[34]

$$\sigma_t^2 = \frac{1}{2U\alpha^2}\left\{\frac{m}{4}(m + 2c)^2\left(1 - \frac{m}{2U}\right)^2 + \frac{m^3}{12}\right\}. \tag{9.23}$$

For case 3, as defined in (9.16), m ranges from 0 when y_t and X_t are such that $y_t - aX_t + U = c$, to $2U$ at $y_t - aX_t - U = c$; and it is easily seen from (9.23) that $\sigma_t^2 = 0$ at $m = 0$ and $\sigma_t^2 = U^2/3\alpha^2$ at $m = 2U$. As can also be seen from (9.18), the *ex ante* probability of realignment increases monotonically from 0 to 1 as m increases from 0 to $2U$.

These results require careful interpretation. If, as one extreme case, the authorities had no freedom to vary X_t, m would vary directly with y_t (given the parameter c and the probability distribution of the shock), and variation over time in the state of the economy would lead to time variation in the probability of realignment and the magnitudes of realignment expectations and the risk premium. There is a clear possibility, moreover, that the magnitude of realignment expectations would be strongly correlated with the perceived risk of realignment and hence with the magnitude

---

[34] See the appendix to this chapter (pp. 166–7) for a derivation.

of the risk premium.[35] At the other extreme, as evident from (9.17)–(9.19) and (9.23), with complete freedom to vary X_t through sterilized intervention, the authorities – if they chose to do so – could prevent time variation in the state of the economy (y_t) from generating time variation in the *ex ante* probability of realignment, the magnitude of realignment expectations, and the perceived risk of realignment. Indeed – although it would generally not be optimal to do so – by keeping $m = 0$, the authorities could maintain a zero *ex ante* probability of realignment in this particular example, thereby also maintaining the magnitudes of realignment expectations and the risk premium at zero.

4   Concluding perspectives

Although the example analyzed in this chapter reflects a highly oversimplified view of macroeconomic behavior and policy objectives, it illustrates that the policy optimization approach yields some useful perspectives. One straightforward result is that, if market participants understand the authorities' incentives and are rational, their realignment expectations, and hence the magnitude of the interest rate differentials that are required to stabilize exchange rates, will depend on the fundamental macroeconomic state variables that enter the policy objective function, quite likely in a nonlinear way. A second result is that the comovements of realignment expectations and the risk premium may be strongly correlated, pointing to a possible bias in the methodology that recent empirical studies of target zones have used to construct measures of realignment expectations, although not necessarily a bias that is quantitatively large.

In addition, the particular policy optimization framework explored in this chapter, which abandons the uncovered interest parity assumption and assumes that exercising the option to realign (the escape clause) is costly, integrates two lines of thinking about the possible causes of forward-rate prediction bias in a rational expectations environment. One of the relevant perspectives is that the incentives of the policy authorities create a peso problem for market participants: in each period the *ex ante* probability of a realignment is generally positive, even though the costs of exercising the escape clause prevent frequent realignments; and persistence in the funda-

---

[35] It can be seen from (9.17) that in case 3 (with $y_t - aX_t + U \geq c > 0$), the magnitude of realignment expectations is a monotonically decreasing function of y_t (given X_t), independently of the parameters c and U. By contrast, the nature of the relationship between realignment risk and the state of the economy depends on the relative magnitudes of these parameters. Computer solutions of (9.23) show, for example, that for $c \leq U$, the magnitude of realignment risk is a near-monotonically increasing function of the probability of realignment $m/2U$, and hence of y_t, whereas for $c = 10U$ a plot of σ_t^2 against m or y_t has an approximately inverted U-shape over the relevant range.

mental macroeconomic state variables that influence the realignment decision leads, during intervals of no realignment, to positive serial correlation in realignment expectations and prediction errors. Thus, when the uncovered interest parity assumption is abandoned, the analytic framework characterizes the risk premium in a manner that integrates traditional concepts based on portfolio stocks and wealth variables with insights about the determinants of time variation in the risk of realignment within a peso-problem environment.

The extent to which such perspectives also apply to flexible exchange rate systems is debatable. If the policy problem analyzed in this chapter was reformulated symmetrically for a flexible rate system, the single-period policy objective function could still attribute costs to changes in the exchange rate (relative, for symmetry, to the level at which it would have been fixed in the adjustable peg regime). Accordingly, the authorities could still have incentives to delay or move gradually in adjusting their policy instruments to shocks, which could generate positive serial correlation in exchange rate movements in a risk averse environment. But with no policy commitment to maintain a fixed rate, the costs of an exchange rate movement would presumably be a continuous function of the size of the change, rather than a step function that jumped discontinuously at the edges of the band. Notably, the difference in the cost functions associated with exchange rate changes under the two regimes would induce the authorities to set their policy instruments at levels that, in a rational expectations environment, would tend to generate greater real and nominal exchange rate variability under a flexible rate regime than under a fixed rate regime. As the other side of the coin, there would tend to be less persistence in deviations from full employment output under the flexible rate regime.[36]

The policy optimization framework provides several useful perspectives on the effectiveness of sterilized intervention. It clarifies the fact that the influence of intervention on the risk premium (the portfolio-balance effect) and the influence on expectations about future exchange rates (the signaling effect) are not independent of each other. It also suggests the importance, in analyzing these effects, of specifying whether market participants are assumed to have complete information about the incentives of the policy authorities. Under the assumptions of complete information and rational expectations, sterilized intervention cannot signal new information about the authorities' ultimate policy objectives, but it can signal that the authorities have taken on a larger exposure to foreign exchange valuation

---

[36] It may be noted here that Flood and Rose (1993), in examining data from major industrial countries during the period 1975–90, find evidence of a significant negative simple correlation between the variances of month-to-month changes in nominal exchange rates and industrial production levels.

losses and, in doing so, can rationally be regarded to have strengthened endogenously their incentives to resist a realignment.

As a corollary to the latter point, the signaling effect of intervention on exchange rate expectations, and the associated effect on the perceived risk of realignment, depend critically on the costs of foreign exchange valuation losses relative to the costs of deviations from full employment output, as reflected in the coefficients of the policy objective function. The appropriate interpretation of this theoretical result, however, requires care in distinguishing between the relative welfare costs perceived by society and the relative costs perceived by policymakers. If society – acting against its own best interests – wanted to make sterilized intervention very effective (whenever it was relied upon) in influencing market assessments of realignment prospects, it could simply design accountability procedures and reward/penalty structures that made it very costly for the authorities to incur valuation losses, thereby making them very reluctant to realign the exchange rate following an increase in their exposure to valuation losses. By the same token, if the authorities perceived that valuation losses had no costs, sterilized intervention would have no effect on realignment expectations in an environment in which market participants had complete information about the authorities' incentives and formed their expectations rationally. Alternatively, the policy authorities may be motivated to minimize a loss function that reflects the relative welfare costs actually perceived by society. In this case, the coefficients of the policy objective function are not parameters to be manipulated, but rather reflect the inherent preferences of society.[37]

When valuation losses are perceived to be costly and sterilized intervention is effective in influencing market assessments of realignment prospects, the time variation of realignment expectations and the risk premium may depend importantly on the extent to which there are explicit or implicit quantitative constraints on the use of sterilized intervention as a policy instrument. In the unrealistic, hypothetical case in which there were no quantitative restrictions on the scale of sterilized intervention, the authorities would have the potential to prevent time variation in the state of the economy from having any effect on realignment expectations or the risk premium.[38]

---

[37] In an analytic framework that explicitly recognized the government budget constraint, valuation losses on foreign exchange reserves would translate directly into higher tax rates (other things being equal), and the coefficients of the specific policy objective function (9.1) could be interpreted in terms of the relative social welfare costs of deviations from full employment and variations in tax rates.

[38] Full use of that potential would not be optimal, however, since the costs of large deviations from full employment output make it important for the authorities to retain some willingness to realign in response to large shocks.

The hypothetical case illustrates an important point for empirical research: namely, that success in relating realignment expectations or the risk premium to macroeconomic state variables may depend critically on efforts to take account of institutional considerations governing the use of sterilized intervention.[39] This, unfortunately, poses a difficult challenge. In reality, countries generally do not set explicit quantitative limits *ex ante* on the scale of sterilized intervention. Experience suggests, however, that beyond some point, the monetary authorities – or the elected officials to whom they are accountable – inevitably find continuing intervention intolerable.[40]

Appendix

To derive (9.23), define:

$$z = y_t - aX_t + u_{t+1} \tag{A1}$$

$$\bar{z} = y_t - aX_t + U \tag{A2}$$

$$m = \bar{z} - c \tag{A3}$$

$$h = \frac{1}{4U}(\bar{z}^2 - c^2). \tag{A4}$$

Then, using (9.15) and (9.17)

$$s_{t+1}^0 = s_t - z/\alpha \tag{A5}$$

$$E_t s_{t+1} = s_t - h/\alpha. \tag{A6}$$

So

$$\sigma_t^2 = E_t\{(s_{t+1} - E_t s_{t+1})^2\} = \frac{1}{2U\alpha^2} \int_c^{\bar{z}} (h-z)^2 dz \tag{A7}$$

$$= \frac{1}{2U\alpha^2} \left[h^2 z - hz^2 + \frac{z^3}{3} \right]_c^{\bar{z}}$$

$$= \frac{1}{2U\alpha^2} \left\{ \frac{1}{16U^2}(\bar{z}-c)^3(\bar{z}+c)^2 - \frac{1}{4U}(\bar{z}-c)^2(\bar{z}+c)^2 + \frac{\bar{z}^3 - c^3}{3} \right\}$$

[39] In principle, such considerations should be reflected in the policy objective function.
[40] The events of September 1992 revealed that even the "unlimited" facilities for providing short-term credit to support intervention within the European Monetary System were curtailed when the scale of intervention was perceived to be a threat to price stability in Germany; see Eichengreen and Wyplosz (1993, pp. 109–13).

$$= \frac{1}{2U\alpha^2} \left\{ (\bar{z}-c)(\bar{z}+c)^2 \left(\frac{\bar{z}-c}{4U} - \frac{1}{2} \right)^2 + \frac{(\bar{z}-c)(\bar{z}+c)^2}{12} - \frac{\bar{z}c(\bar{z}-c)}{3} \right\}$$

$$= \frac{1}{2U\alpha^2} \left\{ \frac{m}{4} (m+2c)^2 \left(1 - \frac{m}{2U} \right)^2 + \frac{m^3}{12} \right\}.$$

10 New directions for conceptual models of flexible exchange rates

The modern theory of flexible exchange rates, with its emphasis on asset markets and the role of forward-looking expectations, represents a "critically important intellectual advance" over the models that existed 20 years ago.[1] With this advance has come an understanding that:

the largely random character of exchange rate fluctuations under floating exchange rate regimes is explained by the prevalence of "news" in inducing most exchange rate changes; the tendency for nominal and real exchange rates to move together under a floating rate regime is explained by the contrast between the behaviour of nominal exchange rates as randomly fluctuating asset prices and the behaviour of national price levels as relatively sluggishly adjusting variables; and with respect to the influence of economic policies on exchange rates, what matters is not simply what policies governments pursue today, but also to an important extent, the policies they are expected to pursue in the future.[2]

Nevertheless, research during the past two decades has been largely unsuccessful in explaining the observed behavior of exchange rates, suggesting the need for better models. This chapter focuses on new directions for conceptual models of flexible rates, returning to several issues that were raised in previous chapters. The first section considers the agenda for research under the maintained hypothesis that market participants have complete information and form rational expectations. The second section focuses on models in which market behavior is assumed to reflect either a substantial irrational component or a process in which rational but incompletely informed market participants extract relevant information from the history of trading. The third section provides concluding perspectives.

1 Models with rational expectations and complete information

As noted in previous chapters, the short-term variability of real and nominal exchange rates has been substantially higher in flexible rate

[1] Mussa (1993, p. 27).   [2] Mussa (1993, p. 24).

systems than in fixed rate regimes. Moreover, the volatility characteristics of the macroeconomic variables that are generally regarded as fundamentals in exchange rate analysis do not seem to change very much across different exchange rate regimes.[3] This suggests that different "structural models" of exchange rates are relevant under the two different types of regimes. The most obvious structural difference between the two types of regimes relates to the policy commitment to keep the exchange rate within a fixed fluctuation band.[4]

Although the willingness of the authorities to commit to a system of fixed exchange rates may not be an entirely exogenous factor, the existence of such a commitment, even when its credibility is limited, provides market participants in a fixed rate regime with an anchor for one-period ahead exchange rate expectations. Some implications of such an anchor for modeling behavior under a fixed rate system were explored in chapter 9 under the assumption that the policy authorities optimize over a one-period horizon. In concluding the chapter, it was suggested that a parallel analysis of behavior under a flexible rate regime would be based on one-period policy optimization with an objective function that attributed relatively low costs (in comparison with the policy objective function for the fixed rate case) to small-to-moderate changes in the exchange rate. Such analysis could explain the relatively high short-term variability of the exchange rate under flexible rate regimes, and would imply a negative correlation between short-term exchange rate variability and the short-term variability of output. Consistently, the one macroeconomic variable with short-term variability characteristics that has been found to be significantly and negatively correlated empirically with the volatility of the exchange rate is the level of real economic activity[5] – an ultimate target variable that the authorities try hard to keep stable through the adjustment of their policy instruments.

That being noted, analysis based on one-period optimization seems difficult to accept as an approach to modeling the behavior of flexible exchange rates, where there is no explicit policy commitment to stabilize the one-period ahead exchange rate. Accordingly, this chapter employs a multiperiod framework in considering new directions for explaining exchange rate behavior within a flexible rate system.

---

[3] Baxter and Stockman (1989), Flood and Rose (1993).

[4] In this connection, Rose (1994) finds empirical evidence of a positive and significant relationship between the degree of short-term exchange rate variability and the width of the official fluctuation band.

[5] Flood and Rose (1993). See also Eichengreen (1994).

An accounting framework

As a skeleton for conceptual models of flexible exchange rates, it is useful to return briefly to the types of approximate definitional identities described in chapters 5–7. Analogous to (5.1) and (5.2), the condition of covered interest parity between times t and $t + T$ can be written as

$$F_{t,T}R_{t,T}^* = S_t R_{t,T} \tag{10.1}$$

and

$$s_t \approx r_{t,T}^* - r_{t,T} + f_{t,T} \tag{10.2}$$

where S is the level of the spot exchange rate in domestic currency per unit of foreign currency, $R_{t,T}$ and $R_{t,T}^*$ are compound nominal interest factors between times t and $t + T$ on assets denominated in domestic and foreign currencies, $F_{t,T}$ is the forward exchange rate at t for delivery at $t + T$, and s_t, $r_{t,T}$, $r_{t,T}^*$, $f_{t,T}$ are the logarithms of S_t, $R_{t,T}$, $R_{t,T}^*$, $F_{t,T}$. In parallel with (5.11) and (5.12), the T-period premium for bearing exchange risk can be defined as

$$\xi_{t,T} = f_{t,T} - E_t s_{t+T} \tag{10.3}$$

implying

$$s_t \approx r_{t,T}^* - r_{t,T} + \xi_{t,T} + E_t s_{t+T}. \tag{10.4}$$

The analogous expression involving real exchange rates and real interest factors is

$$q_t \approx (i_{t,T}^* - i_{t,T}) + \xi_{t,T} + E_t q_{t+T} \tag{10.5}$$

where: $Q_t = S_t P_t^*/P_t$ is the real exchange rate at t; $I_{t,T} = R_{t,T}(P_t/E_t P_{t+T})$ and $I_{t,T}^* = R_{t,T}^*(P_t^*/E_t P_{t+T}^*)$ are compound real interest factors; $E_t Q_T$ is approximately equal to $(E_t S_{t+T})(E_t P_{t+T}^*/E_t P_{t+T})$; and q, $i_{t,T}$, $i_{t,T}^*$ denote the logarithms of Q, $I_{t,T}$, $I_{t,T}^*$.

Notably, (10.4) and (10.5) are valid for any length of the time horizon T. However, most models of exchange rate dynamics under a flexible exchange rate regime rely on the assumption that the real exchange rate is expected to converge to an equilibrium level over the long run,[6] implying that a long-run horizon is generally regarded as the most appropriate choice.

Under the choice of a long-run time horizon, the framework for explaining the observed behavior of exchange rates can be divided into an "anchor" that pins down the expected long-run real exchange rate and a "rope" that links observed exchange rates to the expected long-run real

---

[6] For example, Dornbusch (1976).

exchange rate via the interest rate parity framework, as modified to allow for risk premiums.[7] Alternatively, in terms of the individual components on the right-hand side of approximate identity (10.5), the pressures that cause the observed variability of real exchange rates can be transmitted through three channels: variability in real interest differentials, variability in the risk premium, or variability in the expected future real exchange rate.

The empirical evidence bearing on one of the channels has been analyzed using cointegration tests. In particular, as mentioned in chapter 8, Meese and Rogoff (1988) used cointegration tests to explore the possibility that a common factor could explain the time series behavior of real exchange rates and long-term real interest rate differentials. Their tests found that little of the variance of real exchange rate changes can be accounted for by real interest differentials, and other econometric studies have not been able to reject this finding.[8] Notably, these studies have restricted attention to data observed under flexible exchange rate arrangements.[9]

This line of investigation has not yet been exhausted,[10] and important advances in econometric methodology over the past decade may significantly facilitate empirical attempts to identify simultaneously the long-run and dynamic relationships between exchange rates and other macroeconomic variables. To date, however, the evidence suggests fairly strongly – given the approximate identity (10.5) – that progress in modeling the observed behavior of flexible exchange rates (under the maintained hypothesis of rational expectations and complete information) may largely depend on progress in modeling the long-run equilibrium real exchange rate and the risk premium.

The long-run equilibrium real exchange rate

Models of the long-run equilibrium real exchange rate can be divided into two approaches. Some models simply characterize the equilibrium long-run real exchange rate as a time-invariant purchasing power parity level. As discussed in chapter 4, however, there is not a general consensus on the validity of this assumption. The alternative approach is to characterize

[7] Isard (1983).
[8] Campbell and Clarida (1987), Edison and Pauls (1993) and references cited therein. Edison and Pauls report on more powerful tests for cointegration using error correction models and suggest that additional research in this direction may be warranted.
[9] If pressures on spot exchange rates are transmitted largely through revisions in expectations about long-run equilibrium real exchange rates, and if the distribution of shocks to long-run equilibrium real exchange rates is insensitive to the nature of the nominal exchange rate regime, then the observed regime-sensitivity of the short-term variability of real spot exchange rates (recall the discussion in chapter 4) implies that the behavior of either long-term real interest rate differentials or risk premiums must be regime-sensitive.
[10] Baxter (1994), Clarida and Gali (1994).

long-run exchange rate equilibrium in terms of the joint requirements for maintaining internal and external balance.[11]

In empirical applications, proponents of the latter approach have defined equilibrium real exchange rates as those consistent with equilibrating the current account to some concept of "underlying capital flows" or desired capital flows under various definitions of internal balance.[12] Current account imbalances that were inconsistent with desired capital flows would be unsustainable, generating pressures for exchange rate adjustment. Rough calculations based on this conceptual approach confirm that estimated changes in equilibrium real exchange rates, in association with international disparities in cumulative real output growth, can plausibly explain much of the long-run trends in observed exchange rates.[13]

This approach, however, encounters a number of major difficulties. One difficulty is that it does not lend itself to much precision empirically. In particular, to the extent that the values of equilibrium real exchange rates calculated from quantitative models are quite sensitive to the specification and estimated parameter values of the models, the confidence bands on empirical estimates of equilibrium exchange rates may be quite wide. As some have said, this essentially limits the relevance of the methodology to the identification of "wrong" exchange rates but not the "right" exchange rate. A more serious difficulty is the lack of a clear consensus on the appropriate definition of "external balance." On the one hand, it is not very appealing to define "external balance" as an arbitrary level of current account (or capital) flows; but, on the other hand, conceptual notions of external equilibrium, whether described in terms of current account flows or focused on desired stocks of net international debt, do not yet reflect an adequate understanding of the factors that determine the degree to which claims on different countries are imperfect substitutes.[14] In general, more-

---

[11] The outlines of this approach can be found in Nurkse (1945) and International Monetary Fund (1970); the evolution is reflected in Artus (1978), Williamson (1983), International Monetary Fund (1984b), and Bayoumi et al. (1994).

[12] Williamson (1983, 1994), Wren-Lewis et al. (1991), Stein (1994), Bayoumi et al. (1994). The various ways of defining the external balance consistent with internal balance include: the average external balance over the business cycle, the external balance consistent with maintaining unemployment at an equilibrium rate, and the external balance consistent with maintaining a constant ratio of net foreign assets to full-employment output.

[13] Obstfeld (1985, pp. 414–15) provides an integrated elasticities–absorption model of the current account for which calculations based on reasonable parameter values suggest that a 10 percent increase in the relative demand for one country's output can change the equilibrium real exchange rate by nearly 30 percent. Consistently, the ratio of Japan's real GNP to that of the United States increased by nearly 40 percent from 1972 to 1992, while the real bilateral exchange rate (based on consumer price indices) changed by a little over 100 percent.

[14] This issue is discussed further in the next subsection.

over, it is hard to defend the assumption that external balance can be defined independently of the real exchange rate.

A more encouraging perspective is that recent advances in time series and analysis have substantially expanded the scope for testing simultaneous hypotheses about the long-run and short-run behavior of real exchange rates and current accounts. In particular, the development of the concept of cointegration has led to methodological advances in using error correction models to identify simultaneously the dynamic and long-run relationships between real exchange rates, current accounts, and other macroeconomic variables.[15]

Real intertemporal equilibrium models

At the beginning of the 1980s, the external sectors of most macroeconometric models could be classified as integrated elasticities–absorption models based on static Keynesian-type relationships between consumption (or saving) and income.[16] These models reflected notable advances during the 1960s and 1970s in disaggregating import and export equations for goods and services and achieving greater precision in estimating income and relative price elasticities.[17] Since the early 1980s, intertemporal optimizing models have gained widespread appeal in conceptual analysis of external balance.[18] The intertemporal approach builds on microeconomic foundations in viewing the current account as the outcome of rational forward-looking decisions about saving and investment, and as a channel through which a country can optimally modify the time path of its absorption relative to its production in response to various types of demand or supply shocks.

In essence, the intertemporal equilibrium approach amounts to the dynamic extension of the static Mundell–Fleming model: it transforms the concept of external balance by providing a framework within which cumulative current account balances are constrained over the long run by intertemporal budget constraints, while emphasizing that current account balance in the short run is generally not an optimal outcome. The early vintages of intertemporal models have been limited in their distinctions between different categories of goods, but have begun to provide new

---

[15] See Ericsson (1992a) for an overview of the concept of cointegration and its implications for statistical inference.   [16] Recall chapter 6 (pp. 95–6).

[17] Goldstein and Khan (1985), Helkie and Hooper (1988), Hooper and Márquez (1995).

[18] Lucas (1978, 1982) helped catalyze the equilibrium approach. For surveys see Razin (1995) and Obstfeld and Rogoff (1995). Bosworth (1993) suggests that jointly, the elasticities–absorption and intertemporal approaches do surprisingly well in explaining current account developments during the 1980s.

insights on the comovements of current accounts and real exchange rates, *inter alia*, in response to various transitory and permanent shocks. In the years ahead, improvements in large-scale macroeconometric models may well move further in the direction of integrating the intertemporal analysis of a country's net savings position with an elasticities-type analysis of the composition of its expenditure and production, which may contribute to future advances in explaining the behavior of exchange rates empirically.

Various classes of real intertemporal equilibrium models have emerged since the early 1980s. In the most simplified models, all countries produce the same composite tradable good;[19] other models distinguish among at least two goods, with all goods tradable;[20] and in a third class of models, the menu of goods includes nontradables as well as tradables.[21] Some empirical assessments of the intertemporal approach have consisted of simulation experiments exploring the extent to which the theoretical models can replicate observed comovements of macroeconomic variables under exogenously specified but realistic parameter values.[22] Other studies have implemented direct empirical tests of intertemporal current account models.[23]

Several general insights from intertemporal optimizing models can be developed using the following simple example.[24] Consider a two-country world in which each country produces a single good; let each good have a price of unity in terms of the producing country's currency; and let Q be the relative price or real exchange rate, measured as the amount of the home-country good (H) required to purchase one unit of the foreign-country good (F). C_H, C_F denote the real amounts of each good consumed by the home country; Y is the real output of H; B denotes the home country's net capital inflow, and hence its balance of trade surplus, measured in terms of the home good; and $A = Y + B$ is the level of absorption in the home country. C_H^*, C_F^*, Y^*, $B^* = -B/Q$, and $A^* = Y^* + B^*$ are the analogous flows for the foreign country, with Y^*, B^*, and A^* measured in terms of the foreign good. It is conventional to assume that utility functions have the Cobb–Douglas forms

$$U = (C_H)^{1-m}(C_F)^m, \qquad U^* = (C_H^*)^{m^*}(C_F^*)^{1-m^*} \qquad (10.6)$$

such that the utility maximizing levels of consumption are

[19] Hodrick (1982) and Greenwood (1983) present early examples.
[20] See Stockman (1980), Obstfeld (1982c), Sachs (1982), and Svensson and Razin (1983) for early examples.
[21] Dornbusch (1983a) provides an early example. See also Froot and Rogoff (1991) and Rogoff (1992b).
[22] For example, Stockman and Tesar (1990), Mendoza (1992a, 1992b), Macklem (1993), Backus, Kehoe, and Kydland (1994).
[23] For example, Ahmed (1987), Glick and Rogoff (1992), Ghosh and Ostry (1993, 1994).
[24] The model specification builds on Krugman and Baldwin (1987).

$$C_H = (1-m)(Y+B), \qquad C_F = m(Y+B)/Q \qquad (10.7)$$

and

$$C_H^* = Qm^*(Y^* - B/Q), \qquad C_F^* = (1-m^*)(Y^* - B/Q). \qquad (10.8)$$

The market-clearing conditions are

$$C_H + C_H^* = Y, \qquad C_F + C_F^* = Y^*. \qquad (10.9)$$

Hence, from (10.7)–(10.9), the market-clearing level of the real exchange rate is

$$Q = \frac{mY - (1-m-m^*)B}{m^* Y^*} \qquad (10.10)$$

where it is reasonable to assume that residents of the foreign country exhibit a weaker preference for the home good than home-country residents, or that $m^* < 1-m$. Thus, an increase in net capital flows into the home country, other things being equal, gives rise to an increase in the relative price of the home good (that is, a reduction in Q, the home-good price of the foreign good)

$$\frac{\partial Q}{\partial B} = -\frac{(1-m-m^*)}{m^* Y^*} < 0 \qquad (10.11)$$

since the share of additional home-country absorption that is directed toward the home good exceeds the home-good share of relinquished foreign-country absorption.

This framework leads to perspectives on the relationship between real exchange rate variability and the degree of capital mobility, and on the comovements of real exchange rates and current accounts in response to various types of shocks.[25] Note that for any shock θ, differentiation of (10.10) implies

$$\frac{dQ}{d\theta} = \frac{m}{m^* Y^*}\frac{dY}{d\theta} - \frac{Q}{Y^*}\frac{dY^*}{d\theta} - \frac{(1-m-m^*)}{m^* Y^*}\frac{dB}{d\theta}. \qquad (10.12)$$

The response of the real exchange rate to any type of shock thus depends, in general, on the degrees to which the levels of home and foreign outputs and net capital flows respond to the shock, as well as on the home and foreign ratios of trade to output (m and m^*).

Consider the case of a shock that reduces the level of home-country output with no impact on foreign output, and suppose, as an initial condition, that prior to the shock the balance of trade is zero, such that $m^* Y^* = mY/Q$. Then from (10.12),

[25] The discussion that follows has been stimulated by Michael Dooley.

$$\frac{\Delta Q}{Q} = \frac{\Delta Y}{Y} - \frac{1-m-m^*}{m}\frac{\Delta B}{Y}.$$

(10.13)

Thus, with no capital mobility (that is, $\Delta B = 0$), the increase in the relative price of the home good is equiproportionate to the fall in output of the home good; whereas if access to international borrowing is perfectly elastic and the home country chooses to prevent the loss of output from reducing its current absorption (that is, $\Delta A = \Delta Y + \Delta B = 0$ or $\Delta B = -\Delta Y$), the increase in the relative price of the home good is larger by a factor of $(1-m^*)/m$. Note also that, for any nonnegligible degree of capital mobility, countries with relatively low trade-to-output ratios (m) experience relatively larger changes in their real exchange rates, all else being equal.

(10.13) can be used to compare the effects of transitory and permanent supply shocks (or changes in Y) under different degrees of capital mobility. First, with zero capital mobility ($\Delta B = 0$), the impact effect of a supply shock on the real exchange rate is not influenced by capital flows and, hence, is independent of the persistence of the shock. Second, the impact effect of a supply shock that is perceived to be permanent can be presumed to show little sensitivity to the degree of capital mobility, since the home country would presumably choose to reduce its absorption permanently by the magnitude of its output loss ($\Delta A = \Delta Y$ implying $\Delta B = 0$). Even with a high degree of international capital mobility, it is only attractive to borrow internationally in response to an output loss if the decline in output is temporary. In particular, while borrowing to smooth the time stream of home absorption relative to the time stream of home output tends to be welfare enhancing, a shock that reduces the level of home output permanently without generating any time variation in output generates a situation in which borrowing to raise current absorption at the sacrifice of future absorption would lead to greater time variation in absorption, thereby tending to reduce welfare.

A third point revealed by (10.13) is that transitory supply shocks, in contrast to permanent supply shocks, generate dynamic responses in which the amplitudes of real exchange movements reflect both the degree of capital mobility and the ratio of trade to output. Consider, for example, the case of a transitory decline in home output. During the period in which net capital inflows mitigate the effects of output shortfalls on absorption ($0 < \Delta B < -\Delta Y$), the relative price of home output remains above its preshock level ($\Delta Q < 0$); subsequently, after the negative output shock ends, home absorption is held below home output while international borrowings are repaid, moving the relative price of home output below its preshock level. More generally, the comovements of net capital flows and the real exchange rate relative to preshock levels reflect the time profile of the deviation of output from its preshock level. Furthermore, the amplitudes of the swings in both net capital flows and the real exchange rate reflect the degree of capital mobility, and the amplitude of the swing in the real exchange rate also reflects the ratio of trade to output.

For demand shocks, with home and foreign outputs unchanged, the analog of (10.13) is

$$\frac{\Delta Q}{Q} = -\frac{1 - m - m^*}{m} \frac{\Delta B}{Y}. \tag{10.14}$$

With no capital mobility, real absorption cannot exceed output by definition; thus, if nominal demand growth overheats the home economy (for example, because of unexpected wartime expenditures or policy errors), the only safety valve is for the home-price level to rise, matched by a nominal exchange rate change that keeps the real exchange rate constant. By contrast, if a temporary increase in home demand is accommodated by net capital inflows (to be subsequently repaid with net capital outflows), real absorption can exceed output, and the real exchange rate will change. In this case the amplitude of the real exchange rate movement is directly proportional to the size of the net capital inflow (ΔB) and inversely proportional to the ratio of trade to output (m).

The patterns of exchange rate dynamics implied by this simple example indicate that the intertemporal approach offers new empirically-testable hypotheses, providing hope that analysis based on this approach will improve our ability to explain the behavior of flexible exchange rates. In this connection, however, and despite considerable progress over the past decade, the development of intertemporal optimizing models has a long way to go.[26] Most intertemporal models with more than one good (and hence with relative prices that extend beyond the nominal exchange rate) reflect the unrealistic assumption that goods prices are perfectly flexible; and one major challenge is to relax that assumption.[27] As discussed in chapter 4, a recognition that national price levels adjust sluggishly relative to nominal exchange rates seems important for explaining why the variability of real exchange rates is sensitive to the nominal exchange rate regime.

A second major challenge for intertemporal optimizing models is to develop a deeper understanding of net saving in the context of imperfect capital mobility, in parallel with a deeper understanding of risk premiums. Many intertemporal models of the external balance are based on the hypothesis that countries can borrow and lend in unlimited amounts at an

---

[26] Krugman (1993a), Obstfeld and Rogoff (1995).
[27] See Obstfeld and Rogoff (1994) for a novel approach with sticky prices based on monopolistic competition.

exogenously given world interest rate, subject to intertemporal budget constraints.[28] Needless to say, for many industrial countries and virtually all of the developing countries, the perfect capital mobility assumption is difficult to defend.[29] Notably, empirical estimates of intertemporal current account models suggest that, even for the largest industrial countries, the observed scale of consumption smoothing is significantly smaller than that predicted to occur under perfect capital mobility.[30]

The most streamlined framework for seeking a deeper understanding of intertemporal consumption smoothing under imperfect capital mobility (along with a parallel understanding of risk premiums) is the one-good two-country case in which savings can be held in two different forms, corresponding to contingent claims on the outputs of the two different countries.[31] Although more elaborated analytic models may also be tractable, simply distinguishing between claims on different countries, and on the sources of uncertainty about the yields on these claims, is suggestive. The relevant sources of uncertainty about the yields on the two types of assets can be classified under two broad headings: uncertainty about physical productivity in each country, and uncertainty about tax rates and other political factors relevant to the distribution of output among competing groups of claimants. The perceived magnitudes of these uncertainties are likely to be different for creditors residing in different countries, reflecting, *inter alia*, the facts that creditors may not be able to monitor the actions of nonresident borrowers as effectively as those of resident borrowers,[32] that creditors generally have more legal power to collect payments from debtors residing in their own country than from nonresident debtors, and that governments have power to discriminate against various classes of investors and may view the incomes of nonresident creditors as a more attractive tax base than the incomes of resident voters. Consistent with these considerations, empirical evidence on portfolio

---

[28] In reality, current account imbalances sometimes become constrained by short-run political factors in addition to intertemporal budget constraints. In this connection, Funabashi (1989) and Volcker and Gyohten (1992) emphasize that, prior to the sharp depreciation of the US dollar beginning in early 1985, strong political forces were mounting within the United States to address the large US current account deficit by raising protectionist barriers against imports. See also Takacs (1981) and Stallings (1993).

[29] For perspectives see Gertler and Rogoff (1990) and International Monetary Fund (1991).

[30] Glick and Rogoff (1992) find that country-specific shocks to productivity appear to affect the current accounts of OECD countries by significantly less than they affect investment. Bayoumi and Klein (1994) find evidence of close to perfect capital mobility among Canadian provinces and substantially lower capital mobility between Canada and the rest of the world. See also Obstfeld (1995), Atkeson and Bayoumi (1993), Bayoumi and MacDonald (1994a, 1994b), Lewis (1994).

[31] Gertler and Rogoff (1990) develop such a model.   [32] Gertler and Rogoff (1990).

diversification reveals that market participants exhibit a strong "home bias."[33]

Needless to say, the challenges of extending theoretical models of intertemporal consumption smoothing to the cases of sluggish price adjustment and imperfect capital mobility are difficult. The hope is to gain insights for improving the macroeconometric models used to explain the external balance. Advances in capturing the dynamic behavior of external balances and real exchange rates can help indirectly to identify permanent shifts in long-run equilibrium real exchange rates, and to make the macroeconometric models more appealing as a basis for constructing measures of equilibrium real exchange rates. The consumption/saving decisions that influence the external balance involve decisions about the intertemporal path of consumption, the intratemporal composition of consumption, and the asset composition of savings. Ideally, macroeconometric models of the external balance should capture the principal determinants of each of these types of decisions, as well as the determinants of production and investment decisions.

2   Models with irrationality or limited information

Although attractive directions can be identified for attempting to improve upon existing models of exchange rates without relinquishing the assumption that expectations are rational, a growing body of evidence challenges this central assumption – both for exchange rates and for other asset prices.[34] Among the evidence that model builders must confront are survey data revealing that many market participants condition their behavior to a large extent on "technical analysis" of very recent trends or other patterns in the observed behavior of exchange rates.[35] Consistent with this survey evidence, simulation experiments have confirmed that various types of trading strategies based on technical analysis generate statistically significant profits,[36] and studies of the intra-day behavior of exchange rates have found that volatility spills over from one market to the next, like meteor

---

[33] French and Poterba (1991), Tesar and Werner (1992). Tesar and Werner conjecture that differences in the composition of resident and nonresident portfolios may partly relate to the fact that some sources of country-specific disturbances to residents' nonportfolio income – such as fluctuations in labor's share over the business cycle – can be partially diversified by holding domestic securities; see, however, Atkeson and Bayoumi (1993). Obstfeld (1995) summarizes the literature on "home bias" and discusses a wider range of possible explanations.   [34] Shleifer and Summers (1990).

[35] Taylor and Allen (1992), Group of Ten Deputies (1993). Such technical analysis typically involves the use of charts or more formal statistical techniques to predict future exchange rate movements on the basis of past exchange market developments.

[36] Dooley and Shafer (1983), Sweeney (1986), Cumby and Modest (1987).

showers, as trading days open and close around the globe.[37] Dramatic events – such as the 20 percent drop in the stock-market value of the US corporate sector on October 19, 1987 – also present a major problem for traditional theories of asset prices. In particular, theories postulating that market participants form rational expectations based on complete information have difficulty explaining what new information about relevant economic fundamentals could have prompted such a large revision in either expectations or risk premiums.[38]

With the growing awareness of the shortcomings of models based on rational expectations and complete information, some economists have turned attention to building models in which "fundamentalists" coexist with "feedback traders" (or "chartists") whose behavior is conditioned by the recent history of exchange rates (or other asset prices), rather than by expectations about future economic fundamentals.[39] In these models, the first group of traders, who behave on the basis of expectations about future fundamentals, have the predominant influence on exchange rates over the long run. But risk aversion and substantial uncertainties can make the fundamentalists less influential than feedback traders during periods in which there are no major revisions in expectations about future fundamentals.[40] Accordingly, in the presence of feedback traders, the reluctance of fundamentalists to take large risks allows exchange rates to vary much more widely than is warranted by changes in fundamentals, thereby providing a rationale for the authorities to try to limit exchange rate fluctuations by establishing a target zone.[41] Consistent with this analytic framework, regression analysis of survey data on exchange rate expectations at various horizons suggests that expectations for horizons of up to a few weeks tend to extrapolate recent observed changes in exchange rates, while expectations for horizons of several months or longer tend to forecast a reversal of recent observed changes.[42]

A central issue that arises in this context is whether feedback traders are irrational in the sense of behaving in ways that fail to maximize their risk-compensated expected returns. Because many economists have strong

---

[37] Engle, Ito, and Lin (1990).

[38] Cutler, Poterba, and Summers (1989) examine the 50 largest daily changes in stock prices during 1946–87, finding that in the majority of cases the price changes cannot easily be linked to news about economic fundamentals.

[39] Kyle (1985), Frankel and Froot (1988), Goodhart (1988), Cutler, Poterba, and Summers (1990).

[40] The degree of uncertainty, and hence the influence of fundamentalists, may also depend on the policy authorities' attitude toward the exchange rate. Thus, the dramatic appreciation of the US dollar from early 1981 through early 1985 may have been facilitated, in part, by the US policy of "benign neglect" vis-à-vis dollar exchange rates.

[41] Krugman and Miller (1993).

[42] Frankel and Froot (1988, 1990), Ito (1990, 1994).

objections to models in which market participants behave irrationally, some have started to explore whether feedback trading can be viewed as a rational form of behavior in an environment of limited information.[43] In the empirical domain, a number of economists have started to study the properties of ultra high frequency (e.g., minute-by-minute) data on exchange rates, and to test "microstructural hypotheses" about the behavior of bid–asked spreads, trading volumes, and so forth based on models of how market participants should rationally behave.[44] It is too early to tell how much the microstructure literature will advance our understanding of the degree to which market participants are rational, or of the ways in which the assimilation of information can usefully be modeled.

The point of departure in conceptual attempts to rationalize feedback trading is the postulate that market participants often cannot immediately comprehend the full implications for exchange rates (or other asset prices) of "outside news" about economic fundamentals, and are thus engaged in a continuing inference process. Rather than defining feedback traders as a subset of market participants, it is assumed that traders in general have different information sets, are heterogeneous in their abilities to process information, and are uncertain about the quality of their own processed information relative to that possessed by others. It is also assumed that, over time, market prices will somehow gravitate to levels consistent with complete (or superior) information, and that market participants know this. Accordingly, given knowledge that superior information will prevail in the long run, it can be rational for traders to revise their assessments continuously based on "inside information" generated by the market trading process, which provides them with relevant feedback on the assessments of other market participants.[45]

Whether feedback trading is viewed as irrational in the context of complete information, or rational in the context of incomplete information and a continuous learning process, its presence implies that changes in asset prices over short periods of time are not necessarily related closely to outside news about economic fundamentals. Under the first view – that feedback trading is irrational – the scope for asset prices to diverge from values that rational "fundamentalists" regard as appropriate essentially depends on the widths of the confidence bands that fundamentalists place around their assessments of appropriate prices. If fundamentalists had

---

[43] Gennotte and Leland (1990), Romer (1993).

[44] See, for example, Goodhart and Figliuoli (1991), Lyons (1993), and the volume edited by Frankel, Galli, and Giovannini (1995).

[45] To explain how asset prices can jump by large amounts in the absence of "outside news," one still needs to model the process that traders use to draw inferences from inside information. See Romer (1993).

reason to be highly confident of their point estimates of appropriate asset prices, their pursuit of low-risk expected returns would presumably keep asset prices within a relatively small neighborhood of those point estimates. Under the second view – that feedback trading is rational in the context of limited information – the scope for asset prices to diverge from appropriate levels depends on how quickly market participants can correctly assess the implications of outside news about economic fundamentals.

3   Concluding perspectives

Most economists today believe that

foreign exchange markets behave more like the unstable and irrational asset markets described by Keynes than the efficient markets described by modern finance theory.[46]

While many who reject the traditional efficient markets paradigm cling to the hypothesis that market participants behave rationally, few still believe that the behavior of flexible exchange rates can be accurately described by a model based on the hypothesis that market participants are both fully rational and completely informed about the structure of the model and the behavior of relevant macroeconomic fundamentals.

This situation, however, does not imply that economists should abandon efforts to model how flexible exchange rates would behave in a world of fully rational and completely informed market participants. Indeed, there is reason to conjecture that the behavior of market participants would change endogenously – leading to reductions over time in the short-term variability of flexible exchange rates – if economists ever reached a consensus on an analytic framework that generated relatively precise quantitative estimates of equilibrium exchange rates.

This conjecture reflects the following considerations. There is now fairly strong evidence that the behavior of real exchange rates cannot be adequately explained by the behavior of real interest rate differentials or their underlying determinants, suggesting that progress in explaining observed exchange rates may largely depend on progress in modeling the variability of expected future real exchange rates and the risk premium. Yet, at present, the limitations of both conceptual and empirical models of external balance make it difficult to place much confidence in quantitative estimates of expected future (equilibrium) exchange rates. Thus, economists today still have very limited information about the relationship between equilibrium exchange rates and macroeconomic fundamentals. Accordingly, it is hardly conceivable that rational market participants with

[46] Krugman (1989b, p. 61).

complete information about macroeconomic fundamentals could use that information to form precise expectations about the future market-clearing levels of exchange rates. Until economists can tell market participants with a reasonable degree of precision what they ought to believe about where exchange rates are headed, and can point to a track record of accuracy in doing so, there is little reason to believe that rational market participants will trade currencies on the basis of expectations formed only from assessments of macroeconomic fundamentals.

In addition to what it may imply for research on exchange rate behavior, the latter point has implications for stabilization policy. To the extent that feedback trading has a magnifying effect on exchange rate variability that society perceives to be costly, it raises questions concerning the degree to which, and the conditions under which, countries with flexible exchange rate arrangements should attempt to actively manage their exchange rates. For that matter, the existence of feedback trading may also have a bearing on the choice between fixed and flexible arrangements. These issues are addressed in chapters 11 and 12, which turn to a discussion of exchange rate policy.

As a preface to the discussion in part III of the book, the concluding point here is that the rationale for policy actions to try to stabilize currency values hinges critically on whether economists and policymakers can correctly identify when exchange rates are "inconsistent with macroeconomic fundamentals." Correct identification requires an understanding of how exchange rates would behave in a world of rational market participants with complete information and no feedback trading. Accordingly, further analysis of flexible exchange rate systems with rational expectations and complete information – abstracting from feedback trading and focusing in particular on the issues discussed in the first section of this chapter – remains an important agenda for research.

Part III

Exchange rate policies

11   The choice of exchange rate arrangements

In part III of the book, the focus shifts from the analysis of exchange rate behavior to the design of exchange rate policies. Among the policy issues are questions about the appropriate choice of exchange rate arrangements, the subject of this chapter.

Most of the conceptual literature relating to the choice of exchange rate arrangements is cast in terms of a dichotomy between fixed and flexible exchange rates. In practice, however, systems of rigidly fixed or perfectly flexible rates are hardly ever observed. The Bretton Woods system, for example, was one of fixed-but-adjustable rates, whereas the present system of generalized floating rates has on many occasions involved extensive official intervention to limit exchange rate fluctuations. Moreover, a number of countries have adopted gliding peg arrangements, in which exchange rates are maintained within fixed fluctuation margins during each trading day, while the central parities and fluctuation bands are adjusted on a regular basis, often at a rate that reflects the differential between domestic and foreign inflation rates.

In the official classification by the IMF, exchange rate arrangements are divided into three broad categories: pegged or fixed arrangements, flexible arrangements, and an in-between category of arrangements with "limited flexibility."[1] National choices reveal a lack of consensus in the world today. Among 180 countries classified by the International Monetary Fund at the end of 1993, 77 countries were listed as having fixed exchange rate arrangements, 91 maintained flexible arrangements (including gliding pegs), and 12 were regarded as having arrangements with "limited flexibility."[2] Notably, the proportion of IMF members with flexible exchange arrangements has increased markedly over the past quarter

---

[1] International Monetary Fund (1994); recall the discussion in chapter 3 (pp. 25–6).
[2] International Monetary Fund (1994). The 12 included eight participants in the Exchange Rate Mechanism of the European Monetary System and four Middle Eastern countries with adjustable pegs but wide fluctuation margins ($7\frac{1}{4}$ percent on each side of the central parities).

century.[3] Among nearly 30 countries that joined the IMF between mid-1990 and end-1993, approximately two-thirds have opted for flexible exchange rate arrangements. Moreover, during the last four months of 1992, 5 western European countries (Finland, the United Kingdom, Italy, Sweden, and Norway) were induced by strong market pressures to abandon fixed exchange rate arrangements and let their currencies float, while at the beginning of August 1993, the 8 countries still participating in the fixed rate arrangements of the European Monetary System responded to persistent market pressures by widening substantially (to 15 percent on each side of the central parities) the bands within which their currency values were permitted to fluctuate.

These perspectives illustrate two general themes that emerge from the literature reviewed in this chapter. First, different types of exchange rate arrangements may be appropriate for different countries, depending on their structural characteristics, external environments, and macroeconomic and political circumstances. Second, as structural characteristics, external environments, or macroeconomic and political circumstances change over time, market pressures on exchange rates may sometimes become so overwhelming that they essentially force changes in exchange rate arrangements.

Discussions of optimal currency arrangements have changed considerably over the past half century. The debate over fixed versus flexible exchange rates around 1960, as summarized in the first section, centered on the issue of whether international capital flows would be stabilizing under flexible rates. A new literature emerged during the 1960s, analyzing the types of structural characteristics that made it optimal for a country to choose one type of arrangement or the other. As reviewed in the second section, this literature has focused on a number of relevant structural characteristics of economies, including size and openness, diversity of production activities and occupational skills, geographic factor mobility, fiscal redistribution mechanisms, policy preferences, wage and price flexibility, exposure to shocks, and financial development. The third section discusses several important directions in which the analysis of optimal exchange arrangements was extended during the 1980s and early 1990s, largely in association with deliberations over the move toward monetary

---

[3] At the end of 1969, among 115 countries that were then members of the IMF, only Lebanon maintained a flexible exchange rate; at end-1979, nearly one-quarter of the membership had flexible exchange rates; at end-1989, about one-third; and at end-1993, one-half. These figures treat cases of "limited flexibility" (including participants in the European ERM) as countries with fixed exchange rates, and treat cases of gliding parities or crawling pegs as countries with flexible rates. See International Monetary Fund (1994) and previous issues.

integration in Europe, which is described in the fourth section. The extensions emphasize the relevance of such issues as the adverse effects of exchange rate uncertainty, the credibility of monetary policy, the option value of the inflation tax, the scope for international policy cooperation, and the endogeneity of factor mobility or other structural characteristics. The fifth section returns to questions about speculative capital flows, discussing the trend toward increased international capital mobility and its implications for the choice of exchange rate arrangements, with particular reference to the European exchange market crisis of 1992–93. The sixth section provides concluding perspectives.

1 Fixed versus flexible rates: perspectives around 1960

At the start of the 1960s, the literature on optimal exchange rate arrangements was cast as a general debate over the choice between fixed or flexible rates. Notably, the most contentious issues in that debate related to the functioning of the two types of arrangements. There was broad agreement that exchange rate adjustment had advantages and disadvantages. The perceived advantages stemmed from the realization that the international monetary system could not perform well unless there was scope for balance of payments adjustment through changes in relative national price levels over time. From this perspective, the argument in favor of exchange rate adjustment was seen as analogous to the argument for daylight saving time:

it is much simpler to change the clock that guides all than to have each individual separately change his reaction to the clock ... [Similarly, i]t is far simpler to allow one price to change, namely, the price of foreign exchange, than to rely upon changes in the multiple of prices that together constitute the internal price structure.[4]

Yet it was also recognized that the exchange rate adjustment process could function poorly under either fixed-but-adjustable or flexible exchange rate arrangements, potentially leading to inappropriate changes in households' purchasing power, excessive costs of adjustment or windfalls for firms, unwanted unemployment or inflation, misdirected investment, and intensified pressures for trade restrictions. Indeed, the architects of the Bretton Woods system, as noted in chapter 3, had been influenced

---

[4] Friedman (1953, p. 173). Even advocates of fixed exchange arrangements point to the high potential costs of trying to avoid exchange rate adjustments in some circumstances. For example, Krugman (1989b, p. 70) argues that bringing the underlying inflation rate down in the United States from about 10 percent to about 5 percent over the period 1979–87 had a cumulative output cost of at least 20 percent of annual GNP, suggesting that a country whose relative prices are, say, 10 percent out of line would pay a huge price to preserve a fixed exchange rate.

considerably by the fact that both freely floating and fixed-but-uncoordinated exchange rate arrangements had functioned poorly during the
interwar period. Thus, there were strong perceptions of

[t]he dangers of ... cumulative and self-aggravating movements under a regime of
freely fluctuating exchanges ... Exchange rates in such circumstances are bound to
become highly unstable, and the influence of psychological factors may at times be
overwhelming.[5]

At the same time, with respect to fixed-but-adjustable exchange rate
arrangements, there were clear perceptions of both the dangers of unwar-
ranted competitive devaluations and the occasional appropriateness of
devaluations to restore competitiveness:

It ought to be an elementary principle of international monetary relations that
exchange rates should not be altered by arbitrary unilateral action. The Tripartite
Agreement was a belated and half-hearted admission of this principle.
    But the difficulty of fixing appropriate exchange rates in the first instance is so
great that there should be a reasonable willingness to adjust them in the light of
experience.[6]

The Bretton Woods system moved well beyond the Tripartite Agreement
in establishing an international monetary regime that limited the scope for
altering exchange rates through "arbitrary unilateral action." The International Monetary Fund was created to monitor national policies and,
inter alia, to provide a forum for multilateral consultations on exchange
rate adjustments. The experience of the 1950s and 1960s, however, brought
growing disenchantment with the rigidity of exchange rates under the
Bretton Woods system.[7] Except for the floating of the Canadian dollar
from 1950 to 1962, the system operated from September 1949 until
November 1967 with only two realignments of the par values of major
currencies: the 1958 devaluation of the French franc, and the upward
revaluations of the German mark and the Dutch guilder in 1961.[8]

    In his celebrated arguments for flexible rates, Friedman (1953) not only
emphasized the efficiency of exchange rate flexibility as a mechanism for
achieving adjustments in international cost/price competitiveness when
domestic wages and prices were sticky, but also contended that private
speculation would be stabilizing:

People who argue that speculation is generally destabilizing seldom realize that this
is largely equivalent to saying that speculators lose money, since speculation can be

[5] Nurkse (1944, p. 118), who also disputed (p. 119) "the simple view that exchange ... [rate
    adjustment acts to equilibrate] the balance of trade."
[6] Nurkse (1944, p. 141).   [7] Kenen (1985, pp. 656–7).
[8] De Vries (1985, Vol. I, p. 96). Haberler (1966, p. 135) refers to a tendency for countries "to
    devalue too much and too late and to appreciate too late and too little."

destabilizing in general only if speculators on the average sell when the currency is low in price and buy when it is high.[9]

This assertion provoked a sharp debate.[10] As subsequent experience revealed, the proponents of flexible rates during the Bretton Woods period, in their belief that international capital flows would be stabilizing under such a system, committed the common error of comparing the perceived shortcomings of the prevailing exchange rate regime with an idealization of an alternative.[11]

2   Relevant structural characteristics

While the debate within international policy circles was preoccupied with the question of whether speculation would be destabilizing, a new conceptual framework for analyzing optimal exchange arrangements – abstracting from speculative capital flows – was formulated by Mundell (1961b), with important subsequent extensions by McKinnon (1963) and Kenen (1969).[12] Stressing that

periodic balance-of-payments crises will remain an integral feature of the international economic system as long as fixed exchange rates and rigid wage and price levels prevent the terms of trade from fulfilling a natural role in the adjustment process,[13]

Mundell nevertheless rejected the view that flexible rates were appropriate in all cases and shifted attention to defining the structural characteristics that determined whether it was "optimal" for two or more countries to fix the exchange rates between their currencies. Although Mundell referred to his analysis as a theory of "optimum currency areas," he defined a currency area as "a domain within which exchange rates are fixed,"[14] rather than as an area with a single currency.

Factor mobility

Mundell's analysis started from the presumption that the broad goal of policy was to achieve the best possible reconciliation of two sometimes-

---

[9] Friedman (1953, p. 175).

[10] See Baumol (1957), Telser (1959), and Johnson (1976) on the relationship between profitability and stability. See Kindleberger (1970) for the arguments of those who continued to favor fixed exchange rates.

[11] Kenen (1988, 1994) emphasizes this type of pitfall. McKinnon (1976), reflecting on the first few years of experience with floating rates during the 1970s, characterized the presumption of stabilizing speculation as a vision wrapped in "the Emperor's new clothes."

[12] Corden (1972) evaluated and extended the literature from the perspective of the movement toward economic and monetary union in the European Economic Community. Ishiyama (1975) and Tower and Willett (1976) provided surveys of the literature as of the mid-1970s.

[13] Mundell (1961b, p. 657).   [14] Mundell (1961b, p. 657).

conflicting objectives: maintaining external balance; and minimizing the deviation from "full employment," which was interpreted as the level of employment that achieved the most desirable feasible combination of unemployment and wage inflation. Based on this premise, Mundell argued that the degree of factor mobility was a key determinant of the optimal choice of exchange arrangement, citing both sides of the debate over economic integration in Western Europe.[15] Fixed exchange rates were seen as more conducive than flexible rates to the maintenance of stable relative prices and, thus, to the promotion of economic integration, while flexible rates provided a mechanism for relatively rapid adjustment of economic activity through changes in the relative prices of home and foreign goods. The latter mechanism was particularly important when the degree of factor mobility was relatively low. With relatively low factor mobility, the unemployment or inflationary costs of maintaining a fixed exchange rate could be relatively severe and persistent in an environment subject to unpredictable disturbances to aggregate demand.

Size and openness

Mundell also emphasized the absurdity of suggesting that every region with a minor pocket of unemployment should have its own separate currency. Citing John Stuart Mill (1894) and others, he noted that an increase in the number of separate currencies reduces the usefulness of money as a unit of account and medium of exchange. Analogously, for a small country that had a separate currency, the usefulness of the national money could be enhanced by maintaining a fixed exchange rate.

McKinnon pushed this line of analysis further, focusing on the relevance of openness, as measured by the ratio of tradable goods production to nontradable goods production. Openness was regarded as a determinant of the extent to which "money illusion would ... help in getting labor to accept a cut in real wages,"[16] and hence of the comparative advantages of relative price changes and contractionary or expansionary monetary–fiscal policies as instruments for maintaining internal and external balance. McKinnon argued that, other things being equal, the greater the openness of an economy, the greater would be the responsiveness of domestic wages and prices to a change in the nominal exchange rate, so the stronger was the case for a fixed exchange rate: as openness increases,

flexible exchange rates become both less effective as a control device for external balance and more damaging to internal price-level stability.[17]

---

[15] Mundell (1961b, pp. 661–2). Earlier recognition of the importance of factor mobility can be found in Lerner (1951, pp. 258–60).
[16] McKinnon (1963, p. 723).   [17] McKinnon (1963, p. 719).

This reasoning was similar to the arguments that Mundell had used in suggesting that the smaller the size of the economy, other things being equal, the stronger the case for a fixed exchange rate.[18]

Diversity in production and occupational skills

Kenen (1969) shifted attention to another structural characteristic relevant to the choice of exchange rate arrangements, essentially by distinguishing between two concepts of factor mobility.[19] In addition to depending on the degree of geographic factor mobility, on which Mundell (1961b) had focused, the optimal exchange arrangement depended on the degree of inter-industry factor mobility: the greater the diversity of an economy's production activities and occupational skills, other things being equal, the less severe and persistent would be the unemployment or inflationary costs of unpredictable disturbances to the economy, so the stronger was the case for fixed exchange rates.

Fiscal redistribution mechanisms

Although nonpolitical characteristics such as size, openness, diversity of production, and factor mobility were regarded as relevant considerations in the choice of exchange rate arrangements, it was also recognized that appropriate decisions on exchange rate policy depended importantly on the nature of the broader policy environment. Thus, Kenen (1969) stressed that the optimal currency area – perceived as an area over which it was optimal to assign monetary policies to maintaining fixed exchange rates – depended on the domains for fiscal policies and the scope for using fiscal systems to compensate for regional differences in deviations from full employment.

Policy preferences

An additional perspective on the relevance of the policy environment was provided by Haberler (1966), who emphasized that:

The satisfactory operation of a system of fixed exchanges requires a certain amount of international harmonization of monetary, fiscal, and wage policies, and this, in turn, presupposes that the various countries have broadly similar views on the weight they put on potentially conflicting policy objectives, such as stable prices, level of employment, and rate of growth.[20]

---

[18] Mundell (1961b, p. 663). Although Mundell and McKinnon stressed different factors, each suggested that size and openness were both relevant.

[19] McKinnon (1963) also emphasized the distinction between the two concepts of factor mobility, but without elaborating the implications.   [20] Haberler (1966, p. 133).

Wage and price flexibility

The early literature on optimum currency areas regarded the degree of wage and price flexibility as an implication of other structural characteristics, such as openness and size. Following Mundell (1961b), it was generally assumed that nominal wages and prices could not be reduced in the short run without creating unemployment, but the early literature did not extensively analyze the types of structural policies that might be considered for changing the slope of the short-run Phillips curve.[21]

Exposure to shocks

In various places, the early literature recognized that the relative costs and benefits of different exchange rate arrangements depended on the nature of disturbances to the domestic and foreign economies.[22] Subsequent literature has given more extensive attention to the question of the optimal degree of exchange rate flexibility for coping with various types of shocks (real or nominal; domestic, foreign, or global; permanent or temporary), drawing inferences from both simple theoretical models[23] and stochastic simulations of empirically-based macroeconomic models.[24]

Notably, the conjecture that flexible exchange rates exacerbate output volatility and mitigate the international transmission of business cycles – an unconditional statement that pays no attention to the composition of economic shocks – does not hold up well to empirical scrutiny.[25] Countries experience many types of real shocks, including shocks to productivity, real wages, money velocity, and the stability of financial institutions. Other things being equal, the less symmetric is the distribution of real shocks across countries, the greater is the cost of forgoing the option of exchange rate adjustment in response to shocks. With respect to asymmetric nominal shocks, the pros and cons of fixed exchange rates depend on the source of the shocks. Flexible exchange rates can insulate against spillover effects

---

[21] See, however, the discussion in Tower and Willett (1976). Meanwhile, Friedman (1968) argued that the trade-off between inflation and unemployment was temporary, thus challenging the traditional notion of the Phillips curve.

[22] For example, Kenen (1969), Corden (1972). The formal approach to analyzing the relevance of the nature of economic shocks for the choice among alternative monetary policy regimes in a closed economy, which is usually attributed to Poole (1970) but received earlier attention by Bailey (1962), was extended to the choice of exchange rate regimes by Roper and Turnovsky (1980).

[23] For example, Boyer (1978), Henderson (1979), Flood and Marion (1982), Aizenman and Frenkel (1985), Marston (1985).

[24] For example, Frenkel, Goldstein, and Masson (1989).

[25] Eichengreen (1994).

from nominal shocks emanating from abroad, while fixed exchange rates can neutralize domestic monetary shocks.[26]

Financial development

During the 1950s and 1960s, a central issue in the debate over fixed versus flexible exchange rates, as noted earlier, was the question of whether private capital flows were stabilizing or destabilizing. Since that time, the stock of internationally mobile private capital has grown enormously, and the constraints on capital mobility have been greatly reduced; see the fifth section below. Meanwhile, the debate about the relevance of international capital mobility for the choice of exchange rate regime has focused on new considerations, as also discussed below.

The degree of financial sector development can be distinguished from the international mobility of capital as a structural characteristic relevant to the choice of exchange rate regime. Abstracting from changes in financial portfolio holdings over time – and hence from international financial capital flows – a greater degree of financial development allows market participants, through portfolio diversification at any point in time, to cushion their income and consumption possibility streams more completely against adverse shocks. Thus, for given *ex ante* probability distributions of different types of shocks, an increase in the degree of financial development presumably reduces the relative advantages of one type of exchange rate arrangement over another.

3   Other considerations

Reflecting its primary focus on the structural characteristics of economies, the early literature on optimum currency areas was dismissed in some quarters as "primarily a scholastic discussion which contributes little to practical problems of exchange rate policy and monetary reform."[27] Consistently, empirical studies suggest that the structural characteristics of economies perform very modestly in predicting the types of exchange rate arrangements that countries have actually chosen.[28]

During recent years, the theory of optimum currency areas has been

---

[26] These views are oversimplified, however, to the extent that the policy regime choice is not simply between fixed and flexible rates, but also involves a choice between several possible combinations of home-country and foreign-country monetary policy operating procedures under each type of exchange rate system; see Henderson and McKibbin (1993).

[27] Ishiyama (1975, p. 378).

[28] Honkapohja and Pikkarainen (1992), Edison and Melvin (1990).

resuscitated,[29] greatly benefitting from, and contributing to, the consideration of various practical issues associated with the move toward monetary integration in Europe. To a large extent, these additional considerations can be described under five headings: adverse effects of exchange rate uncertainty, the credibility of monetary policy, the option value of the inflation tax, the scope for international policy cooperation, and the endogeneity of the structural characteristics of economies.[30]

Adverse effects of exchange rate uncertainty

A long-debated issue in the literature on optimal currency arrangements is the question of whether flexible exchange rate systems have strongly adverse consequences for international trade and investment. According to one prominent view, exchange rate flexibility creates

a major new source of uncertainty in making contracts and in investing on the basis of future expected demand ... Movements in exchange rates can wipe out – or double – a 5 percent profit margin in a week.[31]

Consistently, large and persistent changes in exchange rates often catalyze strong political pressures for import protection in countries that have had their international competitiveness eroded.[32]

The opponents of flexible exchange rates, however, have had difficulty backing up their arguments about the adverse consequences. In particular, empirical studies have failed to uncover statistical evidence that exchange rate variability has had much of a depressing effect on international trade volumes,[33] and international trade has continued to expand more rapidly than output throughout the past two decades of widely fluctuating exchange rates. Krugman suggests that, in retrospect, this should not be a surprise: "looking at the volume of trade is not the place where one would expect to find the costs of fluctuating exchange rates."[34] Even if the average lag between export orders and deliveries was as long as a year, and the one-

---

[29] Tavlas (1993), Bayoumi (1994).

[30] Without denying the importance of these considerations, it has been emphasized that, in general, the choice of exchange rate regime should have little relevance in the absence of some kind of "market failure," and that the first-best policy for addressing the market failure may not involve the choice of exchange rate regime; see Flood and Marion (1992). See Krugman (1993a) on what we still need to know about choosing an exchange rate regime.   [31] Cooper (1990, p. 105).

[32] Such concerns about the politically divisive and economically costly effects of exchange rate uncertainty have led to the suggestion that it is not premature to begin thinking about the creation of a common currency for industrial countries in the next century; see Cooper (1984).

[33] Edison and Melvin (1990), Gagnon (1993), International Monetary Fund (1984a).

[34] Krugman (1989b, p. 68).

year standard deviation of the exchange rate was 10 percent, the effect of exchange rate uncertainty would be analogous to adding an implicit transportation cost of only 1 percent.[35]

Along with such arguments, a new conceptual framework has emerged for characterizing the adverse effects of exchange rate uncertainty. Based on insights provided by Dixit (1989),[36] it is now argued that exchange rate uncertainty is likely to make itself felt through delaying "real changes in the world economy that should be met by investment and disinvestment."[37] In particular, it is now recognized that uncertainty about future exchange rates gives firms an incentive to postpone any investment (or disinvestment) in export (or import-substitution) capacity that would be difficult to reverse. By making such an investment immediately, a firm runs the risk of incurring long-term costs if the home currency appreciates; by delaying, the firm risks sacrificing profits over the short run if the home currency depreciates, but can still choose to invest later. This new conceptual framework thus provides a new rationalization for the long-standing view that a system of fixed (or stable) exchange rates, other things being equal, is conducive to economic integration, efficient investment, and growth.[38]

The credibility of monetary policy

The early literature on optimum currency areas preceded the literature on time-inconsistent policies.[39] The rational expectations revolution in macroeconomics, as embodied in the time-inconsistency literature, retained the notion that policy authorities could reduce unemployment in the short run through monetary expansion, but only if money growth exceeded the *ex ante* expectations of market participants. The new literature emphasized, moreover, that rational market participants, recognizing the authorities' incentive to reduce unemployment by generating inflationary monetary "surprises," would doubt the credibility of announced monetary policy intentions, expecting actual inflation to be higher than the rate that would prevail in the presence of a "commitment technology" that prevented monetary surprises. Furthermore, the effect on expected inflation of

---

[35] Krugman (1989b, p. 68). This example assumes that the coefficient of relative risk aversion is 2 and that the risk is completely undiversifiable.

[36] See also Krugman (1989a).   [37] Krugman (1989b, p. 69).

[38] In addition to arguing that exchange rate uncertainty may in some cases delay productive investments, Krugman (1989b) notes that, in other cases, firms may be induced to install excess capacity, spread over different countries, in order to be able quickly to switch production to low-cost locations subsequent to any exchange rate movements. See also Aizenman (1994).

[39] Path-breaking articles on time inconsistency were provided by Kydland and Prescott (1977), Calvo (1978), and Barro and Gordon (1983a, 1983b), with notable anticipation by Friedman (1968).

imperfect monetary policy credibility would be self-validating, leading to a higher rate of observed inflation.

By the late 1980s, this line of analysis had led to the argument that an open economy with relatively poor monetary policy credibility could reduce its inflation rate by fixing its exchange rate *vis-à-vis* the currency of a country with relatively high anti-inflation credibility.[40] Fixed exchange rates were thus regarded as a commitment technology that national authorities could employ – if they so chose – to tie their own hands and thereby gain credibility. France and Italy, by joining a monetary union with Germany, could benefit from the anti-inflation credibility that Germany had already acquired.

Yet history provides evidence of episodes in which national authorities have lost credibility by tying their hands too tightly. The potential for fixed exchange rate commitments to lose credibility was dramatically illustrated by the European exchange market crisis of 1992–93, as discussed later in this chapter. In the European case, the commitment to fixed exchange rates had helped achieve substantial benefits in lowering inflation rates by the early 1990s, but by 1992 German unification and other economic shocks had made the prevailing real exchange rates between some European countries unsustainable. In other cases, where inflation has been rapid but nominal contracts are still sufficiently prevalent to establish a substantial degree of inflation inertia, the high real costs of bringing inflation down quickly may make a gliding peg arrangement more credible than a fixed exchange rate.[41]

The option value of the inflation tax

The new literature on optimum currency areas also pointed to an additional cost of relinquishing monetary autonomy completely – that is, of ceding the power to print money – as distinct from simply making a revokable commitment to a fixed exchange rate regime. Monetary sovereignty can have "significant option value to a government," even if seigniorage revenues are normally very small: the seigniorage obtained by issuing money is probably the most flexible form of taxation available to a government.[42] Indeed, the inflation tax can be viewed as "the revenue of last resort"[43] – a mechanism that governments, throughout history, have

---

[40] Giavazzi and Pagano (1988), Mélitz (1988), de Grauwe (1992).

[41] See Helpman, Leiderman, and Bufman (1994) for a discussion of the gliding peg arrangements adopted by Chile, Israel, and Mexico in recent years, and for empirical evidence that the shift from a fixed to a gliding peg may reduce realignment uncertainty and be associated with a reduction in interest rate volatility.

[42] Eichengreen (1995a).   [43] Goodhart (1995).

commonly relied upon to finance wartime needs and other large or unpopular expenditures.

The scope for international policy cooperation

The literature of the 1960s emphasized, among other things, that the case for fixed exchange rates depended on the degree of similarity between the policy preferences (and Phillips curves) of the participating countries. Modern theory has added perspectives on the importance of policy cooperation.

One of the new perspectives points to the negative inflation externalities that can arise from coordination failure in an environment with multiple decisionmakers.[44] In its simplest form, the argument emphasizes that budget deficits tend to fuel inflation. Accordingly, when a country formulates its budget position, it can be viewed as trading off the benefits of higher absorption or lower taxes against the costs of higher inflation. But the benefits typically accrue primarily to the country in question, while in a fixed exchange rate system the inflationary costs spill over significantly onto other countries. Thus, in the absence of a cooperative approach to policy formulation – and, in particular, a mutual willingness of individual countries to give appropriate weight in their policy calculations to the spillover costs of inflation – a fixed exchange rate system will generate excessive budget deficits and excessive inflation. The demise of the ruble area provides a recent example: once the former Soviet Union (FSU) split into fifteen states and intra-FSU policy cooperation broke down, the attractiveness of having a common currency was rapidly eroded.

Other directions in the literature on international policy cooperation, also focusing on the externalities that policymakers generate for each other, have included a game-theoretic approach to analyzing optimal policy strategies in a multicountry world,[45] and the use of multicountry econometric models to simulate the effects of different possible combinations of home-country and foreign-country policy regimes.[46] In general, the different strands of literature have treated the case for international policy cooperation as a broader set of issues than the choice of an exchange rate

---

[44] See, for example, Aizenman and Isard (1993).

[45] See Canzoneri and Henderson (1991) and Rogoff (1992a). Niehans (1968) and Hamada (1974, 1979) were early contributors to this approach. Canzoneri and Gray (1985) focused attention, *inter alia*, on the conditions under which a fixed exchange rate agreement (between a leader country that controlled its money growth and a follower country that kept the exchange rate fixed) allowed countries, without direct cooperation, to achieve superior macroeconomic outcomes. Rogoff (1985a) advanced the proposition that cooperation could be counterproductive in the presence of third-country effects.

[46] See, for example, Bryant, Hooper, and Mann (1993).

arrangement – and in some cases as a set of issues that takes the exchange rate regime as given. The practical interest in international policy cooperation is discussed in chapter 12.

The endogeneity of structural characteristics

Greater recognition has also been given in recent years to arguments suggesting that the structural characteristics of economies are not exogenous to the choice of exchange rate regime. Thus, wage–price flexibility may increase following the adoption of a fixed rate regime.[47] Or the adoption of a flexible rate system may induce greater international diversification of productive capacity, mitigating some of the costs associated with exchange rate variability.[48] And so forth.

4   The evolution of European exchange arrangements

By the end of the 1960s, alternative ways of introducing greater exchange rate flexibility into the Bretton Woods system were being actively discussed in policy circles. The pros and cons of various alternatives, as seen by policymakers at the time, are described in an IMF report issued in August 1970.[49] The report expressed fear that large fluctuations in exchange rates, perhaps exaggerated by speculative capital movements, "would involve damaging uncertainties for international trade." Moreover, there was concern that – were the Bretton Woods system to be abandoned

the absence of par values and of the associated international procedures for adjusting exchange rates would leave a vacuum in the necessary provisions for international coordination of exchange rates.[50]

Opposition to greater flexibility of exchange rates was particularly strong among European countries, which had moved considerably during the 1960s toward the unification of trade and tariff policies and the formulation of the Common Agricultural Policy (CAP). Indeed, the importance attached by European policy authorities to the preservation and strengthening of economic integration and cooperation, and the desirability of stable exchange rates from that perspective, led the European Community (EC) to revive the idea of a monetary union

---

[47] Flood and Marion (1982). As Eichengreen (1995a) notes, for example, Italy succeeded in abolishing its wage indexation scheme (the scala mobile) in anticipation of European monetary unification.   [48] Aizenman (1994).
[49] International Monetary Fund (1970).
[50] International Monetary Fund (1970, p. 304).

involving the reduction and eventual elimination of exchange rate fluctuations between the currencies of the EC countries and the complete liberalization of capital movements between them.[51]

In pursuit of that idea, the EC decided in December 1969 to assemble a group of experts to come up with a detailed plan, which it endorsed in March 1971.

The plan, known as the Werner Report,[52] proposed a three-stage process for implementing monetary union. Stage one, from 1971 to 1974, would "create the machinery for coordinated policy making;" stage two would "make exchange-rate changes depend on explicit member agreements;" and the final stage three would create a "Community central bank shaped after the US Federal Reserve System."[53]

As one of the first significant steps, in March 1972 the six EC members (France, Germany, Italy, Belgium, the Netherlands, and Luxembourg), together with three soon-to-be members (the United Kingdom, Denmark, and Ireland),[54] established an independent currency arrangement – known as the "snake" – with narrower fluctuation margins than the IMF rules then permitted.[55] The international economic environment at the time, however, was unkind to the snake – in much the same manner as it contributed to a turbulent experience with managed floating within the broader international monetary system.[56] Britain, Ireland, and Denmark left the arrangement in June 1972, although Denmark rejoined in October; Italy left in February 1973; France left in January 1974, rejoined in July 1975, and left again in March 1976; and in the meantime, a number of small realignments took place.[57] To an important extent, the difficulties of holding the snake together reflected the fact that different countries – in the wake of the 1972–73 boom and the stagflationary oil price shock of 1973–74 – chose different approaches to macroeconomic stabilization, giving rise, among other things, to different inflation rates. As a consequence, the process of monetary unification stagnated.

In October 1977, the British President of the EC launched a new drive for monetary union.[58] This led to the formation of the European Monetary System (EMS) in March 1979. At the beginning, eight of the nine members of the EC participated in the fixed Exchange Rate Mechanism (ERM) of the EMS. One of the eight participants, Italy, was allowed to adopt wide

---

[51] De Vries (1985, Vol. I, p. 21).   [52] Council of the European Communities (1970).
[53] Fratianni and von Hagen (1992, p. 13).
[54] These three countries joined the Community on January 1, 1973.
[55] The Smithsonian Agreement in December 1971 had widened the IMF margins to 2¼ percent on either side of par values. The United Kingdom did not join the snake until May 1, 1972.
[56] Goldstein (1980).
[57] Solomon (1982), Kindleberger (1984), de Vries (1985). Norway and Sweden joined in March 1973, with Sweden withdrawing in August 1977.   [58] Jenkins (1978).

fluctuation margins of 6 percent on each side of its par values; the others adopted narrow margins of $2\frac{1}{4}$ percent. The United Kingdom remained outside the ERM until October 1990. Three more countries joined the EC during the 1980s – Greece in 1981, followed by Spain and Portugal in 1986 – with Spain entering the ERM as of June 1989 and Portugal as of April 1992.[59] Although the European Currency Unit (ECU)[60] is used as the common numeraire of the ERM and a means of payment among partici- pating monetary authorities, the Deutsche mark has evolved, *de facto*, as the center currency of the ERM to date, and monetary policies in countries other than Germany have been effectively constrained to follow that of the Bundesbank.

Together, the fixed exchange rate system and the macroeconomic environment of the 1980s contributed to a dramatic convergence in inflation rates among countries participating in the ERM (figure 11.1, top panel). The period also brought a steady decrease – until the summer of 1992 – in the frequency of exchange rate adjustments (figure 11.1, lower panel); thus, EMS central rates were realigned seven times between March 1979 and September 1983,[61] four times between October 1983 and March 1988,[62] and once between April 1988 and August 1992.[63] Consistently, the month-to-month variability of nominal and real exchange rates fell dra- matically (table 11.1), even for European countries that sought exchange rate stability but were not participants in the ERM.[64]

These trends toward inflation convergence and exchange rate stability propelled the political process further. In June 1988, a decision was taken to require the lifting of all remaining capital controls by July 1990, and a committee was established to prepare a blueprint for monetary unification. The blueprint, known as the Delors Report,[65] was issued in April 1989 and

[59] The United Kingdom, Spain, and Portugal all adopted the wide 6 percent fluctuation margins.

[60] The ECU is a basket currency defined by fixed quantities of the currencies of participants in the EMS.

[61] During these seven realignments, bilateral central rates against the Deutsche mark were changed six times for the Danish krone, five times each for the Belgian franc and Italian lira, four times each for the French franc and Irish pound, and twice for the Dutch guilder.

[62] On these four occasions, bilateral central rates against the Deutsche mark were changed three times each for the Italian lira and the Irish pound, two times each for the Belgian franc, the Danish krone, and the French franc, and at no time for the Dutch guilder.

[63] On the latter occasion, in January 1990, the central rate of the Italian lira was devalued by 3.7 percent against the Deutsche mark as a "technical realignment" associated with a decision to narrow the fluctuation margins for the lira from 6 percent (on each side of the central rate) to $2\frac{1}{4}$ percent. The new central rate was fixed at approximately the prevailing market rate, and the lower intervention limit was not adjusted.

[64] This reduction in exchange rate volatility did not come at the expense of increased interest rate volatility; see Artis and Taylor (1994).

[65] Commission for the Study of Economic and Monetary Union (1989). See Ungerer et al. (1990) for a review of the EMS experience through October 1990.

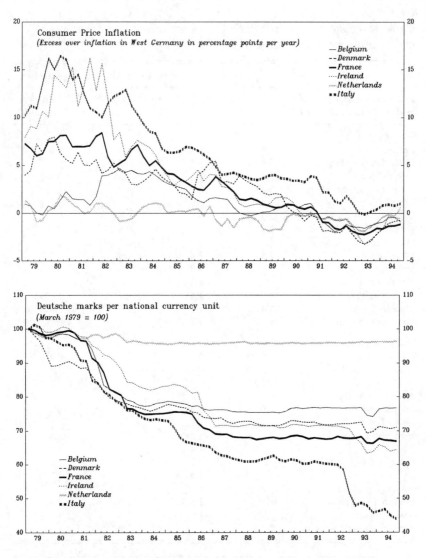

Source: Based on quarterly data from International Monetary Fund, *International Financial Statistics.*

Figure 11.1 Inflation convergence and exchange rate stability for the original ERM members, 1979–94

Table 11.1. *Short-term variability of exchange rates among European currencies, April 1973–August 1992*

	Average absolute values of monthly percentage changes			
Bilateral exchange rates against the Deutsche mark	Apr. 1973–Mar. 1979	Apr. 1979–Sept. 1983	Oct. 1983–Mar. 1988	Apr. 1988–Aug. 1992
Nominal				
Belgian franc	0.6	0.7	0.3	0.2
Netherlands guilder	0.8	0.5	0.3	0.3
Danish krone	0.9	0.7	0.5	0.4
Austrian schilling	0.4	0.2	0.2	0.2
French franc	1.6	0.8	0.6	0.4
Italian lira	2.3	0.9	0.6	0.5
Irish pound	2.2	0.7	0.6	0.3
Swiss franc	1.7	1.4	0.9	1.1
Pound sterling	2.3	2.6	1.8	1.5
Swedish krona	1.2	1.7	1.1	0.9
Norwegian krone	1.1	1.5	1.2	0.8
Finnish markka	1.6	1.4	0.9	1.0
Spanish peseta	2.4	1.8	1.0	1.0
Portuguese escudo	1.9	1.9	1.1	0.9
Real, based on consumer prices				
Belgian franc	0.8	0.8	0.3	0.4
Netherlands guilder	1.0	0.6	0.4	0.4
Danish krone	1.1	0.8	0.7	0.6
Austrian schilling	0.5	0.4	0.4	0.5
French franc	1.6	0.9	0.6	0.5
Italian lira	2.3	1.1	0.7	0.6
Irish pound	2.3	1.0	0.7	0.4
Swiss franc	1.8	1.4	0.9	1.1
Pound sterling	2.2	2.7	1.9	1.5
Swedish krona	1.2	1.9	1.2	1.2
Norwegian krone	1.2	1.7	1.2	1.0
Finnish markka	1.5	1.5	1.0	1.2
Spanish peseta	2.7	1.9	1.1	1.1
Portuguese escudo	2.2	2.1	1.1	1.1

Source: International Monetary Fund, *International Financial Statistics* and Research Department.

adopted in June. Two and a half years later, at the Maastricht Summit in December 1991, the member states of the EC adopted comprehensive amendments to their Charter, the 1957 Treaty of Rome. Although it still had to be ratified by member states, the Maastricht Treaty allowed, *inter alia*, for the transition to a single currency and the establishment of a central monetary policy institution for the Community.

The blueprint provided by the Delors Report and the Maastricht Agreement – including the holes left to be filled in the plan – has elicited much controversy.[66] Moreover, as discussed further on pp. 208–12 below, for those who had disregarded the fault lines *en route* to monetary union, the year-long turbulence in European exchange markets, beginning during the summer of 1992, forced a re-examination of the road map. By the end of January 1993, extremely strong market pressures had led to the withdrawal of the Italian lira and the pound sterling from the ERM; to the devaluations of the Spanish peseta, the Portuguese escudo, and the Irish pound within the ERM; and to the abandonment of the pegs of the Finnish markka, the Norwegian krone, and the Swedish krona against the ECU. By the beginning of August 1993, the peseta and escudo had been devalued further and the fluctuation bands of the ERM had been widened to 15 percent on each side of the central rates.[67]

Despite the turbulence and controversy, the Maastricht Treaty was ratified and entered into force on November 1, 1993, when the European Community was essentially renamed the European Union (EU).[68] The European Monetary Institute – intended as a precursor of the future European central bank – began to operate on January 1, 1994.[69] On January 1, 1995, EU membership was expanded to include Austria, Finland, and Sweden, with Austria also choosing to participate in the ERM.[70]

5   The nature of speculative capital flows: perspectives today

The European exchange market crisis during 1992–93 dramatically focused attention on the fact that the volume of internationally mobile private capital, and the speed with which it can move from currency to currency or country to country, have increased tremendously over recent decades. These developments, in some respects, are very welcome. Just as domestic financial markets provide a mechanism for individual participants in a closed economy, through borrowing and lending, to change the time

[66] Kenen (1992) and Eichengreen (1993b) provide overviews of the blueprint and the main issues, along with lists of other references. See also Giovannini (1990a, 1990b), Fratianni and von Hagen (1992), and Krugman (1992).

[67] Germany and the Netherlands agreed to maintain $2\frac{1}{4}$ percent fluctuation margins with respect to each other's currencies.

[68] The European Community continues to exist as a legal entity within the EU, but "European Union" has become the umbrella term.

[69] See Bank of England (1994).

[70] Norway had been invited to join the EU as well but rejected membership in a national referendum. Austria had, *de facto*, pegged its currency to the Deutsche mark since 1981. Finland, Norway, and Sweden had shifted during 1990–91 from trade-weighted currency pegs to pegs against the ECU, but strong exchange market pressures had led all three countries to abandon their fixed exchange rate commitments by the end of 1992.

profiles of their consumption relative to their output or income, international capital markets greatly expand the set of feasible time profiles for aggregate national consumption. By allowing countries to smooth their consumption streams through periods of recession and boom, international capital mobility provides important welfare gains. In theory, international capital mobility also facilitates the transmission of savings to countries in which the productivity of investment is relatively high, which can provide additional welfare gains for the world as a whole.

At the same time, as has long been recognized, a high degree of capital mobility forces countries participating in a fixed exchange rate system – or wishing to dampen the variability of flexible exchange rates – to sacrifice national autonomy over their monetary policies.[71] More generally, a widely cited "impossibility theorem" maintains that countries cannot simultaneously have free capital mobility, fixed exchange rates, and an independent monetary policy. The theorem exaggerates the impossibilities to the extent that claims on different countries are imperfect substitutes, or that nominal price stickiness provides some scope for monetary independence in the presence of fixed exchange rates and perfect capital mobility.[72] It also ignores the fact that fluctuation margins around fixed exchange rate parities provide scope for a limited degree of monetary independence.[73]

In the European context, following the June 1988 decision to lift all capital controls within the EMS by mid-year 1990, it was generally agreed that free trade, full capital mobility, fixed exchange rates, and independent national monetary policies constituted an "inconsistent quartet" of policy objectives, and that, ultimately,

the only solution to the inconsistency is to complement the internal market with a monetary union.[74]

Accordingly, the policy debate in Europe in recent years – at least until the summer of 1992 – has for the most part accepted the long-run goal of monetary union, focusing primarily on issues relating to the process of transition, including issues relating to the choice of exchange rate arrangements during the transition.

The remainder of this section provides some general background on the

---

[71] Recall from chapter 6 the discussion of the Mundell–Fleming conceptual framework that emerged during the 1960s.   [72] Crockett (1993).

[73] Svensson (1994). Rose (1994) makes a first attempt to evaluate the impossibility theorem empirically, but does not find strong support for mutual incompatibility. His conclusions, however, are based on using a monetary model as the specification hypothesis about the relationship between exchange rates and fundamentals; the discussion in chapter 10 suggests that it might also be interesting to evaluate the impossibility theorem empirically using a real intertemporal optimizing model of exchange rate dynamics.

[74] Padoa Schioppa (1988, p. 376).

increase in international capital mobility during recent decades. It then discusses the factors that led to the year-long episode of strong pressures on European exchange rates during 1992–93.

Trends in international capital mobility

The Articles of Agreement of the International Monetary Fund state explicitly that member countries "may exercise such controls as are necessary to regulate international capital movements," provided the controls do not restrict current account transactions or unduly delay the settlement of international contracts.[75] At the end of 1993, roughly three-quarters of the IMF's member countries maintained restrictions of some sort on international capital flows,[76] although in many cases – including all industrial countries – the remaining controls were relatively minor.[77]

Restrictions on international capital flows take several forms. One form consists of direct quantitative constraints on the external asset and liability positions of domestic residents, sometimes distinguishing financial institutions (especially banks) from other residents. Alternatively, capital flows may be discouraged indirectly, either by maintaining separate exchange rates for commercial and financial transactions (dual or multiple exchange rate systems), or by imposing taxes on international capital transactions or on income from external capital holdings.

The effectiveness of capital controls – whether direct or indirect – obviously depends on the ability of the authorities to prevent capital transactions from flowing through channels that either avoid detection or legitimately escape the coverage of the controls. This ability has been undermined considerably during recent decades by the continuing intro-duction of new financial products and services,[78] the proficiency of financial markets and intermediaries in migrating between different regulatory jurisdictions throughout the world,[79] and the revolution in information-

---

[75] International Monetary Fund (1993a, Article VI, Section 3).

[76] International Monetary Fund (1994, line E26, pp. 88–94).

[77] During the 1970s, extensive capital controls were the rule in most industrial countries, the major exceptions being the United States, Canada, Germany, the Netherlands, and Switzerland.

[78] The process of financial innovation has been closely associated with the extensive liberalization and deregulation of domestic financial markets since the beginning of the 1980s. By the early 1990s, competitive forces had substantially reduced the traditional roles of banks in the provision of financial services, with corporate borrowers in major industrial countries increasingly able to satisfy their liquidity, risk-management, and financing needs directly in markets for liquid securities; see Goldstein et al. (1992).

[79] An inportant example of this phenomenon was the development of the Eurodollar market – specifically, the market in US dollars held on deposit in banks or bank branches located

processing and communication technologies. The case for capital controls as an element of stabilization policy is discussed in chapter 12. Suffice it to say here that, with the erosion of the effectiveness of capital controls – alternatively viewed as a rise in the costs of enforcing them – a number of developing countries have taken steps to liberalize restrictions on international capital flows, and the industrial countries have essentially eliminated them.[80]

Net international capital flows – as reflected in current account imbalances – are generally smaller today relative to gross national products than they were during the gold standard period (1880–1914).[81] However, gross stocks and flows of internationally mobile private capital have increased dramatically, particularly during the last two decades.[82] Growth in cross-border portfolio investment has been concentrated among nonbank institutional investors (such as pension funds, insurance companies, and mutual funds), which have been expanding – and are likely to continue to expand – their roles in the management of savings. Between 1980 and 1990, the total assets of nonbank institutional investors, as a share of household financial assets, grew from 20 percent to 31 percent in the United States, from 42 percent to 59 percent in the United Kingdom, and from 11 percent to 36 percent in France.[83] Characterized in a different way, the total assets of nonbank institutional investors amounted in 1990 to 133 percent of GNP in the United States and 108 percent in the United Kingdom.[84] Non-bank institutional investors in Europe and Japan kept a higher proportion (about 20 percent) of their securities portfolios in holdings of foreign securities, around 1990, than did those in the United States (about 5 to 7 percent); but in general, these shares have been rising and are likely to continue to increase.[85]

Convergence trade and European exchange market developments, 1992–93

The drama that unfolded in European exchange markets during 1992–93 vividly illustrated that a high degree of international capital mobility has

outside the United States – which was stimulated, *inter alia*: by the desires of the Soviet Union and other communist countries during the 1950s to build up holdings of dollars outside the United States; by the US interest equalization tax of 1964, which was designed to discourage foreign borrowers from issuing debt obligations in the US market; and by the rise in Eurodollar interest rates above the ceiling rates that banks in the United States were permitted to pay (under Regulation Q) on certificates of deposit during the tight money years of 1968–69. See Stigum (1990).

[80] Mathieson and Rojas-Suárez (1993) review the experiences and issues.
[81] Fishlow (1985), Bayoumi (1990).
[82] Goldstein *et al.* (1993), Group of Ten Deputies (1993).
[83] Group of Ten Deputies (1993, p. 6).   [84] Group of Ten Deputies (1993, p. 6).
[85] Group of Ten Deputies (1993, p. 4).

important implications for exchange rate policy. Although the year-long crisis did not derail the institutional preparations for European monetary union (EMU), it forced a serious re-evaluation of the plans for the transition.

The factors that led to the crisis can be decomposed into three elements.[86] The first of these was a set of implicit constraints on national policy autonomy during the transition process, reflecting the criteria agreed at Maastricht for assessing the readiness of a country to participate in the monetary union. These criteria stressed inflation convergence and healthy public finances, along with a requirement that countries could not participate in EMU unless they had complied with the "normal" fluctuation margins of the ERM for at least two years without severe tensions and without devaluing on their own initiative.

The second element in the build-up to the crisis was the unification of East and West Germany in October 1990 – commonly viewed as a "shock" – which created difficulties for macroeconomic policy in Germany, with spillover effects on other European countries. In particular, German unification, which required a major increase in fiscal spending at a time when the West German economy was already operating at or near potential, led to a substantial fiscal imbalance and, in turn, induced the Bundesbank to maintain high short-term interest rates to combat inflationary pressures. Although other European countries initially benefitted, through an increase in their exports, from the first-round expansionary effects of the stimulus, for many of them the second-round effects of higher German interest rates posed difficulties. Given their commitments to exchange rate stability vis-à-vis the Deutsche mark – whether within the ERM or (in the cases of Finland, Norway, and Sweden) through pegs to the ECU – the policy mix in Germany essentially forced most other European countries to keep their interest rates above the levels that would have been most appropriate for responding to their own domestic needs. The difficulties were especially harsh for those European countries with economies in recession, or with relatively large stocks of interest bearing public debt.

The third element in the build-up to the crisis was a phenomenon known as "convergence trade." With no general ERM realignment since 1987, and with agreement on the Maastricht Treaty in December 1991, including the criteria for readiness to participate in the monetary union, many investors apparently assumed either that the likelihood of future realignments had become quite small, or that European central banks, at the least, would intervene extensively to resist any pressures for realignment. This spurred sizeable capital inflows into European countries where interest rates

---

[86] See Research Department, IMF (1993) for a more extensive discussion.

(reflecting inflation differentials) were relatively high.[87] The idea of convergence trade was to invest domestic-currency funds, e.g. dollars, in assets denominated in a high-yielding foreign currency, e.g. lire, covering the domestic-currency exchange rate exposure by purchasing dollars forward against sales of Deutsche marks. This left the investor with a long position in lire and a short position in marks, but as long as the lira/mark exchange rate did not change significantly over the horizon of the investment, the investor could earn the lira/mark interest differential on top of the dollar interest return. In the United States the attractiveness of these convergence trades spawned a whole new segment of the mutual fund industry, assisted apparently by the fact that short-term dollar interest rates had plunged to very low levels.[88]

Notably, all of the European currencies with relatively high short-term interest rates came under severe pressure during the late summer of 1992. In all these cases, domestic policy needs dictated that, if exchange rates were to be realigned, the direction of realignment (*vis-à-vis* the Deutsche mark) was a one-way bet. The pressure, which began to build after voters in Denmark narrowly rejected the Maastricht Treaty in early June 1992,[89] strengthened considerably in late August, when opinion poll results started to show a significant chance that French voters might also reject the treaty in a referendum scheduled for September 20. These signals began to erode confidence that

the discipline of commitments to exchange rate parities and to the Maastricht convergence process would continue to induce (or allow) governments to refrain from pursuing policies that gave priority to shorter-term domestic economic objectives.[90]

The erosion of confidence led to an overwhelming response by international investors:

Prudent investors who had earlier sought higher yields by placing funds in potentially vulnerable currencies increasingly saw the merit of covering their exposed positions before the French vote. Speculators who saw the potential for profit from one-way bets against currencies that might be devalued (but would not

---

[87] Net purchases by foreigners of domestic securities in the United Kingdom, Italy, Spain, and Sweden amounted to 140 billion dollars between January 1990 and June 1992; see Group of Ten Deputies (1993, p. 11).

[88] Group of Ten Deputies (1993, p. 11). The value of the US dollar against the Deutsche mark, which had depreciated to an all-time low at the beginning of September 1992, strengthened considerably during the subsequent exchange market turmoil as investors sought to cover their positions (or move into short positions) in potentially vulnerable European currencies.

[89] Subsequently, after being granted certain exemptions, Denmark ratified the treaty in May 1993.   [90] Research Department, IMF (1993, p. 142).

appreciate) increasingly saw the merit of opening short positions in potentially vulnerable currencies. Inevitably, the process snowballed, as sales of potentially vulnerable currencies by private market participants led to growing market tensions, which made prudent investors ever more concerned about the need for defensive cover and speculators ever more confident about the prospects for profit.[91]

The pressures on exchange rates "were broadly based – from the full range of institutional investors as well as from nonfinancial corporations" and "unprecedented in magnitude, to judge from the scale of intervention and the defensive interest rate reactions of some central banks."[92] The first currency unhinged was the Finnish markka, which was floated off its peg to the ECU on September 8. Market pressures then rapidly transferred to the Swedish krona, which was successfully defended (only to succumb to a subsequent attack in November) through announcements of fiscal measures, heavy intervention, and sharp increases in overnight interest rates (to an annualized rate of 500 percent on September 16). On September 13 the lira was devalued by 7 percent. On September 16–17, the pound sterling and lira were withdrawn from participation in the ERM. On September 17, the Spanish peseta was devalued by 5 percent. And despite affirmation of the Maastricht Treaty in the French referendum on September 20, intense pressures continued, off and on, through August 1993, when the fluctuation bands were widened extensively.[93] One striking feature of the episode was "the way that pressures seemed to spread from one currency to another in serial fashion," which many viewed as

reflecting the fact that a large depreciation of one ... currency put further pressure on the already weak competitive position (or economic activity) of the next.[94]

From June through December 1992, total official intervention sales of Deutsche marks by European central banks amounted to DM 284 billion net, of which DM 188 billion was sold in defense of ERM currencies.[95]

The crisis in European exchange markets has given new focus to discussions of optimal exchange rate arrangements.[96] One major issue is whether "hybrid systems" that combine elements of fixity and flexibility are still viable. Has it become virtually impossible to manage floating rates effectively, or to keep rates fixed without relinquishing exchange rates altogether through the adoption of a common currency? A related issue, with particular relevance for Europe, concerns the optimal design of

[91] Research Department, IMF (1993, p. 142).
[92] Group of Ten Deputies (1993, pp. 12–13).
[93] For a chronology through mid-September 1993, see International Monetary Fund (1993b, pp. 42–7).   [94] Group of Ten Deputies (1993, pp. 13–14).
[95] Group of Ten Deputies (1993, p. 25).
[96] Crockett (1993), Eichengreen (1995a), de Grauwe (1994).

exchange rate arrangements during the process of transition to a common currency. Should the move from the present highly flexible arrangements (with fluctuation margins of 15 percent on either side of central parities) to a common currency be a gradual one with progressive narrowing of the scope for exchange rate fluctuations, or should countries aim at establishing the relevant macroeconomic and institutional preconditions for monetary union under highly flexible exchange arrangements, with the intention of then moving from relatively high flexibility to a common currency in a single step?

These questions may be debated for some time. Regarding the issue of whether hybrid systems are still viable, it is notable that the 1992–93 experience was not an attack against a hybrid exchange rate system that European countries were seeking to sustain, but rather an attack precipitated by the shortcomings of the process for making the intended transition from a hybrid system to a common currency area. In particular, during the years leading up to the 1992 crisis, the transition process in Europe had the shortcoming that the degree of resistance to exchange rate adjustment was not kept consistent with the degree of convergence in macroeconomic performances and domestic policy needs. Also notable is the fact that the eruption of the crisis did not immediately follow the shock that, to many, looms large in its explanation – namely, the unification of Germany during 1990. Thus, according to one view, the crisis might have been avoided if the build-up of foreign exchange exposure through convergence trades had been discouraged by policies and policy attitudes that were less resistant to exchange rate realignments in the aftermath of German unification.[97]

6   Concluding perspectives

According to the "impossibility theorem," in the modern era of high international capital mobility, countries that have relinquished capital controls cannot simultaneously have fixed exchange rates and independent monetary policies. This point, while somewhat overstated, does not imply, however, that the only choices are the two extreme cases of completely fixed exchange rates and completely independent monetary policies.

In reality, few countries have chosen to form common currency areas or

[97] Along these lines, Fratianni and von Hagen (1992), in a proposal that went to press before the European crisis, suggested that the transition to currency union should include the institution of regular decisions on whether to undertake exchange rate realignments at the policy meetings of the council of EMS central bank governors:

Making realignment decisions regular and formal events would reduce ... the symbolic and political content of these decisions ... [and] destroy the current, unfortunate perception in some EMS countries of a trade-off between political commitment to EMU and desirable exchange-rate flexibility (p. 224).

to adopt freely floating exchange rates, and for understandable reasons. Exchange rate adjustment is an efficient mechanism for achieving the changes in relative national price levels that are often desirable to facilitate balance-of-payments adjustment over time, so countries that form common currency areas relinquish an important degree of freedom.[98] Yet, too much exchange rate variability, which generally results in capricious variability in the profit margins and sales of domestic producers, and in the nominal magnitudes and real purchasing powers of domestic incomes, is widely perceived to be highly undesirable. Policy authorities, aware of the economic interests of their constituents, have thus usually gravitated toward hybrid systems that occupy the middle ground between exchange rate rigidity and freely floating exchange arrangements.

In practice, hybrid systems fall into two broad categories: fixed, but adjustable, exchange rate arrangements; and flexible, but managed, exchange rate arrangements. For individual countries, a variety of structural characteristics and other considerations – as discussed on pp. 191–200 above – may be relevant in selecting the preferable type of arrangement. Thus, within many European countries, the prospect of substantial economic and political gains from closer integration has generated strong sentiment for moving toward a common currency area in the long run and for maintaining fixed (but adjustable) exchange rate arrangements in the interim. At the same time, there is presently little genuine support in the United States, Japan, and Germany for a system of fixed exchange rates between the dollar, the yen, and the mark; in particular, while loud complaints about exchange rate movements periodically make the headlines in these countries, there is little political support for exchange rate arrangements that would require, *de facto*, the relinquishment of national autonomy over monetary policies.

For many countries, the choice between fixed and flexible exchange rates is not a clear cut decision. Thus, the Baltic countries chose different routes for breaking away from the ruble area during 1992, with Estonia fixing the exchange rate of the kroon to the Deutsche mark through a currency board arrangement,[99] while Latvia and Lithuania opted initially for floating

---

[98] This is not to argue against the movement toward European Monetary Union or to suggest that existing common currency areas, such as the United States of America, should not be preserved. Although relinquishing an independent currency to join a common currency area has its costs, a common currency area can also provide major benefits to its member states.

[99] Bennett (1993, 1994). Under a currency board arrangement, the board normally agrees to supply or redeem domestic base money against a foreign currency without limit at a fixed exchange rate. Thus, a pure currency board arrangement is essentially equivalent to a fixed exchange rate arrangement in which sterilization is prohibited and the monetary authorities have no autonomy over interest rates.

exchange rates.[100] Moreover, in some cases, the nature of existing exchange rate arrangements is best understood as part of an evolutionary process of oscillation between fixed and flexible regimes.[101]

The increasing international mobility of capital has provided substantial benefits for the world economy, expanding the scope for countries to change the time profiles of their consumption and investment paths relative to their output streams, encouraging the flow of savings to countries in which the productivity of investment is relatively high, and opening the way for the international dissemination of production processes and managerial, marketing, and technological skills. Yet the accumulation of huge stocks of internationally mobile private capital has also magnified the challenges for macroeconomic stabilization and exchange rate policies, as illustrated by the overwhelming pressures that attempts to adjust the currency composition of these stocks brought to bear on European exchange rates during 1992–93.

While the latter experience has led some to question whether hybrid exchange rate arrangements remain viable today, it is misleading to attribute the European crisis to weaknesses inherent in fixed but adjustable exchange rates. In particular, the 1992–93 crisis was not an attack on a hybrid arrangement that European countries sought to sustain over the long run, but rather an attack precipitated by inconsistency between, on the one hand, the degree of official commitment to avoiding exchange rate adjustment during the transition to a common currency and, on the other, the degree of progress in achieving macroeconomic convergence.

That being recognized, however, it is generally agreed that the increased international mobility of capital has made the maintenance of macroeconomic stability in individual countries highly dependent on the consistency of exchange rates with macroeconomic policy objectives, and on successful international policy cooperation, regardless of the type of exchange rate arrangements that countries choose. Hybrid exchange rate arrangements have become much more challenging to preserve – but so have freely floating arrangements and common currency areas. The challenges for making exchange rate arrangements consistent with the broad objectives of national macroeconomic policies, and for achieving an appropriate degree of international policy cooperation, are considered in chapter 12.

Although discussions of the difficulties associated with international capital mobility often focus on stabilization policies in the industrial

---

[100] Lithuania shifted to a currency board arrangement in April 1994, partly to provide the central bank with a shield for resisting political pressures to extend credit in amounts exceeding its monetary policy targets.

[101] Flood, Bhandari, and Horne (1989), Eichengreen (1995b). For example, under adjustable peg regimes, efforts to convince market participants of the authorities' commitment to the peg have sometimes led to rigidity, crisis, and an eventual shift to a flexible rate regime.

countries, the increase in international capital mobility has had major implications for the developing countries as well. Indeed, for a number of developing countries, inflows of capital surged during the early 1990s, exceeding 10 percent of GDP in some years.[102] For these countries, too, policy toward the exchange rate involves a much broader set of issues than the choice of exchange rate arrangements; and the costs of inappropriate policies have been magnified by increased international capital mobility.[103] The issues that have become prominent for developing countries are also considered in chapter 12.

---

[102] Schadler *et al.* (1993, Table 1).
[103] This was vividly illustrated by the financial crisis that erupted in Mexico during December 1994.

12 Policy-oriented perspectives on exchange rate stability

Previous chapters have emphasized that exchange rate adjustment can be a desirable way to achieve needed changes in relative national price levels over time, but that, in addition to achieving desirable adjustments, flexible exchange rate arrangements in practice have led to occasional large misalignments of exchange rates, and have generally bred relatively high short-term variability. Fixed exchange rate arrangements, in many cases, have also left much to be desired, occasionally giving rise to episodes in which policy authorities have essentially lost control over the process of exchange rate adjustment. Because most economic participants are exposed in one way or another to the effects that exchange rate changes have on economic activity and relative prices and costs, and because most people dislike economic uncertainty, policymakers have often expressed strong desires for a greater degree of exchange rate stability. Notably, as demonstrated by Austria, it is possible to succeed in achieving a relatively high degree of exchange rate stability without making a formal commitment to a fixed exchange rate arrangement.

This chapter focuses on several policy issues that have an important bearing on exchange rate stability, regardless of whether countries choose fixed or flexible exchange rate arrangements. The issues are grouped under four headings. The first section discusses the importance of fiscal and monetary policy discipline as a precondition for both price level stability and nominal exchange rate stability. The second section considers the conceptual case for, and the practicality of, imposing controls on international capital flows for the purpose of stabilizing exchange rates. The third section turns to one of the manifestations of international capital mobility that a number of developing countries have experienced during recent years – "the capital inflows problem" – and addresses its policy implications, including its implications for exchange rate stabilization. The fourth section discusses the role and limitations of international policy cooperation in stabilizing exchange rates between the currencies of the major industrial countries. The fifth section provides concluding perspectives.

216

1   The role of fiscal and monetary discipline

Exchange rates are difficult to stabilize in an inflationary environment. More precisely, when the price levels (and unit costs of production) of two countries are trending upward at rates that differ significantly, it is difficult to stabilize the nominal exchange rate between their currencies for very long. Any country that seeks to keep the foreign exchange value of its currency relatively stable must therefore provide a macroeconomic environment conducive to maintaining a relatively stable domestic price level.

Almost all economists regard fiscal discipline as an essential precondition for price level stability. There is considerable debate over the appropriate interpretation of fiscal discipline – in particular, over the conceptually-appropriate measure of fiscal balance and the prudentially-appropriate upper bound on the size of fiscal deficits – but there is virtually no disagreement with the view that large fiscal deficits are inconsistent with price-level stability.

Economists also recognize that price stability is difficult to maintain or restore unless the credibility of policy commitments is sufficiently high to create *ex ante* expectations of price stability. An announced policy intention of maintaining fiscal discipline may thus not be very credible *ex ante* without institutional arrangements that effectively shield the policy authorities from strong political pressures either to exceed fiscal spending targets or to reduce tax rates to levels inconsistent with revenue needs. In this connection, the credibility of announced fiscal intentions may be particularly dependent on the existence of institutional mechanisms to limit the monetary financing of fiscal deficits by the central bank.

Historical support for such accepted wisdom comes partly from studies of attempts to end episodes of high inflation. For example, a widely-cited study of successful stabilization programs in several European countries during the 1920s concluded:

The essential measures that ended hyperinflation in each of Germany, Austria, Hungary, and Poland were, first, the creation of an independent central bank that was legally committed to refuse the government's demand for additional unsecured credit and, second, a simultaneous alteration in the fiscal policy regime ... In each case ... once it became widely understood that the government would not rely on the central bank for its finances, the inflation terminated and the exchanges stabilized.[1]

Similarly, a study of the macroeconomic experiences during 1965–90 of 18 developing countries, including almost all the large developing market

[1] Sargent (1982, p. 89).

economies, concluded that "the crucial element [in stabilization from high inflation] is fiscal discipline."[2]

The literature on stopping high inflations also emphasizes that fiscal adjustment may not be a sufficient condition for restoring price level and nominal exchange rate stability.[3] Somewhat ironically, it is easier to stop inflation cold – perhaps relying only on fiscal adjustment and an announced target for the nominal exchange rate – after rates of inflation have become astronomical. During such episodes of hyperinflation, market participants become virtually unwilling to bind themselves to any nominal contracts (such as nominal wage agreements) that extend over significant time horizons. All prices in the economy thus typically become indexed *de facto* to the nominal exchange rate, the economy becomes devoid of backward-looking behavior,[4] and when fiscal reform is sufficiently extensive and credible, the announcement of a fixed nominal exchange rate can provide an anchor for all prices in the economy.[5] By contrast, when inflation is not sufficiently high to completely discourage long-term nominal contracts and thereby eliminate backward-looking inertia in the inflation process, fiscal adjustment is unlikely to be sufficient for restoring price level and nominal exchange rate stability.[6]

2   The pros and cons of capital controls

In recent decades, even countries with relatively stable price levels have sometimes experienced large and persistent exchange rate movements that have been difficult to explain in terms of undisciplined macroeconomic policies or any changes in "underlying economic fundamentals." Such evidence of "misalignments" under flexible exchange rate arrangements – in conjunction with parallel episodes of overwhelming pressures on fixed exchange rates, and with survey findings that market participants often take positions on the basis of technical analysis of exchange rate trends,

---

[2] Corden (1993, p. 206).
[3] Dornbusch (1992a), Végh (1992), Santaella (1993), and references cited therein.
[4] Cagan (1992), Végh (1992).
[5] See Corden (1993) and Aghevli, Khan, and Montiel (1991) for further discussion of the economic arguments for adopting a nominal exchange rate anchor to try to solve the coordination problems that are involved in price-level stabilization efforts. Note also, as a different perspective, that political support for stabilization efforts is likely to be stronger when the initial degree of instability is very high.
[6] The successes and failures of various attempts to stop high inflations in Latin America and Israel since the 1960s have led some economists, such as Dornbusch (1982), to conclude that wage and price controls should be part of a stabilization package. Végh (1992) provides stylized facts on these stabilization efforts.

rather than on the basis of economic fundamentals alone – has elicited various proposals for reforming the international monetary system.[7]

The suggestions for reform have included proposals for introducing explicit or implicit taxes to discourage short-term international capital flows. Specifically, in a suggestion first advanced in 1978, Tobin recommended:

An international uniform tax would be levied on spot transactions in foreign exchange (including of course deliveries pursuant to futures contracts and options). The proposal has two major motivations. One purpose is to increase the weight market participants give to long-range fundamentals relative to immediate speculative opportunities. The second is to allow greater autonomy to national monetary policies, by creating a larger wedge between short interest rates in different currencies.[8]

And along similar lines, others have suggested that

financial institutions purchasing foreign exchange with domestic currency for their own account or on behalf of customers [be required] to make noninterest bearing deposits with the central bank.[9]

Notably, such proposed devices for throwing "sand in the wheels" of cross-currency capital flows have little support among policy authorities in the industrial countries today.[10] Yet such devices would be much less restrictive than the capital controls that many of these countries maintained through the 1970s. The more traditional and restrictive approach, in particular, has been to prohibit most types of capital movements altogether, at least for domestic residents, and to require specific authorization for any exceptions. In addition, as a mechanism for enforcing controls on capital account transactions, exporters have been required, traditionally, to surrender or repatriate their foreign exchange earnings on current account transactions; and customs documents on exports have been monitored by the authorities responsible for enforcing the surrender or repatriation requirements.

To a large extent, the lack of enthusiasm for capital controls among the industrial countries today probably reflects an awareness of how easily a transactions tax (and most other forms of capital controls) could be evaded in the modern financial environment:[11]

---

[7] Summary discussions are provided by Dornbusch and Frankel (1988) and Goldstein and Isard (1992).   [8] Tobin (1991, p. 4).
[9] Eichengreen and Wyplosz (1993, p. 120), who note that the Bank of Italy pioneered such policies in the 1970s. See also Eichengreen, Rose, and Wyplosz (1994a).
[10] Group of Ten Deputies (1993).   [11] Recall the discussion in chapter 11 (pp. 207–8).

At the least, implementation would require extensive monitoring of transactions and sizable expenditures for administrative staff. More serious still, the tax would not be effective unless major countries and the offshore financial centers all agreed to implement it. If only a few nations (for example, one or two offshore financial centers) refused to cooperate, financial transactions could be shifted into those jurisdictions to escape the tax, thereby largely negating the effects of the tax even for those countries implementing the proposal.[12]

Similarly, a noninterest bearing deposit requirement on bank lending to nonresidents could easily be evaded by redirecting capital flows through other channels.[13]

By essentially abolishing their capital controls over the past two decades, the industrial countries have returned today to the situation that prevailed at the beginning of the century. Prior to World War I, exchange restrictions were "almost entirely unknown."[14] Even during World War I, official reserve holdings and credit operations were adequate for avoiding persistent exchange market pressures, and the implementation of exchange controls went little further than the introduction of restrictions on the convertibility of paper money into gold and on the free international movement of gold. Thus, the British Treasury during the period 1916–19 had little difficulty stabilizing the sterling/dollar exchange rate by arranging for J.P. Morgan & Co., acting on its behalf, to provide dollars "on tap" against sterling in unlimited amounts at the rate of 4.7640 dollars per pound.[15] The task of stabilizing exchange rates was no doubt facilitated by the fact that historical experience at the time did not provide memorable evidence that wars tended to cause large exchange rate realignments:

The only modern war on a large scale within living memory was the Franco–German war of 1870; it left the currency of the victorious nation unaffected, while the depreciation of the currency of the vanquished was merely $3\frac{1}{2}$ percent.[16]

The interwar experience catalyzed a strong shift in sentiment toward trade restrictions and capital controls. By the early 1930s, following unsuccessful attempts to re-establish international monetary stability under both floating and fixed exchange rates (recall the discussion in chapter 3), resort to exchange restrictions was widespread. The recent history of exchange rate instability had heightened perceptions of currency risk and created a climate in which shifts in confidence could easily trigger large private capital flows. Thus, "to a great number of countries in the 1930s, exchange control seemed the only solution."[17]

Policy attitudes toward exchange controls remained strongly favorable

---

[12] Bryant (1987, p. 157).
[13] See the discussion in Eichengreen, Rose, and Wyplosz (1994a).   [14] Einzig (1934, p. 20).
[15] Einzig (1934, p. 24).   [16] Einzig (1934, p. 23).   [17] Nurkse (1944, p. 163).

in the aftermath of World War II. Indeed, the postwar international monetary system gave its blessing to transitory restrictions on current account transactions, as well as to controls on capital movements, and throughout Western Europe the war-damaged countries relied on extensive trade restrictions. The first and only attempt to abolish current account restrictions soon after the war – by the United Kingdom, in 1947 – quickly turned into "a colossal failure."[18] Based partly on the lessons from that experience, the countries of Western Europe waited until the end of 1958 to relinquish their controls on current account transactions,[19] and most industrial countries continued to rely on extensive capital controls through the 1970s.

Today the industrial countries, as noted, generally regard capital controls as ineffective and counterproductive, given the size of private financial capital stocks relative to official international reserve holdings, and also considering the many channels through which financial portfolio holdings can be shifted rapidly at low transactions costs in and out of currencies and across borders. Policy attitudes toward capital controls in the industrial countries have thus flip-flopped radically with the evolution of the international monetary system.

The case against capital controls today is less clear cut for those developing countries in which the scope for conducting international financial transactions is still limited and the costs of arranging such transactions still high. Even in those countries, however, the scope for evading capital controls may be substantial. One widely-acknowledged avenue for circumventing capital controls in practice is through leads or lags in the timing, or distortions in the invoicing, of current account transactions.

In theory, the case for capital controls must be based on an assessment that the costs associated with unrestricted capital movements would be likely to outweigh the benefits. For developing countries, the ability to attract inflows of foreign direct investment capital, which often bring managerial and technological resources as well, can be particularly benefic-ial; and for that reason it may be undesirable to place restrictions on direct investment inflows, or to discourage such inflows by restricting the repa-triation of earnings on domestic investments by nonresidents.[20]

[18] Haberler (1954, p. 16). In particular, after securing a 3.75 billion dollar loan from the United States, Britain restored full convertibility for "current transactions" on July 15, 1947, only to have to suspend convertibility again five weeks later after the proceeds from the loan had been virtually exhausted.

[19] Greene and Isard (1991) discuss the preconditions for establishing current account convertibility and provide a capsule review of relevant historical experience.

[20] In practice, the economic benefits of allowing foreign direct investment to proceed without restriction are sometimes outweighed by political desires to limit foreign ownership of domestic factors of production.

Accordingly, capital controls are often limited to restrictions on capital outflows by domestic residents.[21] Proponents of such restrictions have argued that the success of development efforts depends critically on the strength of domestic investment, and that domestic residents, at least in theory, may therefore be better off individually when they are collectively prevented from moving capital abroad.[22] Thus, to the extent that controls on capital outflows are effective, they provide a mechanism for internalizing the externalities from domestic investment and thereby promoting economic development. According to this view, even countries pursuing sound fiscal and monetary policies may benefit from restrictions on capital outflows if the nonpolicy-related risks to their development efforts are high. It has also been argued that, in addition to facilitating the attainment of medium-term development objectives, restrictions on short-term capital flows can reduce the scope for speculative pressures to undermine a country's efforts to maintain relatively stable exchange and interest rates.[23]

Such arguments, however, are controversial. One of the main theoretical counterarguments is that, in the absence of capital controls, the very threat of capital outflows, and of short-term capital flows in either direction, can have an important disciplining effect, heightening the authorities' concern to keep their macroeconomic policies sound. Other arguments against capital controls point to: the economic efficiency losses from "taxing" or prohibiting certain classes of international financial transactions, or international financial transactions by certain classes of market participants; the fact that the administration of controls often leads to bribery and other undesirable "rent-seeking activities;" and the prospect that the techniques that are likely to develop for evading capital controls, as well as the spread of evasion-oriented and rent-seeking mentalities, may have spillover effects on the tax system and provide an impetus for the expansion of the underground economy.[24]

Obviously, the strength of incentives for moving capital abroad in the presence of controls depends on the prospective gains from doing so, on the ability to do so without being detected, and on the costs of being detected. Abstracting from the latter two factors, economic theory suggests that the incentives to move capital abroad tend to strengthen when a country's macroeconomic policies and prospects deteriorate; and indeed, experience confirms that controls tend to be particularly ineffective in limiting capital

---

[21] However, the outbreak of the Mexican currency crisis in December 1994, following a period of large capital inflows, has rekindled discussion of restrictions on nondirect investments by nonresidents.   [22] Greene and Isard (1991).

[23] The need for fiscal revenues may provide another motive for capital controls in the specific form of taxes.

[24] Mathieson and Rojas-Suárez (1993, p. 18).

movements and maintaining exchange rate stability when macroeconomic policies are unsound.[25] Thus, despite continuing debate over the case for capital account restrictions in countries that do not yet have highly developed financial markets, few economists regard capital controls as a substitute for fiscal and monetary discipline.

3   The capital inflows problem

Many developing countries, including some with extensive capital controls in place, have experienced dramatic shifts in the volume of capital flows during the past two decades, which have generally put substantial pressures on nominal and real exchange rates. The rapid build-up of external debt by developing countries during the 1970s and early 1980s, and the widespread debt-servicing difficulties encountered after mid-1982, have been widely discussed.[26]

In the early 1990s, after about a decade in which the developing countries attracted little capital from abroad, a shift in the tide once again restored the "normal pattern" of substantial flows from industrial countries to developing countries where "the marginal productivity of capital should be higher, other things equal."[27] Net capital inflows[28] to Latin America quadrupled from an average annual rate below 11 billion dollars during 1985–89 to more than 60 billion dollars in 1992–94, while net capital inflows to Asia rose from an average of less than 20 billion dollars per year during 1985–89 to more than 50 billion dollars per year in 1992–94.[29] For a number of these countries, the shifts in net capital flows exceeded $2\frac{1}{2}$ percent of GDP, and in at least a half dozen cases the shifts exceeded 5 percent of GDP.[30] Such large surges in capital inflows posed a problem for economic policy.[31] By the end of 1994, a change in sentiment had turned internationally mobile capital away from investments in Mexico, which snowballed

---

[25] Mathieson and Rojas-Suárez (1993) review the experiences and issues associated with the liberalization of capital controls.

[26] For historical perspectives see de Vries (1987, chapters 10–12). On the analytic issues see Frenkel, Dooley, and Wickham (1989) and International Monetary Fund (1991, chapter V).

[27] Goldstein and Mussa (1993, p. 40). The normal pattern was dominant during the gold standard era, in the flows from the United States to Europe following World War II, and in flows into developing countries during the 1960s and 1970s.

[28] A country's net capital inflow – here defined as the increase in the net international indebtedness of its private residents and its public sector excluding the monetary authorities – corresponds (except for errors and omissions) to the sum of its current account surplus plus the change in the official international reserve holdings of its monetary authorities.

[29] International Monetary Fund, World Economic Outlook data bank.

[30] Calvo, Leiderman, and Reinhart (1994, p. 25).

[31] Calvo, Leiderman, and Reinhart (1993, 1994), Goldstein and Mussa (1993), Schadler et al. (1993).

into a sharp depreciation of the Mexican peso and a crisis for the Mexican economy that had contagion effects on other currencies and countries.[32]

Analysis of the so-called "capital inflows problem" sheds light on the difficulties of designing policies conducive to exchange rate stability. It also raises questions about the wisdom of attempting to stabilize exchange rates.

The starting point for such analysis is to recognize that the capital inflows problem comes in several varieties, related in part to different causal factors. In some cases, capital inflows may be induced to a large extent by factors beyond the control of the countries experiencing the inflows, such as external recessions that reduce the returns on investments in other countries, or external events that stimulate global demand for a country's major exports. In other cases, the capital inflows may be primarily a response to domestic causal factors, such as a major shift in the balance of political power, an increase in domestic interest rates resulting from monetary tightening, the implementation of an attractive and credible stabilization program, a reduction in the rate of taxation of capital income, or significant steps to deregulate and liberalize the domestic financial system.

Different causal factors can have different implications for the nature of the capital inflows. Where the causes are cyclical or reversible, the capital inflows are likely to have short-term horizons. Where the causes are perceived to imply permanent changes in the domestic climate for investment, the capital inflows are more likely to have long-term horizons.

Similarly, differences in causal factors, along with differences in the initial macroeconomic conditions and policy responses of the countries experiencing surges in capital inflows, can lead to different types of changes in macroeconomic variables. Capital inflows can be very beneficial when the causal factors, initial macroeconomic conditions, and policy responses together provide inducements for a high proportion of the inflows to finance productive investments, while also keeping the economy from overheating. Obversely, when capital inflows are used to finance additional consumption rather than new capacity to generate output, they can result in future debt-servicing difficulties; and when policy responses are not appropriate, capital inflows can overheat the economy and precipitate a shift in investor sentiment that leads to financial turmoil and macroeconomic instability.

In general, the appropriate policy response to a surge in capital inflows depends on a number of considerations; a study of six recent experiences reveals considerable diversity in the policy responses that different countries have chosen.[33] In principle, an assessment of the causes of the capital

---

[32] The Mexican crisis and its implications receive little attention in this book, which was in the final stages of editing when the crisis broke.   [33] Schadler et al. (1993).

inflows – and, in particular, of whether the causes suggest that the inflows have a short-term or a long-term horizon – should play a major role in shaping the policy response. In practice, however, it may be difficult to attach much confidence to such assessments.

Apart from taking any measures that may be appropriate to increase the absorptive capacity of the economy and otherwise to encourage use of the inflows to finance productive investments, the policy authorities must make decisions in four areas: (i) whether to let the exchange rate adjust and, if so, by how much; (ii) how completely, and with what instruments, to sterilize any build-up of foreign exchange reserves; (iii) whether to combine the monetary and exchange rate policy reactions with adjustments in fiscal policy or trade policy; and (iv) to what extent it is appropriate to strengthen prudential supervision of the domestic financial sector.[34]

By choosing to float the exchange rate freely, without any official intervention, the authorities could choke off or dampen the capital inflow and any effects on either the domestic money supply or the stock of domestic credit. In addition to restraining money and credit expansion, however, the authorities would be following a strategy that let the incipient capital inflow result in an appreciation of the domestic currency, thereby reducing the competitiveness of exports and adversely affecting the tradable goods sector.

A decision to manage the exchange rate – whether to keep it rigidly fixed or to limit the appreciation of the domestic currency unit – would lead to an accumulation of official foreign exchange reserves. The counterpart changes on the balance sheet of the monetary authority could include either an increase in central bank liabilities (base money) or a reduction in central bank holdings of domestic assets (typically government securities). Outcomes involving an increase in the supply of base money would correspond, by definition, to unsterilized purchases of foreign exchange reserves; outcomes involving an unchanged monetary base, to sterilized intervention.

A decision to sterilize at least part of the build-up of foreign exchange reserves could be implemented either by raising reserve requirements on bank deposits or by selling domestic securities. The drawback of relying heavily on reserve requirements imposed on a specific group of intermediaries (as, for example, in the extreme case of a 100 percent reserve requirement on increases in bank deposits) is that it tends to encourage the establishment of other intermediaries to circumvent the reserve requirements and effectively undermine the sterilization effort. The drawback of sterilizing through sales of securities is that it tends to push up domestic interest rates, which

---

[34] Calvo, Leiderman, and Reinhart (1994).

raises the cost of servicing the fiscal debt and also provides an additional stimulus to the capital inflows, other things being equal.

A decision not to sterilize the build-up of foreign exchange reserves would have different drawbacks. The expansion of money and credit could raise the risk that the economy would overheat. In addition, allowing the capital inflows to be intermediated through the banking system would run the risk that banks would not find sound investments for their new deposit balances, or would end up with a mismatch between the maturities of their assets and the maturities of their liabilities. The latter problem would be particularly troublesome if the cause of the capital inflow was a transitory phenomenon and the build-up of deposit balances was likely to be soon reversed.

Although none of the options for monetary and exchange rate policy in response to a surge in capital inflows – floating, sterilized intervention, or unsterilized intervention – is without drawbacks, capital inflows that are invested productively can generally be regarded as a blessing. Moreover, countries can look for ways to mitigate the drawbacks of monetary and exchange rate policies through fiscal policy adjustments, trade policy actions, or a strengthening of banking supervision. Although fiscal policy is often difficult to adjust in the short run, fiscal restraint, where feasible, can help counterbalance the effects of monetary expansion on aggregate demand.[35] Similarly, trade policy actions might be considered as a means of mitigating part of the adverse effects on the tradable goods sector.[36] Finally, by expediting steps to strengthen banking supervision, countries can reduce the prospect that the intermediation of capital inflows will lead to serious strains on their financial institutions.

With respect to the maintenance of exchange rate stability, there is every reason to believe that many developing countries will continue to experience occasional strong shifts in the volume and direction of capital flows in the years ahead, reflecting their continuing exposure to various sorts of domestic and external shocks.[37] Indeed, for most developing countries, the policy agenda includes major domestic structural reforms that, if successful, are likely to heighten significantly their attractiveness for capital inflows. In this context, it is generally inappropriate for policy to seek to

[35] Thailand provides an example where, in response to a surge in capital inflows, fiscal policy was shifted from a central government deficit of 4 percent of GDP in the late 1980s to a surplus of nearly 5 percent in the early 1990s; see Schadler et al. (1993).

[36] Calvo, Leiderman, and Reinhart (1994). Such actions, however, could be counterproductive if they resulted in the introduction of permanent distortions or the violation of international trade agreements.

[37] See Khan and Ostry (1992) and references cited therein on the effects of various exogenous disturbances on equilibrium real exchange rates for developing countries.

avoid real and nominal exchange rate adjustment over the medium run.[38] Moreover, even in the short run, given that each of the options for monetary and exchange rate policies has drawbacks, policies that allow exchange rates to fluctuate moderately may be more appropriate for some countries than policies that maintain a high degree of exchange rate stability.

4   The scope for international policy cooperation

In today's world of interdependent national economies, the macroeconomic policies and performances of individual countries can have important spillover effects. Policy decisions taken in one country affect macroeconomic outcomes at home, but also generate "externalities" for other countries. These spillover effects provide a rationale for international policy cooperation. In theory, cooperation among the policymakers of different countries, to take into account the external effects of each other's policies and to exploit these externalities for their mutual benefit, can achieve a Pareto efficient outcome for the world economy – that is, an outcome that exhausts the scope for modifying policies in a way that could make one country better off without leaving any other country worse off. And in practice, even when Pareto efficient outcomes are difficult to identify or achieve, a cooperative approach to policy formulation can sometimes be much more effective than a noncooperative approach in resisting threats to international economic stability.

Reflecting these perceptions, the literature on international policy cooperation has grown rapidly over the past decade, stimulated by an intensification of policy cooperation efforts among the major industrial countries. In practice, policymakers in these countries have tended to refer to their efforts as a process of "coordination," which some have defined as "a significant modification of national policies in recognition of international economic interdependence."[39] Unfortunately, such semantics has generated two types of confusion. For one thing, the efforts referred to as a policy coordination process have in practice consisted largely of information sharing and analytic discussions, with only occasional modifications of national policies; the definition of policy coordination thus does not accurately fit the process that parades under the name of policy coordination. Second, as references to coordination have infiltrated the literature, the term "cooperation" has taken different meanings, sometimes being

---

[38] On the implications of targeting the real exchange rate in developing countries, see Adams and Gros (1986), Lizondo (1991), Montiel and Ostry (1991), Calvo, Reinhart, and Végh (1994).   [39] Wallich (1984, p. 85).

used to refer narrowly to mild forms of collaboration that usually involve information sharing, and sometimes having a broad connotation that includes both "significant modification of national policies" and milder forms of collaboration. To minimize such semantical confusion, this book refers to policy cooperation in the broad sense of the term and makes few references to policy coordination.

For the most part, the academic literature on policy cooperation has found it useful to analyze issues within an optimizing framework in which each country has its own welfare objective function.[40] One branch of the literature has taken a game-theoretic approach to analyzing optimal policy strategies in a multicountry world,[41] while another has used empirical multicountry econometric models to simulate the effects of different possible combinations of home-country and foreign-country policy regimes.[42]

In contrast to the mainstream academic literature, some economists and most policymakers look at policy cooperation as a "regime-preserving" process designed to thwart various threats to international economic stability.[43] The regime-preserving perspective recognizes that wars among nations with the weapons of trade barriers and capital controls are likely to be mutually destructive.[44] It also recognizes that, in practice, policymakers do not rely continuously on formal analysis with macroeconometric models to identify optimal cooperative policy settings, partly because of their limited faith in formal analysis when knowledge about the structure of the international economy and the nature of disturbances is incomplete. Rather, in their efforts at international cooperation, policymakers focus more selectively and less formally on policy issues for which there is broad agreement that failure to cooperate could imply significant welfare losses;[45] for example, the Plaza Agreement of September 1985 was catalyzed by a strong desire to push the US dollar down from the high level to which it had appreciated during the first half of the 1980s.[46]

Of course, cooperative policy actions – just as noncooperative policy measures – may sometimes turn out, in retrospect, to have been misguided by uncertainty about their economic effects, or to be regrettable in the wake of unanticipated events. For example, the stimulative fiscal policy actions

---

[40] For surveys and other insightful discussions, see Bryant (1995b), Cooper (1985, 1990), Artis and Ostry (1986), Fischer (1988), Horne and Masson (1988), Frenkel, Goldstein, and Masson (1990), Kenen (1990), and Currie (1993).   [41] Recall chapter 11, n. 45.

[42] For example, Bryant, Hooper, and Mann (1993).   [43] Kenen (1988).

[44] Tobin (1987, p. 68).   [45] Goldstein and Isard (1992), Summers (1994).

[46] Funabashi (1989), Volcker and Gyohten (1992), Pauls (1990). Part of the rationale for the Plaza Agreement was to deflect protectionist legislation in the United States. Although the dollar had already declined considerably since late February 1985, the depreciation had not yet significantly eased the strains on the US tradable goods sector.

undertaken by Germany in accordance with the Bonn Summit agreement of 1978 were regretted when the world was shocked by inflationary pressures emanating from the sharp increase in oil prices that began at the end of that year.[47] But it is equally possible to point to episodes in which failure to coordinate policies adequately resulted in worse macroeconomic performances than any country wanted.[48] Uncertainty, moreover, may strengthen the case for policy cooperation, which can eliminate that part of the uncertainty related to the actions of other governments.[49]

The history of international monetary stability and instability over the past century provides additional perspectives on why policymakers attach considerable importance to international policy cooperation. Economic historians point to successful international monetary cooperation during times of crisis as an important element in explaining the longevity of the international gold standard prior to World War I.[50] Similarly, the high degree of economic instability that prevailed under a sequence of different short-lived international monetary regimes during the 1920s and early 1930s has been associated in part with a lack of adequate policy cooperation.[51] Following that period of instability, Britain, France, and the United States sought to establish a greater degree of cooperation by entering into the Tripartite Monetary Agreement in 1936; and during World War II, the British and American governments devoted serious attention to the design of rules and institutions for postwar international economic policy cooperation. Notably, the Articles of Agreement of the International Monetary Fund, as adopted in 1944, lists first among the purposes of the IMF:

To promote international monetary cooperation through a permanent institution which provides the machinery for consultation and collaboration on international monetary problems.[52]

Also on the list is the purpose:

To promote exchange stability, to maintain orderly exchange arrangements among members, and to avoid competitive exchange depreciation.[53]

---

[47] Currie, Holtham, and Hughes Hallett (1989).

[48] For example, as documented by Solomon (1991), when most of the Group of Seven countries stimulated their economies in 1972 in response to the slowdown that had occurred in 1970–71, which led to an excessively booming global economy; and similarly, when the industrial countries tightened monetary policy in 1979 and the early 1980s, which led to an excessively weak global economy.

[49] Ghosh and Masson (1993).

[50] Eichengreen (1992). Recall the discussion in chapter 3.

[51] Eichengreen (1992). See also Cooper (1992), who gives inadequate international cooperation less weight than Eichengreen as a factor underlying the interwar instability.

[52] International Monetary Fund (1993a, Article I).

[53] International Monetary Fund (1993a, Article I).

In practice, international policy cooperation has been strengthened over time in important ways. During the gold standard era, monetary cooperation consisted primarily of countries assisting each other – either by extending credit or by standing ready to relinquish gold – when other countries needed to build reserves to defend their parities. Under the Tripartite Agreement, cooperation was expanded to include day-to-day collaboration in making decisions on appropriate levels for exchange rates and in intervening, when so desired, to manage them. Since World War II, the evolution has continued with the creation of the International Monetary Fund and, in 1961, the establishment within the Organization for Economic Cooperation and Development (OECD) of a forum (Working Party 3) for regular discussions of monetary and balance-of-payments problems by policymakers from the largest members of the OECD (the Group of Ten). As a result international policy cooperation has come to include an ongoing process of close consultation (within the OECD, the IMF, and elsewhere) among finance ministry and central bank officials from the largest countries to examine each other's macroeconomic policies, identify inconsistent policies, and encourage appropriate policy adjustments.[54] Over the same period – with the creation and subsequent expansion of the credit facilities of the IMF; with the establishment in 1961–62, and subsequent enlargement, of both a network of "swap" arrangements (reciprocal credit facilities) among major central banks and the General Arrangements to Borrow (GAB);[55] and with the creation and allocation of the special drawing right (SDR) as a new international reserve asset – cooperative mechanisms for the provision of international liquidity and credit have been strengthened.

Nevertheless, international policy cooperation has not generally involved major sacrifices of national autonomy by the largest industrial countries. The process of ongoing policy discussions and occasional cooperative actions by these countries – often referred to, since 1985, as the Group of Seven (G7) policy coordination process[56] – has paid particular

---

[54] Solomon (1982), Crockett (1989). Since 1978, when the Second Amendment to the IMF's Articles of Agreement became effective following the breakdown of the Bretton Woods system, a new Article IV, governing members' obligations regarding exchange arrangements, has given the IMF staff a major role in analyzing the appropriateness of the macroeconomic policies of its member countries, thereby enhancing the importance of the IMF as a forum for international consultations on macroeconomic policy issues.

[55] The GAB, which provided a mechanism for the IMF to supplement its quota-based resources, was designed primarily in anticipation of resource needs that might evolve from the balance-of-payments problems of the two major reserve centers, the United States and the United Kingdom; see Ainley (1984).

[56] The Plaza Agreement in September 1985 involved only the Group of Five (France, Germany, Japan, United Kingdom, United States), but the process was expanded to the Group of Seven (including Canada and Italy) at the Tokyo Economic Summit in May 1986.

attention to the objective of exchange rate stability. But there is currently little inclination in the three key-currency countries (the United States, Japan, and Germany) to give exchange rate objectives higher priority than objectives for domestic economic activity and price stability. This is not to overlook the demonstrated willingness of the largest industrial countries to cooperate in directing monetary policies toward exchange rate objectives at times when exchange rates were viewed to be extraordinarily misaligned, nor to forget the occasions on which they have coordinated changes in their interest rates for purposes of minimizing the effects on exchange rates.[57] In most circumstances, however, there is little willingness to let domestic monetary conditions depart significantly from the settings appropriate for meeting domestic policy objectives.[58] Thus, to the extent that monetary policy is perceived to be the only effective mechanism for stabilizing exchange rates or domestic economic conditions, there is little inclination to make the commitments that would be required to keep exchange rates among the key currencies significantly more stable than they have been since early 1987, when the Louvre Accord implicitly characterized dollar exchange rates as no longer misaligned.

A number of economists have suggested that the key-currency countries, in theory, could strengthen their ability to stabilize exchange rates without sacrificing domestic economic stability by making fiscal policy more flexible.[59] Countries that have adopted fixed exchange rate arrangements, and have thereby ceded much of their scope for directing monetary policy at domestic needs, might also benefit considerably from reforms that made fiscal policy more flexible as a stabilization instrument.

On the surface, this corollary of Tinbergen's (1952) principle – that the successful pursuit of n policy objectives requires n policy instruments – is straightforward:

To manage economies in a half-sensible way – let alone to attempt the sort of cooperation ministers say they want – governments must be willing and able to exert flexible control over both monetary and fiscal policies. They cannot rely on interest rates both to steer exchange rates and to maintain the right amount of domestic demand.[60]

---

[57] Volcker and Gyohten (1992), Pauls (1990).

[58] Mussa et al. (1994). This statement needs qualification in the light of the apparent willingness of the German authorities to concede monetary autonomy during the process leading to European Monetary Union.

[59] Solomon (1991), Goldstein and Isard (1992). It can also be argued that reductions of labor market rigidities and other structural impediments to the maintenance of domestic economic stability would provide greater scope for directing monetary policy at the maintenance of external stability.

[60] The Economist, "Plug for the Dollar," April 16, 1988, p. 15.

With a little probing beneath the surface, however, the proposition becomes questionable. In practice, one of the reasons that fiscal policy is not actively used as a stabilization tool today is that previous attempts to do so, particularly during the 1960s and 1970s, were widely regarded as counterproductive. More generally, economists broadly agree that, even apart from the political and institutional obstacles to implementing fiscal changes in a timely manner, several unresolved conceptual and empirical issues make it difficult to prescribe the right dosage and timing of fiscal policy adjustment. The unresolved issues involve, among other things: distinctions between the effects of temporary and permanent fiscal adjustments; the effect of deficit spending on expectations about future tax rates; and the sensitivity of the time profile of economic activity to the extent to which fiscal adjustments are announced or anticipated in advance of the dates on which they become effective.

Notably, the conceptual and empirical difficulties relating to fiscal activism, as well as historical attempts to use fiscal policy for short-run stabilization purposes, are associated, for the most part, with "fine-tuning" strategies that involve discretionary decisions about the magnitude and timing of changes in fiscal policy instruments. By contrast to discretionary fine-tuning strategies, automatic fiscal stabilizing mechanisms can escape many of the difficulties. Such automatic stabilizers can operate both on fiscal revenues, via automatic adjustments in certain tax rates, and on public expenditures, via acceleration or deceleration of spending. In principle, automatic stabilizers can be designed: to increase or reduce aggregate demand promptly at appropriate points in the business cycle; to trigger automatically on the basis of cyclical indicators, without any discretionary decisions; and to have symmetric effects on the budget balance over the business cycle, without affecting the medium-term orientation of fiscal policy.

Even so, automatic stabilizers must be carefully designed to insure that they do not pose a serious risk to price stability. The danger is that mechanisms that promptly and automatically counteract any declines in private demand with fiscal stimulus – if sufficiently strong – could invite inflationary price and wage setting by the private sector, and could also weaken incentives to work.[61] This danger, however, could be significantly reduced by designing the automatic stabilizers to respond to aggregate demand shortfalls on a scale that depended on the values of several different economic indicators, including the prevailing rate of inflation.

Abstracting from the scope to make national policymaking more effec-

---

[61] Polak (1988, p. 14) regards this inflationary bias as a primary reason that fiscal activism proved unsatisfactory during the 1960s and 1970s.

tive by strengthening automatic fiscal stabilization mechanisms in an appropriately-designed manner, the reluctance of the largest industrial countries to cede monetary autonomy is understandable. Moreover, given their successful track record in achieving relatively low inflation rates, it is difficult to argue persuasively that the performance of the world economy would be improved by diverting monetary policies in these countries from their price stabilization objectives.[62] Indeed, it has been argued that the pursuit of international coordination in exchange markets and in macroeconomic policy management can become counterproductive if it allows policymakers to escape their responsibilities for domestic economic performance by providing an excuse for not pursuing appropriate domestic policies,[63] or if it leads to attempts to stabilize exchange rates at unsustainable levels.

Those dangers being recognized, there is nevertheless considerable sentiment that "our world today would not be manageable without great efforts in international cooperation,"[64] that "there is still great room for improvement in these endeavors,"[65] and that there is "no room for complacency in meeting the challenges of interdependence."[66] Various proposals have thus been put forth for strengthening the capacity of the G7 policy coordination process to identify inconsistent policies, anticipate future developments, and lead to appropriate recommendations for policy adjustments.[67] And the case for target zones to stabilize exchange rates – at sustainable levels supported by policy cooperation – continues to be debated.[68]

5   Concluding perspectives

Other things being equal, exchange rate stability is something that informed people generally regard as desirable. Consistently, many countries, as well as the IMF, include orderly exchange markets or stable exchange rates on their lists of economic policy objectives. Few if any countries, however, put exchange rate stability at the top of their lists.

The macroeconomic policy environment has a major influence on the stability of exchange rates, regardless of whether countries adopt fixed or flexible exchange rate arrangements. Although exchange rates are conti-

---

[62] Goldstein and Isard (1992).   [63] Feldstein (1988, 1990), Krugman (1988a).
[64] Guth (1988, p. 215).   [65] Guth (1988, p. 215).   [66] Dobson (1991, p. 156).
[67] Crockett and Goldstein (1987), Dobson (1991, 1994), Solomon (1991), Goldstein (1992).
These proposals have tended to focus on the set of participants in the process, the analytic orientation and continuity of the process, and the implementation and follow-up of policy recommendations.
[68] Krugman and Miller (1993), Bergsten and Williamson (1994), Kenen (1994), Mussa et al. (1994).

nually perturbed by the flow of news and rumors, and can potentially be driven considerable distances by market momentum, currency stability can be greatly enhanced when countries adhere to disciplined monetary and fiscal policies. A commitment to disciplined macroeconomic policies, and a successful track record in maintaining macroeconomic stability, makes market participants more confident that the macroeconomic environment will remain stable, and therefore more inclined to react to exchange rate movements in a manner that tends to dampen the fluctuations. In this connection, many countries might be able to enhance their macroeconomic stabilization powers, and to make market participants more confident that the macroeconomic environment will remain stable, by undertaking institutional reforms to strengthen their automatic fiscal stabilization mechanisms in a manner designed to relieve the overburdening of monetary policy without introducing an inflationary bias.

Even so, policymakers will continue sometimes to confront situations in which desirable outcomes for domestic economic activity or price stability become difficult to achieve without significant adjustments in exchange rates. In recent years, the manifestation of such difficulties for some of the developing countries has been referred to as the capital inflows problem. For countries with highly developed financial markets, controls on international capital movements have become ineffective and counterproductive as a device for ameliorating conflicts between domestic policy objectives and exchange rate stability. Consequently, when such a conflict arises, the most appropriate policy response generally calls for exchange rate adjustment, with the amount of adjustment depending on the nature of the developments underlying the conflict.

International policy cooperation – when appropriately pursued – can be important in providing an environment conducive to macroeconomic stability in general, and thus to orderly exchange rate developments. Cooperation among the largest countries can be particularly important, since economic performance in these countries has relatively large spillover effects on other countries. Accordingly, it can be constructive for economic policymakers from the largest countries to engage in frank and frequent discussions aimed at cross-examining each other's policies, identifying inconsistencies, anticipating future developments, and considering mutually advantageous policy adjustments. For such discussions to prove constructive, however, it is crucial that they be based on sound policy analysis, and that they do not put individual countries under pressures to pursue policies that are not broadly consistent with their own interests.

Equally, efforts at international policy cooperation – when not appropriately designed and sensibly adapted to unanticipated events – can undermine currency stability. This was illustrated by the European exchange market crisis of 1992–93, which has been widely attributed to the narrowness and rigidity of the target zones within which exchange rates were kept fixed in the wake of events that caused the domestic policy needs of different European countries to diverge substantially. As a general lesson from such experiences, currency stability can be undermined whenever policy authorities seek to stabilize exchange rates at levels that are not conducive to satisfactory macroeconomic outcomes.[69]

Just as the excessive pursuit of exchange rate stability as a policy objective can be self-defeating, currency instability can be fostered by a "hands-off policy" toward the exchange rate. This is particularly the case in a world in which market participants trade partly on the basis of technical analysis of, or feedback from, the recent history of exchange rate behavior. It can be contended, in this regard, that the sharp appreciation of the US dollar from the end of 1980 through early 1985 resulted in part from the fact that the United States rejected exchange rate stability as a policy objective.

The sharp appreciation of the dollar in the early 1980s, and the 1992–93 crisis in European exchange markets, are the most heralded episodes of exchange rate instability over the past two decades. These experiences argue strongly against both hands-off policies toward the exchange rate and too much rigidity in adjustable peg systems. This being said, it should be emphasized that the first experience did not result from the type of flexible but managed exchange rate arrangements that are prevalent in the world today. Today's international monetary system is not characterized by hands-off policies toward key-currency exchange rates, and to that extent, it may be appropriate to regard the misalignment of dollar exchange rates in the early 1980s as a drawing from a different sample.

Whether the three largest industrial countries should make stronger policy commitments to stabilize key-currency exchange rates continues to be actively debated. Looking ahead over the next decade and beyond, it is hard to imagine that these three countries will be prepared to make substantial sacrifices of monetary or fiscal autonomy. Accordingly, efforts at reforming the international monetary system in a manner that required them to do so would likely be fruitless. Moreover, steps to implement international monetary reforms that lacked credibility could well have the counterproductive effect of increasing exchange rate instability.

This suggests that the prospects for achieving greater stability of key-currency exchange rates in the years ahead cannot be much enhanced by changing the nature of exchange rate arrangements *per se*. Such prospects,

[69] Krugman (1988a) and others have suggested, in this connection, that international policy cooperation during 1987, following the Louvre Accord, was badly misguided in resisting further downward pressures on dollar exchange rates via actions that translated into interest rate increases through most of the year, until stock markets crashed in October.

rather, depend largely on improving the quality of national macroeconomic policies and international policy cooperation, which in turn depends both on increasing the effectiveness of policy analysis and on overcoming political impediments to the timely adoption of appropriate policies.

References

Abuaf, Niso and Philippe Jorion 1990. "Purchasing Power Parity in the Long Run," *Journal of Finance* 45, 157–74

Adams, Charles F. and Daniel Gros 1986. "The Consequences of Real Exchange Rate Rules for Inflation: Some Illustrative Examples," International Monetary Fund *Staff Papers* 33, 439–76

Adams, Donald B. and Dale W. Henderson 1983. "Definition and Measurement of Exchange Market Intervention," *Staff Studies* 126, Washington: Board of Governors of the Federal Reserve System

Adler, Michael and Bruce Lehmann 1983. "Deviations from Purchasing Power Parity in the Long Run," *Journal of Finance* 38, 1471–87

Agénor, Pierre-Richard, Jagdeep S. Bhandari, and Robert P. Flood 1992. "Speculative Attacks and Models of Balance of Payments Crises," International Monetary Fund *Staff Papers* 39, 357–94

Aghevli, Bijan B., Mohsin S. Khan, and Peter J. Montiel 1991. "Exchange Rate Policy in Developing Countries: Some Analytical Issues," *Occasional Paper* 78, Washington: International Monetary Fund

Ahmed, Shaghil 1987. "Government Spending, The Balance of Trade and the Terms of Trade in British History," *Journal of Monetary Economics* 20, 195–220.

Ainley, Michael 1984. *The General Arrangements to Borrow*, Pamphlet Series 41, Washington: International Monetary Fund

Aizenman, Joshua 1994. "Monetary and Real Shocks, Productive Capacity and Exchange Rate Regimes," *Economica* 61, 407–34

Aizenman, Joshua and Jacob A. Frenkel 1985. "Optimal Wage Indexation, Foreign Exchange Intervention, and Monetary Policy," *American Economic Review* 75, 402–23

Aizenman, Joshua and Peter Isard 1993. "Externalities, Incentives, and Failure to Achieve National Objectives in Decentralized Economies," *Journal of Development Economics* 41, 95–114

Alexander, Sidney S. 1952. "Effects of a Devaluation on a Trade Balance," International Monetary Fund *Staff Papers* 2, 263–78.

Aliber, Robert Z. (ed.) 1974. *National Monetary Policies and the International Financial System*, Chicago: University of Chicago Press

1973. "The Interest Parity Theorem: A Reinterpretation," *Journal of Political Economy* 81, 1451–9

Allen, Polly R. and Peter B. Kenen 1980. *Asset Markets, Exchange Rates, and Economic Integration: A Synthesis*, Cambridge: Cambridge University Press

Argy, Victor 1994. *International Macroeconomics: Theory and Policy*, London: Routledge

1981. *The Post War International Monetary Crisis: An Analysis*, London: George Allen & Unwin

Argy, Victor and Pentti J.K. Kouri 1974. "Sterilization Policies and the Volatility in International Reserves," in Aliber (ed.), 209–30

Argy, Victor and Michael G. Porter 1972. "The Forward Exchange Market and the Effects of Domestic and External Disturbances Under Alternative Exchange Rate Systems," International Monetary Fund *Staff Papers* 19, 503–32

Artis, Michael J. and Sylvia Ostry 1986. "International Economic Policy Coordination," *Chatham House Papers* 30, Royal Institute of International Affairs, London: Routledge & Kegan Paul

Artis, Michael J. and Mark P. Taylor 1994. "The Stabilizing Effect of the ERM on Exchange Rates and Interest Rates: An Empirical Investigation," International Monetary Fund *Staff Papers* 41, 123–48

Artus, Jacques R. 1978. "Methods of Assessing the Long-Run Equilibrium Value of an Exchange Rate," *Journal of International Economics* 8, 277–99

1976. "Exchange Rate Stability and Managed Floating: The Experience of the Federal Republic of Germany," International Monetary Fund *Staff Papers* 23, 312–33

Atkeson, Andrew and Tamim Bayoumi 1993. "Do Private Capital Markets Insure Regional Risk? Evidence from the United States and Europe," *Open Economies Review* 4, 303–24

Backus, David K. 1984. "Empirical Models of the Exchange Rate: Separating the Wheat from the Chaff," *Canadian Journal of Economics* 17, 824–46

Backus, David K., Patrick J. Kehoe, and Finn E. Kydland 1994. "Relative Price Movements in Dynamic General Equilibrium Models of International Trade," in van der Ploeg (ed.), 62–96

Bailey, Martin J. 1962. *National Income and the Price Level*, New York: McGraw-Hill

Baillie, Richard T. and Patrick C. McMahon 1989. *The Foreign Exchange Market: Theory and Econometric Evidence*, Cambridge: Cambridge University Press

Balassa, Bela 1964. "The Purchasing-Power Parity Doctrine: A Reappraisal," *Journal of Political Economy* 72, 584–96

Bank of England 1994. "The Role of the European Monetary Institute," *Bank of England Quarterly Bulletin* 34, 51–4

Bank for International Settlements 1993. *Central Bank Survey of Foreign Exchange Market Activity in April 1992*, Basle

Barro, Robert J. 1989. "Introduction," in Barro (ed.), *Modern Business Cycle Theory*, Cambridge, Mass.: Harvard University Press, 1–15

Barro, Robert J. and David B. Gordon 1983b. "A Positive Theory of Monetary Policy in a Natural-Rate Model," *Journal of Political Economy* 91, 589–610

1983a. "Rules, Discretion, and Reputation in a Model of Monetary Policy," *Journal of Monetary Economics* 12, 101–21

Bartolini, Leonardo 1993. "Devaluation and Competitiveness in a Small Open Economy: Ireland 1987–1993," *Working Paper* WP/93/82, International Monetary Fund

Baumol, William J. 1957. "Speculation, Profitability, and Stability," *Review of*

Economics and Statistics 39, 263–71

Baxter, Marianne 1994. "Real Exchange Rates and Real Interest Rates: Have We Missed the Business-Cycle Relationship?," *Journal of Monetary Economics* 33, 5–37

Baxter, Marianne and Alan C. Stockman 1989. "Business Cycles and the Exchange-Rate Regime: Some International Evidence," *Journal of Monetary Economics* 23, 377–400

Bayoumi, Tamim 1994. "A Formal Model of Optimum Currency Areas," International Monetary Fund *Staff Papers*, 41, 537–54

1990. "Saving-Investment Correlations," International Monetary Fund *Staff Papers* 37, 360–87

Bayoumi, Tamim and Barry Eichengreen 1994. "Macroeconomic Adjustment Under Bretton Woods and the Post-Bretton-Woods Float: An Impulse–Response Analysis," *Economic Journal* 104, 813–27

Bayoumi, Tamim and Michael W. Klein 1994. "A Provincial View of Capital Mobility," draft

Bayoumi, Tamim and Ronald MacDonald 1994b. "On the Optimality of Consumption Across Canadian Provinces," *Discussion Paper* 1030, Centre for Economic Policy Research

1994a. "Consumption, Income, and International Capital Market Integration," *Discussion Paper* 1028, Centre for Economic Policy Research

Bayoumi, Tamim, Peter Clark, Steve Symansky, and Mark Taylor 1994. "Robustness of Equilibrium Exchange Rate Calculations to Alternative Assumptions and Methodologies," in Williamson (ed.), 19–59

Bennett, Adam G.G. 1994. "Currency Boards: Issues and Experiences," *Papers on Policy Analysis and Assessment* PPAA/94/18, International Monetary Fund

1993. "The Operation of the Estonian Currency Board," International Monetary Fund *Staff Papers* 40, 451–70

Bergsten, C. Fred and John Williamson 1994. "Is the Time Ripe for Target Zones or the Blueprint?," in Bretton Woods Commission, C21–30

Bertola, Guiseppe and Ricardo J. Caballero 1992. "Target Zones and Realignments," *American Economic Review* 82, 520–36

Bertola, Guiseppe and Lars E.O. Svensson 1993. "Stochastic Devaluation Risk and the Empirical Fit of Target Zone Models," *Review of Economic Studies* 60, 689–712

Bickerdike, C.F. 1920. "The Instability of Foreign Exchange," *Economic Journal* 30, 118–22

Bilson, John F.O. 1981. "The Speculative Efficiency Hypothesis," *Journal of Business* 54, 435–51

1978b. "Rational Expectations and the Exchange Rate," in Frenkel and Johnson (eds.), 75–96

1978a. "The Monetary Approach to the Exchange Rate: Some Evidence," International Monetary Fund *Staff Papers* 25, 48–75

Bilson, John F.O. and Richard C. Marston (eds.) 1984. *Exchange Rate Theory and Practice*, Chicago: University of Chicago Press

Bingham, T.R.G. 1992. "Foreign Exchange Markets," in Newman *et al.* (eds.), Vol. 2, 154–7

Black, Stanley W. 1973. "International Money Markets and Flexible Exchange

Rates," *Princeton Studies in International Finance* 32, Princeton: International Finance Section, Department of Economics, Princeton University

Blackburn, Keith and Martin Sola 1993. "Speculative Currency Attacks and Balance of Payments Crises," *Journal of Economic Surveys* 7, 119–44

Blanchard, Olivier J. 1979. "Speculative Bubbles, Crashes and Rational Expectations," *Economics Letters* 3, 387–9

Bloomfield, Arthur I. 1959. *Monetary Policy Under the International Gold Standard: 1880–1914*, New York: Federal Reserve Bank of New York

Blundell-Wignall, Adrian (ed.) 1993. *The Exchange Rate, International Trade and the Balance of Payments*, Sydney: Reserve Bank of Australia

Board of Governors of the Federal Reserve System 1943. *Banking and Monetary Statistics*, Washington

Bordo, Michael D. 1993b. "The Bretton Woods International Monetary System: A Historical Overview," in Bordo and Eichengreen (eds.), 3–98

    1993a. "The Gold Standard, Bretton Woods and Other Monetary Regimes: An Historical Appraisal," *Working Paper* 4310, National Bureau of Economic Research

    1992b. "Gold Standard: Theory," in Newman *et al.* (eds.), Vol. 2, 267–71

    1992a. "Bimetallism," in Newman *et al.* (eds.), Vol. 1, 208–10

Bordo, Michael D. and Barry Eichengreen (eds.) 1993. *A Retrospective on the Bretton Woods System: Lessons for International Monetary Reform*, Chicago: University of Chicago Press

Borensztein, Eduardo R. 1987. "Alternative Hypotheses About the Excess Return of Dollar Assets," International Monetary Fund *Staff Papers* 34, 29–59

Bosworth, Barry P. 1993. *Saving and Investment in a Global Economy*, Washington: The Brookings Institution

Boucher Breuer, Janice 1994. "An Assessment of the Evidence on Purchasing Power Parity," in Williamson (ed.), 245–77

Boughton, James M. 1988. "The Monetary Approach to Exchange Rates: What Now Remains?," Essays in *International Finance* 171, Princeton: International Finance Section, Department of Economics, Princeton University

    1984. "Tests of the Performance of Reduced-Form Exchange Rate Models," *Journal of International Economics* 31, 41–56

Boyer, Russell A. 1978. "Optimal Foreign Exchange Market Intervention," *Journal of Political Economy* 86, 1045–55

Boyer, Russell A. and Charles F. Adams 1988. "Forward Premia and Risk Premia in a Simple Model of Exchange Rate Determination," *Journal of Money, Credit and Banking* 20, 633–44

Branson, William H. 1969. "The Minimum Covered Interest Differential Needed for International Arbitrage Activity," *Journal of Political Economy* 77, 1028–35

    1968. *Financial Capital Flows in the U.S. Balance of Payments*, Amsterdam: North-Holland

Branson, William H. and Dale W. Henderson 1985. "The Specification and Influence of Asset Markets," in Jones and Kenen (eds.), 749–805

Branson, William H., Jacob A. Frenkel, and Morris Goldstein (eds.) 1990. *International Policy Coordination and Exchange Rate Fluctuations*, Chicago: University of Chicago Press

Branson, William H., Hannu Halttunen, and Paul Masson 1979. "Exchange Rates in the Short Run: Some Further Results," *European Economic Review* 12, 395–402

1977. "Exchange Rates in the Short Run: The Dollar Deutsche Mark Rate," *European Economic Review* 10, 303–24

Bretton Woods Commission 1994. *Bretton Woods: Looking to the Future*, Washington: Bretton Woods Committee

Brock, William A. 1974. "Money and Growth: The Case of Long-run Perfect Foresight," *International Economic Review* 15, 750–77

Brown, William Adams Jr. 1940. *The International Gold Standard Reinterpreted, 1914–1934*, New York: National Bureau of Economic Research

Bryant, Ralph C. 1995b. "International Cooperation for National Macroeconomic Policies: Where Do We Stand?," in Kenen (ed.)

1995a. "The 'Exchange Risk Premium', Uncovered Interest Parity, and the Treatment of Exchange Rates in Multicountry Macroeconomic Models," unpublished paper

1987. *International Financial Intermediation*, Washington: The Brookings Institution

Bryant, Ralph C., Gerald Holtham, and Peter Hooper (eds.) 1988. *External Deficits and the Dollar: The Pit and the Pendulum*, Washington: The Brookings Institution

Bryant, Ralph C., Peter Hooper, and Catherine Mann (eds.) 1993. *Evaluating Policy Regimes: New Research in Empirical Macroeconomics*, Washington: The Brookings Institution

Bryant, Ralph C., David A. Currie, Jacob A. Frenkel, Paul R. Masson, and Richard Portes (eds.) 1989. *Macroeconomic Policies in an Interdependent World*, Washington: International Monetary Fund

Bryant, Ralph C., Dale W. Henderson, Gerald Holtham, Peter Hooper, and Steven A. Symansky (eds.) 1988. *Empirical Macroeconomics for Interdependent Economies*, Washington: The Brookings Institution

Buiter, Willem H. and Marcus Miller 1982. "Real Exchange Rate Overshooting and the Output Cost of Bringing Down Inflation," *European Economic Review* 18, 85–123

Cagan, Phillip 1992. "Hyperinflation: Theory," in Newman *et al.* (eds.), Vol. 2, 323–5

Calvo, Guillermo 1978. "On the Time Consistency of Optimal Policy in a Monetary Economy," *Econometrica* 46, 1411–28

Calvo, Guillermo and Carlos A. Rodríguez 1977. "A Model of Exchange Rate Determination under Currency Substitution and Rational Expectations," *Journal of Political Economy* 85, 617–25

Calvo, Guillermo, Leonardo Leiderman, and Carmen M. Reinhart 1994. "The Capital Inflows Problem: Concepts and Issues," *Contemporary Economic Policy* 12, 54–66

1993. "Capital Inflows and Real Exchange Rate Appreciation in Latin America," *International Monetary Fund Staff Papers* 40, 108–51

Calvo, Guillermo, Carmen M. Reinhart, and Carlos A. Végh 1994. "Targeting the Real Exchange Rate: Theory and Evidence," *Working Paper* WP/94/22, International Monetary Fund

Campbell, John Y. and Richard H. Clarida 1987. "The Dollar and Real Interest Rates," *Carnegie–Rochester Conference Series on Economic Policy* 27, 103–40

Cantillon, Richard 1755. *Essai sur la Nature du Commerce en Général*, London: Fletcher Iyles (translated by H. Higgs (ed.), New York: Augustus M. Kelley, 1964)

Canzoneri, Matthew B. and Jo Anna Gray 1985. "Monetary Policy Games and the Consequences of Non-Cooperative Behavior," *International Economic Review* 26, 547–64

Canzoneri, Matthew B. and Dale W. Henderson 1991. *Monetary Policy in Interdependent Economies: A Game Theoretic Approach*, Cambridge, Mass.: MIT Press

Caramazza, Francesco 1993. "French–German Interest Rate Differentials and Time-Varying Realignment Risk," International Monetary Fund *Staff Papers* 40, 567–83

Cassel, Gustav 1922. *Money and Foreign Exchange After 1914*, New York: Constable & Co

1918. "Abnormal Deviations in International Exchanges," *Economic Journal* 28, 413–5

Chen, Zhaohui and Alberto Giovannini 1993. "The Determinants of Realignment Expectations Under the EMS: Some Empirical Regularities," *Working Paper* 4291, National Bureau of Economic Research

Clarida, Richard and Jordi Gali 1994. "Sources of Real Exchange Rate Fluctuations: How Important are Nominal Shocks?," *Working Paper* 4658, National Bureau of Economic Research

Clarke, Stephen V.O. 1967. *Central Bank Cooperation: 1924–31*, New York: Federal Reserve Bank of New York

Clinton, Kevin 1988. "Transactions Costs and Covered Interest Arbitrage: Theory and Evidence," *Journal of Political Economy* 96, 358–70

Commission for the Study of Economic and Monetary Union 1989. *Report* ["Delors Report"], Luxembourg: Office for Official Publications of the European Communities

Committee on Reform of the International Monetary System and Related Issues ["Committee of Twenty"] 1974. *International Monetary Reform: Documents of the Committee of Twenty*, Washington: International Monetary Fund

Cooper, Richard N. 1992. "Fettered to Gold? Economic Policy in the Interwar Period," *Journal of Economic Literature* 30, 2120–8

1990. "Comment," in Branson *et al.* (eds.), 102–5

1985. "Economic Interdependence and Coordination of Economic Policies," in Jones and Kenen (eds.), 1195–1234

1984. "A Monetary System for the Future," *Foreign Affairs* 63, 166–84

Corden, W. Max 1993. "Exchange Rate Policies for Developing Countries," *Economic Journal* 103, 198–207

1972. "Monetary Integration," *Essays in International Finance* 93, Princeton: International Finance Section, Department of Economics, Princeton University

Council of the European Communities 1970. *Interim Report on the Establishing by Stages of Economic and Monetary Union* ["Werner Report"], Luxembourg: Office for Official Publications of the European Communities

Crockett, Andrew 1993. "Monetary Policy Implications of Increased Capital Flows," Bank of England *Quarterly Bulletin* 33, 492–504

 1989. "The Role of International Institutions in Surveillance and Policy Coordination," in Bryant *et al.* (eds.), 343–64

Crockett, Andrew and Morris Goldstein 1987. "Strengthening the International Monetary System: Exchange Rates, Surveillance, and Objective Indicators," *Occasional Paper* 50, Washington: International Monetary Fund

Cukierman, Alex, Miguel A. Kiguel, and Leonardo Leiderman 1994. "Choosing the Width of Exchange Rate Bands – Credibility vs. Flexibility," *Discussion Paper* 907, Centre for Economic Policy Research.

Cumby, Robert E. 1988. "Is It Risk? Explaining Deviations from Uncovered Interest Parity," *Journal of Monetary Economics* 22, 279–99

Cumby, Robert E. and David M. Modest 1987. "Testing for Market Timing Ability: A Framework for Forecast Evaluation," *Journal of Financial Economics* 19, 169–89

Cumby, Robert E. and Maurice Obstfeld 1984. "International Interest Rate and Price Level Linkages Under Flexible Exchange Rates: A Review of Recent Evidence," in Bilson and Marston (eds.), 121–51

Currie, David 1993. "International Cooperation in Monetary Policy: Has it a Future?," *The Economic Journal* 103, 178–87

Currie, David, Gerald Holtham, and Andrew Hughes Hallett 1989. "The Theory and Practice of International Policy Coordination: Does Coordination Pay?," in Bryant *et al.* (eds.), 14–46

Cutler, David M., James M. Poterba, and Lawrence H. Summers 1990. "Speculative Dynamics and the Role of Feedback Traders," *American Economic Review* 80, 63–8

 1989. "What Moves Stock Prices?," *Journal of Portfolio Management* 15, 4–12

Danker, Deborah J., Richard D. Haas, Dale W. Henderson, Steven A. Symansky, and Ralph W. Tryon 1987. "Small Empirical Models of Exchange Market Intervention: Applications to Germany, Japan, and Canada," *Journal of Policy Modeling* 9, 143–73

De Grauwe, Paul 1994. "Towards European Monetary Union without the EMS," *Economic Policy* 9, 147–74

 1992. *The Economics of Monetary Integration*, Oxford: Oxford University Press

De Gregorio, José and Holger C. Wolf 1994. "Terms of Trade, Productivity, and the Real Exchange Rate," *Working Paper* 4807, National Bureau of Economic Research

De Kock, Gabriel and Vittorio Grilli 1993. "Fiscal Policies and the Choice of Exchange Rate Regime," *Economic Journal* 103, 347–58

Despres, Emile, 1973. *International Economic Reform: Collected Papers of Emile Despres*, ed. by Gerald M. Meier, New York: Oxford University Press

Despres, Emile, Charles P. Kindleberger, and Walter S. Salant 1969. "The Dollar and World Liquidity: A Minority View," *The Economist* (February 1, 1966), 526–9. Reprinted with minor additions in Lawrence H. Officer and Thomas D. Willett (eds.), *The International Monetary System: Problems and Proposals*, Englewood Cliffs, N.J.: Prentice-Hall, 41–52.

De Vries, Margaret Garritsen 1987. *Balance of Payments Adjustment 1945 to 1986: The IMF Experience*, Washington: International Monetary Fund

1985. *The International Monetary Fund, 1972–1978: Cooperation on Trial*, Washington: International Monetary Fund

1976. *The International Monetary Fund, 1966–1971: The System Under Stress*, Washington: International Monetary Fund

Diebold, Francis X., Steven Husted, and Mark Rush 1991. "Real Exchange Rates Under the Gold Standard," *Journal of Political Economy* 99, 1252–71

Diebold, Francis X. and James A. Nason 1990. "Nonparametric Exchange Rate Prediction?," *Journal of International Economics* 28, 315–32

Dixit, Avinash 1989. "Entry and Exit Decisions Under Uncertainty," *Journal of Political Economy* 97, 620–38

Dobson, Wendy 1994. "Economic Policy Coordination Institutionalized? The G-7 and the Future of the Bretton Woods Institutions," in Bretton Woods Commission, C143–8

1991. *Economic Policy Coordination: Requiem or Prologue?*, Washington: Institute for International Economics

Domínguez, Kathryn M. and Jeffrey A. Frankel 1993b. "Does Foreign-Exchange Intervention Matter? The Portfolio Effect," *American Economic Review* 83, 1356–69

1993a. *Does Foreign Exchange Intervention Work?*, Washington: Institute for International Economics

Dooley, Michael P. 1989. "Discussion," in Federal Reserve Bank of Boston, *International Payments Imbalances in the 1980s*, Boston, 189–94

Dooley, Michael P. and Peter Isard 1991. "A Note on Fiscal Policy, Investment Location Decisions, and Exchange Rates," *Journal of International Money and Finance* 10, 161–8

1987. "Country Preferences, Currency Values and Policy Issues," *Journal of Policy Modeling* 9, 65–81

1983. "The Portfolio-Balance Model of Exchange Rates and Some Structural Estimates of the Risk Premium," International Monetary Fund *Staff Papers* 30, 683–702

1982b. "The Role of the Current Account in Exchange-Rate Determination: A Comment on Rodríguez," *Journal of Political Economy* 90, 1291–4

1982a. "A Portfolio-Balance Rational-Expectations Model of the Dollar–Mark Exchange Rate," *Journal of International Economics* 12, 257–76

1980. "Capital Controls, Political Risk and Deviations from Interest-Rate Parity," *Journal of Political Economy* 88, 70–84

Dooley, Michael P. and Jeff Shafer 1983. "Analysis of Short-Run Exchange Rate Behavior: March 1973 to November 1981," in David Bigman and Teizo Taya (eds.), *Exchange Rate and Trade Instability: Causes, Consequences and Remedies*, Cambridge, Mass.: Ballinger, 43–69

Dornbusch, Rudiger 1992b. "Purchasing Power Parity," in Newman *et al.* (eds.), Vol. 3, 236–44

1992a. "Lessons from Experiences with High Inflation," *World Bank Economic Review* 6, 13–31

1983b. "Exchange Risk and the Macroeconomics of Exchange Rate Determination," in Robert G. Hawkins, Richard M. Levich, and Clas G. Wihlborg (eds.), *The Internationalization of Financial Markets and National Economic Policy*, Greenwich, Conn.: JAI Press, 3–27

1983a. "Real Interest Rates, Home Goods, and Optimal External Borrowing," *Journal of Political Economy* 91, 141–53

1982. "Stabilization Policies in Developing Countries: What Have We Learned?," *World Development* 10, 701–8

1980. "Exchange Rate Economics: Where Do We Stand?," *Brookings Papers on Economic Activity*, 143–85

1976. "Expectations and Exchange Rate Dynamics," *Journal of Political Economy* 84, 1161–76

1975. "Exchange Rates and Fiscal Policy in a Popular Model of International Trade," *American Economic Review* 65, 859–71

Dornbusch, Rudiger and Stanley Fischer 1980. "Exchange Rates and the Current Account," *American Economic Review* 70, 960–71

Dornbusch, Rudiger and Jeffrey Frankel 1988. "The Flexible Exchange Rate System: Experience and Alternatives," in Silvio Borner (ed.), *International Finance and Trade in a Polycentric World*, New York: St. Martin's Press, 151–97

Dornbusch, Rudiger and Jacob A. Frenkel 1984. "The Gold Standard Crisis of 1847," *Journal of International Economics* 16, 1–27

Drazen, Allan and Paul R. Masson 1994. "Credibility of Policies versus Credibility of Policymakers," *Quarterly Journal of Economics* 109, 735–54

Edison, Hali J. 1993. "The Effectiveness of Central-Bank Intervention: A Survey of the Literature After 1982," *Special Papers in International Economics* 18, Princeton: International Finance Section, Department of Economics, Princeton University

1987. "Purchasing Power Parity in the Long Run: A Test of the Dollar/Pound Exchange Rate (1890–1978)," *Journal of Money, Credit, and Banking* 19, 376–87

1985. "Purchasing Power Parity: A Quantitative Reassessment of the 1920s Experience," *Journal of International Money and Finance* 4, 361–72

1981. *Short Run Dynamics and Long Run Equilibrium Behavior in Purchasing Power Parity: A Quantitative Reassessment*, unpublished Ph.D. dissertation, London School of Economics

Edison, Hali J. and Jan Tore Klovland 1987. "A Quantitative Reassessment of the Purchasing Power Parity Hypothesis: Evidence from Norway and the United Kingdom," *Journal of Applied Econometrics* 2, 309–33

Edison, Hali J. and Michael Melvin 1990. "The Determinants and Implications of the Choice of an Exchange Rate System," in William S. Haraf and Thomas D. Willett (eds.), *Monetary Policy for a Volatile Global Economy*, Washington: AEI Press, 1–44

Edison, Hali J. and B. Dianne Pauls 1993. "A Re-Assessment of the Relationship Between Real Exchange Rates and Real Interest Rates: 1974–1990," *Journal of Monetary Economics* 31, 165–87

Edison, Hali J., Joseph E. Gagnon, and William R. Melick 1994. "Understanding the Empirical Literature on Purchasing Power Parity: The Post-Bretton Woods Era," *International Finance Discussion Paper* 465, Federal Reserve Board

Edison, Hali J., Jaime R. Márquez, and Ralph W. Tryon 1987. "The Structure and Properties of the Federal Reserve Board Multicountry Model," *Economic*

Modelling 4, 115–315

Edwards, Sebastian 1982. "Exchange Rates and 'News': A Multi-Currency Approach," *Journal of International Money and Finance* 1, 211–24

Eichenbaum, Martin and Charles Evans 1992. "Some Empirical Evidence on the Effects of Monetary Policy Shocks on Exchange Rates," *Working Paper* WP-92–32, Federal Reserve Bank of Chicago

Eichengreen, Barry 1995b. "The Endogeneity of Exchange Rate Regimes," in Kenen (ed.)

1995a. *International Monetary Arrangements for the 21st Century*, Washington: The Brookings Institution

1994. "History of the International Monetary System: Implications for Research in International Macroeconomics and Finance," in van der Ploeg (ed.), 153–91

1993b. "European Monetary Unification," *Journal of Economic Literature* 31, 1321–57

1993a. "Epilogue: Three Perspectives on the Bretton Woods System," in Bordo and Eichengreen (eds.), 621–57

1992. *Golden Fetters: The Gold Standard and the Great Depression*, Oxford: Oxford University Press

1989. *Elusive Stability: Essays in the History of International Finance, 1919–1939*, Cambridge: Cambridge University Press

(ed.) 1985. *The Gold Standard in Theory and History*, New York: Methuen

1985. "Editor's Introduction," in Eichengreen (ed.), 1–35

Eichengreen, Barry and Peter B. Kenen 1994. "Managing the International Economy under the Bretton Woods System: An Overview," in Kenen (ed.), 3–57

Eichengreen, Barry and Charles Wyplosz 1993. "The Unstable EMS," *Brookings Papers on Economic Activity*, 51–143

Eichengreen, Barry, Andrew K. Rose, and Charles Wyplosz 1994b. "Speculative Attacks on Pegged Exchange Rates: An Empirical Exploration with Special Reference to the European Monetary System," *Working Paper* 4898, National Bureau of Economic Research

1994a. "Is There a Safe Passage to EMU? Evidence on Capital Controls and a Proposal," *Discussion Paper* 1061, Centre for Economic Policy Research

Einzig, Paul 1970. *The History of Foreign Exchange*, London: Macmillan

1949. *Primitive Money*, London: Eyre & Spottiswoode

1934. *Exchange Control*, London: Macmillan

Engel, Charles M. and Robert P. Flood 1985. "Exchange Rate Dynamics, Sticky Prices and the Current Account," *Journal of Money, Credit and Banking* 17, 312–27

Engel, Charles M. and John H. Rogers 1994. "How Wide is the Border?," *Working Paper* 4829, National Bureau of Economic Research

Engle, Robert F., Takatoshi Ito, and Wen-Ling Lin 1990. "Meteor Showers or Heat Waves? Heteroskedastic Intra-Daily Volatility in the Foreign Exchange Market," *Econometrica* 58, 525–42

Ericsson, Neil R. 1992b. "Parameter Constancy, Mean Square Forecast Errors, and Measuring Forecast Performance: An Exposition, Extensions, and Illustration," *Journal of Policy Modeling* 14, 465–95

1992a. "Cointegration, Exogeneity, and Policy Analysis: An Overview," *Journal of Policy Modeling* 14, 251–80

Evans, Martin D.D. and Karen K. Lewis 1992b. "Trends in Expected Returns in Currency and Bond Markets," *Working Paper* 4116, National Bureau of Economic Research

1992a. "Peso Problems and Heterogeneous Trading: Evidence From Excess Returns in Foreign Exchange and Euromarkets," *Working Paper* 4003, National Bureau of Economic Research

Feldstein, Martin S. 1990. "Comment," in Branson *et al.* (eds.), 55–9

(ed.) 1988. *International Economic Cooperation*, Chicago: University of Chicago Press

1988. "Distinguished Lecture on Economics in Government: Thinking About International Economic Coordination," *Journal of Economic Perspectives* 2, 3–13

Finn, Mary G. 1986. "Forecasting the Exchange Rate: A Monetary or Random Walk Phenomenon?," *Journal of International Money and Finance* 5, 181–93

Fischer, Stanley 1994. "Modern Central Banking," paper presented at the Bank of England's Tercentenary Celebration.

1988. "International Macroeconomic Policy Coordination," in Feldstein (ed.), 11–43

Fisher, P.G., S.K. Tanna, D.S. Turner, K.F. Wallis, and J.D. Whitley 1990. "Econometric Evaluation of the Exchange Rate in Models of the U.K. Economy," *Economic Journal* 100, 1230–44

Fishlow, Albert 1985. "Lessons From the Past: Capital Markets During the 19th Century and the Interwar Period," *International Organization* 39, 383–439

Fleming, J. Marcus 1962. "Domestic Financial Policies Under Fixed and Under Floating Exchange Rates," International Monetary Fund *Staff Papers* 12, 369–80

Flood, Robert P., Jagdeep S. Bhandari, and Jocelyn P. Horne 1989. "Evolution of Exchange Rate Regimes," International Monetary Fund *Staff Papers* 36, 810–35

Flood, Robert P. and Peter M. Garber 1991. "The Linkage Between Speculative Attack and Target Zone Models of Exchange Rates," *Quarterly Journal of Economics* 106, 1367–72

1984b. "Collapsing Exchange Regimes: Some Linear Examples," *Journal of International Economics* 17, 1–13

1984a. "Gold Monetization and Gold Discipline," *Journal of Political Economy* 92, 90–107

1980. "Market Fundamentals versus Price-Level Bubbles: The First Tests," *Journal of Political Economy* 88, 745–70

Flood, Robert P. and Robert J. Hodrick 1990. "On Testing for Speculative Bubbles," *Journal of Economic Perspectives* 4, 85–101

Flood, Robert P. and Peter Isard 1989. "Monetary Policy Strategies," International Monetary Fund *Staff Papers* 36, 612–32

Flood, Robert P. and Nancy P. Marion 1992. "Exchange Rate Regime Choice," in Newman *et al.* (eds.), Vol. 1, 829–31

1982. "The Transmission of Disturbances Under Alternative Exchange-Rate Regimes with Optimal Indexing," *Quarterly Journal of Economics* 97, 43–66

Flood, Robert P. and Andrew K. Rose 1993. "Fixing Exchange Rates: A Virtual

Quest for Fundamentals," *Working Paper* 4503, National Bureau of Economic Research

Flood, Robert P. and Mark P. Taylor 1995. "Exchange Rate Economics: What's Wrong with the Conventional Macro Approach?," in Frankel *et al.* (eds.)

Flood, Robert P., Andrew K. Rose and Donald J. Mathieson 1991. "An Empirical Exploration of Exchange-Rate Target-Zones," *Carnegie–Rochester Conference Series on Public Policy* 35, 7–65

Frankel, Jeffrey A. 1986. "International Capital Mobility and Crowding Out in the U.S. Economy: Imperfect Integration of Financial Markets or of Goods Markets?," in Rik W. Hafer (ed.), *How Open Is the U.S. Economy?*, Lexington, Mass.: Lexington Books, 33–67

1984. "Tests of Monetary and Portfolio Balance Models of Exchange Rate Determination," in Bilson and Marston (eds.), 239–60

1982c. "In Search of the Exchange Risk Premium: A Six-Currency Test Assuming Mean–Variance Optimization," *Journal of International Money and Finance* 1, 255–74

1982b. "A Test of Perfect Substitutability in the Foreign Exchange Market," *Southern Economic Journal* 49, 406–16

1982a. "The Mystery of the Multiplying Marks: A Modification of the Monetary Model," *Review of Economics and Statistics* 64, 515–19

1979. "On the Mark: a Theory of Floating Exchange Rates Based on Real Interest Differentials," *American Economic Review* 69, 610–22

Frankel, Jeffrey A. and Kenneth A. Froot 1990. "Exchange Rate Forecasting Techniques, Survey Data, and Implications for the Foreign Exchange Market," *Working Paper* 3470, National Bureau of Economic Research

1988. "Chartists, Fundamentalists and the Demand for Dollars," *Greek Economic Review* 10, 49–102

1987. "Using Survey Data to Test Standard Propositions Regarding Exchange Rate Expectations," *American Economic Review* 77, 133–53

1986. "Understanding the U.S. Dollar in the Eighties: The Expectations of Chartists and Fundamentalists," *Economic Record* 62, Supplementary Issue, 24–38

Frankel, Jeffrey A. and Andrew K. Rose 1995. "A Survey of Empirical Research on Nominal Exchange Rates," in Grossman and Rogoff (eds.)

Frankel, Jeffrey A., Gaimpaolo Galli, and Alberto Giovannini (eds.) 1995. *The Microstructure of Foreign Exchange Markets*, Chicago: University of Chicago Press

Fratianni, Michele and Jürgen von Hagen 1992. *The European Monetary System and European Monetary Union*, Boulder, Col.: Westview Press

French, Kenneth R. and James M. Poterba 1991. "Investor Diversification and International Equity Markets," *American Economic Review* 81, 222–6

Frenkel, Jacob A. (ed.) 1983. *Exchange Rates and International Macroeconomics*, Chicago: University of Chicago Press

1981. "Flexible Exchange Rates, Prices, and the Role of 'News': Lessons from the 1970s," *Journal of Political Economy* 89, 665–705

1978. "Purchasing Power Parity: Doctrinal Perspective and Evidence from the 1920s," *Journal of International Economics* 8, 169–91

1976. "A Monetary Approach to the Exchange Rate: Doctrinal Aspects and

Empirical Evidence," *Scandinavian Journal of Economics* 78, 200–24

Frenkel, Jacob A. and Morris Goldstein 1986. "A Guide to Target Zones," International Monetary Fund *Staff Papers* 33, 633–73

Frenkel, Jacob A. and Harry G. Johnson (eds.) 1978. *The Economics of Exchange Rates: Selected Studies*, Reading, Mass.: Addison-Wesley

1976. *The Monetary Approach to the Balance of Payments*, Toronto: University of Toronto Press

Frenkel, Jacob A. and Richard M. Levich 1977. "Transactions Costs and Interest Arbitrage: Tranquil Versus Turbulent Periods," *Journal of Political Economy* 85, 1209–26

1975. "Covered Interest Arbitrage: Unexploited Profits?," *Journal of Political Economy* 83, 325–38

Frenkel, Jacob A. and Michael L. Mussa 1985. "Asset Markets, Exchange Rates and the Balance of Payments," in Jones and Kenen (eds.), 679–747

1980. "The Efficiency of the Foreign Exchange Market and Measures of Turbulence," *American Economic Review* 70, 374–81

Frenkel, Jacob A. and Assaf Razin 1987. "The Mundell–Fleming Model A Quarter Century Later: A Unified Exposition," International Monetary Fund *Staff Papers* 34, 567–620

Frenkel, Jacob A., Michael P. Dooley, and Peter Wickham (eds.) 1989. *Analytical Issues in Debt*, Washington: International Monetary Fund

Frenkel, Jacob A., Morris Goldstein, and Paul Masson 1990. "The Rationale for, and Effects of, International Economic Policy Coordination," in Branson *et al.* (eds.), 9–55

1989. "Simulating the Effects of Some Simple Coordinated Versus Uncoordinated Policy Rules," in Bryant *et al.* (eds.), 203–39

Friedman, Milton 1968. "The Role of Monetary Policy," *American Economic Review* 58, 1–17

1953. "The Case for Flexible Exchange Rates," in Friedman, *Essays in Positive Economics*, Chicago: University of Chicago Press, 157–203

Froot, Kenneth A. and Jeffrey A. Frankel 1989. "Forward Discount Bias: Is it an Exchange Risk Premium?," *Quarterly Journal of Economics* 104, 139–61

Froot, Kenneth A. and Takatoshi Ito 1989. "On the Consistency of Short-Run and Long-Run Exchange Rate Expectations," *Journal of International Money and Finance* 8, 487–510

Froot, Kenneth A. and Kenneth Rogoff 1995. "Perspectives on PPP and Long-Run Real Exchange Rates," in Grossman and Rogoff (eds.)

1991. "The EMS, the EMU, and the Transition to a Common Currency," in Olivier Blanchard and Stanley Fischer (eds.), *1991 NBER Macroeconomics Annual*, Cambridge, Mass.: MIT Press, 269–317

Froot, Kenneth A. and Richard H. Thaler 1990. "Foreign Exchange," *Journal of Economic Perspectives* 4, 179–92

Funabashi, Yoichi 1989. *Managing the Dollar: From the Plaza to the Louvre*, Washington: Institute for International Economics

Gagnon, Joseph E. 1993. "Exchange Rate Variability and the Level of International Trade," *Journal of International Economics* 34, 269–87

Gandolfo, Giancarlo, Pietro Carlo Padoan, and Giovanna Paladino 1990. "Exchange Rate Determination: Single-Equation or Economy-Wide Models?

A Test Against the Random Walk," *Journal of Banking and Finance* 14, 965–92

Garber, Peter M. and Michael G. Spencer 1994. "The Dissolution of the Austro-Hungarian Empire: Lessons for Currency Reform," *Essays in International Finance* 191, Princeton: International Finance Section, Department of Economics, Princeton University

Gennotte, Gerard and Hayne Leland 1990. "Market Liquidity, Hedging, and Crashes," *American Economic Review* 80, 999–1021

Gertler, Mark and Kenneth Rogoff 1990. "North–South Lending and Endogenous Domestic Capital Market Inefficiencies," *Journal of Monetary Economics* 26, 245–66

Ghosh, Atish R. 1992. "Is It Signalling? Exchange Intervention and the Dollar–Deutschemark Rate," *Journal of International Economics* 32, 201–20

Ghosh, Atish R. and Paul R. Masson 1993. *Economic Cooperation in an Uncertain World*, Oxford: Basil Blackwell

Ghosh, Atish R. and Jonathan D. Ostry 1994. "External Instability and the External Balance in Developing Countries," International Monetary Fund *Staff Papers* 41, 214–35

   1993. "Do Capital Flows Reflect Economic Fundamentals in Developing Countries?," *Working Paper* WP/93/34, International Monetary Fund

Giavazzi, Francesco and Marco Pagano 1988. "The Advantage of Tying One's Hands: EMS Discipline and Central Bank Credibility," *European Economic Review* 32, 1055–82

Giavazzi, Francesco, Stefano Micossi, and Marcus Miller (eds.) 1988. *The European Monetary System*, Cambridge: Cambridge University Press

Gilbert, Milton and Irving B. Kravis 1954. *An International Comparison of National Products and the Purchasing Power of Currencies*, Paris: Organization for European Economic Cooperation

Giovannini, Alberto 1990b. "The Transition to European Monetary Union," *Essays in International Finance* 178, Princeton: International Finance Section, Department of Economics, Princeton University

   1990a. "European Monetary Reform: Progress and Prospects," *Brookings Papers on Economic Activity*, 217–91

   1988. "Exchange Rates and Traded Goods Prices," *Journal of International Economics* 24, 45–68

Giovannini, Alberto and Bart Turtelboom 1994. "Currency Substitution," in van der Ploeg (ed.), 390–436.

Girton, Lance and Dale Henderson 1976. "Financial Capital Movements and Central Bank Behavior in a Two Country, Short-Run Portfolio Balance Model," *Journal of Monetary Economics* 2, 33–61

   1973. "A Two Country Model of Financial Capital Movements as Stock Adjustments with Emphasis on the Effects of Central Bank Policy," *International Finance Discussion Paper* 24, Federal Reserve Board

Girton, Lance and Don Roper 1981. "Theory and Implications of Currency Substitution," *Journal of Money, Credit and Banking* 13, 12–30

   1977. "A Monetary Model of Exchange Market Pressure Applied to the Postwar Canadian Experience," *American Economic Review* 67, 537–48

Glen, Jack D. 1992. "Real Exchange Rates in the Short, Medium, and Long Run," *Journal of International Economics* 33, 147–66

Glick, Reuven and Kenneth Rogoff 1992. "Global Versus Country-Specific Productivity Shocks and the Current Account," *Working Paper* 4140, National Bureau of Economic Research

Goldstein, Morris 1992. "Improving Economic Policy Coordination: Evaluating Some New and Not-So-New Proposals," paper delivered at the Rinaldo Ossola Memorial Conference on "The International Monetary System," sponsored by the Banca d'Italia, Perugia

1984. "The Exchange Rate System: Lessons of the Past and Options for the Future," *Occasional Paper* 30, Washington: International Monetary Fund

1980. "Have Flexible Exchange Rates Handicapped Macroeconomic Policy?," *Special Papers in International Economics* 14, Princeton: International Finance Section, Department of Economics, Princeton University

Goldstein, Morris and Peter Isard 1992. "Mechanisms for Promoting Global Monetary Stability," in Morris Goldstein *et al.*, "Policy Issues in the Evolving International Monetary System," *Occasional Paper* 96, Washington: International Monetary Fund, 1–36

Goldstein, Morris and Mohsin S. Khan 1985. "Income and Price Effects in Foreign Trade," in Jones and Kenen (eds.), 1041–1105

Goldstein, Morris and Michael Mussa 1993. "The Integration of World Capital Markets," *Working Paper* WP/93/95, International Monetary Fund

Goldstein, Morris, David Folkerts-Landau, Mohamed El-Erain, Steven Fries, and Liliana Rojas-Suárez 1992. *International Capital Markets: Development, Prospects and Policy Issues*, Washington: International Monetary Fund

Goldstein, Morris, David Folkerts-Landau, Peter Garber, Liliana Rojas-Suárez, and Michael Spencer 1993. *International Capital Markets: Part I. Exchange Rate Management and International Capital Flows*, Washington: International Monetary Fund

Goodhart, Charles A.E. 1995. "The Political Economy of Monetary Union," in Kenen (ed.)

1988. "The Foreign Exchange Market: A Random Walk with a Dragging Anchor," *Economica* 55, 437–60

Goodhart, Charles A.E. and Lorenzo Figliuoli 1991. "Every Minute Counts in Financial Markets," *Journal of International Money and Finance* 10, 23–52

Grabbe, J. Orlin 1991. *International Financial Markets*, second edition, New York: Elsevier

Gray, Jo Anna 1976. "Wage Indexation: A Macroeconomic Approach," *Journal of Monetary Economics* 2, 221–35

Greene, Joshua E. and Peter Isard 1991. "Currency Convertibility and the Transformation of Centrally Planned Economies," *Occasional Paper* 81, Washington: International Monetary Fund

Greenwald, Bruce and Joseph Stiglitz 1993. "New and Old Keynesians," *Journal of Economic Perspectives* 7, 23–44

Greenwood, Jeremy 1983. "Expectations, the Exchange Rate, and the Current Account," *Journal of Monetary Economics* 12, 543–69

Grice-Hutchinson, Marjorie 1952. *The School of Salamanca*, Oxford: Clarendon Press

Grilli, Vittorio and Graciela Kaminsky 1991. "Nominal Exchange Rate Regimes and the Real Exchange Rate," *Journal of Monetary Economics* 27, 191–212

Grossman, Gene and Kenneth Rogoff (eds.) 1995. *Handbook of International Economics*, Vol. 3, Amsterdam: North-Holland

Group of Ten Deputies 1993. *International Capital Movements and Foreign Exchange Markets*, Rome

1985. *The Functioning of the International Monetary System*, reprinted in Crockett and Goldstein, 1987, 44–59

Guth, Wilfred (ed.) 1988. *Economic Policy Coordination*, Washington: International Monetary Fund

1988. "Summary and Conclusions," in Guth (ed.), 201–16

Haas, Richard D. and William E. Alexander 1979. "A Model of Exchange Rates and Capital Flows: The Canadian Floating Rate Experience," *Journal of Money, Credit and Banking* 11, 467–82.

Haberler, Gottfried 1966. "Adjustment, Employment, and Growth," in William Fellner *et al.*, *Maintaining and Restoring Balance in International Payments*, Princeton: Princeton University Press, 123–35

1961. "A Survey of International Trade Theory," *Special Papers in International Economics* 1, Princeton: International Finance Section, Department of Economics, Princeton University

1954. "Currency Convertibility," *National Economic Problems Series* 451, New York: American Enterprise Association

Hacche, Graham and John Townend 1981. "Exchange Rates and Monetary Policy: Modelling Sterling's Effective Exchange Rate: 1972–80," *Oxford Economic Papers* 33, Supplement, 201–47

Hahn, Frank H. 1959. "The Balance of Payments in a Monetary Economy," *Review of Economic Studies* 26, 110–25

Hakkio, Craig S. 1984. "A Re-examination of Purchasing Power Parity: A Multi-country and Multi-period Study," *Journal of International Economics* 17, 265–77

Halikias, Ioannis 1994. "Testing the Credibility of Belgium's Exchange Rate Policy," International Monetary Fund *Staff Papers* 41, 350–66

Hamada, Koichi 1979. "Macroeconomic Strategy Coordination under Alternative Exchange Rates," in Rudiger Dornbusch and Jacob A. Frenkel (eds.), *International Economic Policy*, Baltimore, Md.: The Johns Hopkins University Press, 292–324

1974. "Alternative Exchange Rate Systems and the Interdependence of Monetary Policies," in Aliber (ed.), 13–33

Hansen, Lars Peter and Robert J. Hodrick 1980. "Forward Exchange Rates as Optimal Predictors of Future Spot Rates: An Econometric Analysis," *Journal of Political Economy* 88, 829–53

Harberger, Arnold C. 1950. "Currency Depreciation, Income, and the Balance of Trade," *Journal of Political Economy* 58, 47–60

Harrod, Roy F. 1939. *International Economics*, London: Nisbet & Co. Ltd

Helkie, William L. and Peter Hooper 1988. "An Empirical Analysis of the External Deficit, 1980–86," in Bryant, Holtham, and Hooper (eds.), 10–56

Helpman, Elhanan, Leonardo Leiderman, and Gil Bufman 1994. "A New Breed of Exchange Rate Bands: Chile, Israel and Mexico," *Economic Policy* 19, 259–306

Henderson, Dale W. 1984. "Exchange Market Intervention Operations: Their Role in Financial Policy and Their Effects," in Bilson and Marston (eds.), 357–406

1979. "Financial Policies in Open Economies, "*American Economic Review* 69, 232–9

Henderson, Dale W. and Warwick J. McKibbin 1993. "A Comparison of Some Basic Monetary Policy Regimes for Open Economies: Implications of Different Degrees of Instrument Adjustment and Wage Persistence," *Carnegie–Rochester Conference Series on Public Policy* 39, 221–317

Henderson, Dale W. and Stephanie Sampson 1983. "Intervention in Foreign Exchange Markets: A Summary of Ten Staff Studies," *Federal Reserve Bulletin*, 830–6

Herring, Richard J. and Richard C. Marston 1976. "The Forward Market and Interest Rates in Eurocurrency and National Money Markets," in Carl H. Stem, John H. Makin, and Dennis E. Logue (eds.), *Eurocurrencies and the International Monetary System*, Washington: American Enterprise Institute, 139–63

Hicks, John R. 1937. "Mr. Keynes and the 'Classics': A Suggested Interpretation," *Econometrica* 5, 147–59

Hilley, John L., Carl R. Beidleman, and James A. Greenleaf 1981. "Why There Is No Long Forward Market in Foreign Exchange," *Euromoney* (January), 94–103.

Hodrick, Robert J. 1987. *The Empirical Evidence on the Efficiency of Forward and Futures Foreign Exchange Markets*, Chur, Switzerland: Harwood Academic Publishers

1982. "On the Effects of Macroeconomic Policy in a Maximizing Model of a Small Open Economy," *Journal of Macroeconomics* 4, 195–213

1978. "An Empirical Analysis of the Monetary Approach to the Determination of the Exchange Rate," in Frenkel and Johnson (eds.), 97–116

Hoffman, Dennis L. and Dan E. Schlagenhauf 1985. "The Impact of News and Alternative Theories of Exchange Rate Determination," *Journal of Money, Credit and Banking* 17, 328–46

Honkapohja, Seppo and Pentti Pikkarainen 1992. "Country Characteristics and the Choice of Exchange Rate Regime: Are Mini-Skirts Followed by Maxis?," *Discussion Paper* 744, Centre for Economic Policy Research

Hooper, Peter and Jaime Márquez 1995. "Exchange Rates, Prices, and External Adjustment," in Kenen (ed.)

Hooper, Peter and John Morton 1982. "Fluctuations in the Dollar: A Model of Nominal and Real Exchange Rate Determination," *Journal of International Money and Finance* 1, 39–56.

Horne, Jocelyn and Paul R. Masson 1988. "Scope and Limits of International Economic Cooperation and Policy Coordination," International Monetary Fund *Staff Papers* 35, 259–96

Houthakker, Hendrik S. and Stephen P. Magee 1969. "Income and Price Elasticities in World Trade," *Review of Economics and Statistics* 51, 111–25

Huizinga, John 1987. "An Empirical Investigation of the Long-Run Behavior of Real Exchange Rates," *Carnegie–Rochester Conference Series on Public Policy* 27, 149–214

Hume, David 1752. *On the Balance of Trade*, reprinted in Eichengreen (ed.), 1985, 39–48

Ikenberry, G. John 1993. "The Political Origins of Bretton Woods," in Bordo and Eichengreen (eds.), 155–98

International Monetary Fund 1994. *Exchange Arrangements and Exchange Restrictions: Annual Report 1994*, Washington

1993b. *World Economic Outlook*, Washington

1993a. *Articles of Agreement*, Washington

1991. *International Capital Markets: Developments and Prospects*, Washington.

1984b. "Issues in the Assessment of Exchange Rates of the Industrial Countries," *Occasional Paper* 29, Washington

1984a. "Exchange Rate Volatility and World Trade," *Occasional Paper* 28, Washington

1970. "The Role of Exchange Rates in the Adjustment of International Payments: A Report by the Executive Directors," Washington, reprinted in de Vries, 1976, Vol. II, 273–330

Isard, Peter 1994. "Realignment Expectations, Forward Rate Bias, and Sterilized Intervention in an Optimizing Model of Exchange Rate Adjustment," International Monetary Fund *Staff Papers* 41, 435–59

1988. "Exchange Rate Modeling: An Assessment of Alternative Approaches," in Bryant, Henderson, *et al.* (eds.), 183–201

1983. "An Accounting Framework and Some Issues for Modeling How Exchange Rates Respond to the News," in Frenkel (ed.), 19–56

1980. "Factors Determining Exchange Rates: The Roles of Relative Prices, Balances of Payments, Interest Rates and Risk," Federal Reserve Board, *International Finance Discussion Paper* 171

1978. "Exchange-Rate Determination: A Survey of Popular Views and Recent Models," *Princeton Studies in International Finance* 42, Princeton: International Finance Section, Department of Economics, Princeton University

1977. "How Far Can We Push the 'Law of One Price'?," *American Economic Review* 67, 942–8

Ishiyama, Yoshihide 1975. "The Theory of Optimum Currency Areas: A Survey," International Monetary Fund *Staff Papers* 22, 344–83

Ito, Takatoshi 1994. "Short-Run and Long-Run Expectations of the Yen/Dollar Exchange Rate," *Journal of the Japanese and International Economies*, 8, 119–43

1990. "Foreign Exchange Rate Expectations: Micro Survey Data," *American Economic Review* 80, 434–49

Jastram, Roy W. 1977. *The Golden Constant: The English and American Experience 1560–1976*, New York: John Wiley & Sons

Jenkins, Roy 1978. "European Monetary Union," *Lloyds Bank Review* 127, 1–14

Johnson, Harry G. 1977. "The Monetary Approach to the Balance of Payments: A Nontechnical Guide," *Journal of International Economics* 7, 251–68

1976. "Destabilizing Speculation: A General Equilibrium Approach," *Journal of Political Economy* 84, 101–8

1972. "The Monetary Approach to Balance-of-Payments Theory," *Journal of Financial and Quantitative Analysis* 7, 1555–72

1961. "Towards a General Theory of the Balance of Payments," in Johnson, *International Trade and Economic Growth: Studies in Pure Theory*, Cambridge, Mass.: Harvard University Press, 153–68

Jones, Ronald and Peter B. Kenen (eds.) 1985. *Handbook of International Economics*, Vol. 2, Amsterdam: North-Holland

Kaminsky, Graciela 1993. "Is There a Peso Problem? Evidence from the Dollar/ Pound Exchange Rate, 1976–87," *American Economic Review* 83, 450–72

Kaminsky, Graciela and Karen K. Lewis 1993. "Does Foreign Exchange Intervention Signal Future Monetary Policy?," *Working Paper* 4298, National Bureau of Economic Research

Kemp, Murray C. 1992. "Elasticities Approach to the Balance of Payments," in Newman *et al.* (eds.), Vol. 1, 744–5

Kenen, Peter B. (ed.) 1995. *Understanding Interdependence: The Macroeconomics of the Open Economy*, Princeton: Princeton University Press

(ed.) 1994. *Managing the World Economy: Fifty Years After Bretton Woods*, Washington: Institute for International Economics

1994. "Ways to Reform Exchange Rate Arrangements," in Bretton Woods Commission, C13–20

1992. *EMU After Maastricht*, Washington: Group of Thirty

1990. "The Coordination of Macroeconomic Policies," in Branson *et al.* (eds.), 63–102

1988. *Managing Exchange Rates*, London: Routledge

1985. "Macroeconomic Theory and Policy: How The Closed Economy Model Was Opened," in Jones and Kenen (eds.), 625–77

1969. "The Theory of Optimum Currency Areas: An Eclectic View," in Mundell and Swoboda (eds.), 41–60

Keynes, John Maynard 1936. *The General Theory of Employment, Interest and Money*, New York: Harcourt, Brace & Co.

1925. *The Economic Consequences of Mr. Churchill*, London: Hogarth Press

1923. *A Tract on Monetary Reform*, London: Macmillan

Khan, Mohsin S. and Jonathan D. Ostry 1992. "Response of the Equilibrium Real Exchange Rate to Real Disturbances in Developing Countries," *World Development* 20, 1325–34

Kindleberger, Charles P. 1984. *A Financial History of Western Europe*, London: George Allen & Unwin

1970. "The Case for Fixed Exchange Rates, 1969," in Federal Reserve Bank of Boston, *The International Adjustment Mechanism*, Boston, 93–108

1965. "Balance of Payments Deficits and the International Market for Liquidity," *Essays in International Finance* 46, Princeton: International Finance Section, Department of Economics, Princeton University

Kouri, Pentti J.K. 1976. "The Exchange Rate and the Balance of Payments in the Short Run and in the Long Run: A Monetary Approach," *Scandinavian Journal of Economics* 78, 280–304

Kouri, Pentti J.K. and Michael G. Porter 1974. "International Capital Flows and Portfolio Equilibrium," *Journal of Political Economy* 82, 443–67

Krasker, William S. 1980. "The Peso Problem in Testing the Efficiency of Forward Exchange Markets," *Journal of Monetary Economics* 6, 269–76

Kravis, Irving B., Alan Heston, and Robert Summers 1982. *World Product and Income: International Comparisons of Real Gross Product*, Baltimore, Md.: Johns Hopkins University Press

Kravis, Irving B. and Robert E. Lipsey 1983. "Toward an Explanation of National Price Levels," *Princeton Studies in International Finance* 52, Princeton: International Finance Section, Princeton University

1978. "Price Behavior in the Light of Balance of Payments Theories," *Journal of International Economics* 8, 193–246

Krueger, Anne O. 1983. *Exchange-Rate Determination*, Cambridge: Cambridge University Press

Krugman, Paul 1993c. "Comment," in Bordo and Eichengreen (eds.), 539–40

1993b. "Recent Thinking About Exchange Rate Determination and Policy," in Blundell-Wignall (ed.), 6–21

1993a. "What Do We Need to Know About the International Monetary System?," *Essays in International Finance* 190, Princeton: International Finance Section, Department of Economics, Princeton University

1992. "Second Thoughts on EMU," *Japan and The World Economy* 4, 187–200

1991. "Target Zones and Exchange Rate Dynamics," *Quarterly Journal of Economics* 106, 669–82

1990. "Equilibrium Exchange Rates," in Branson *et al.* (eds.), 159–87

1989b. "The Case for Stabilizing Exchange Rates," *Oxford Review of Economic Policy* 5, 61–72

1989a. *Exchange Rate Instability*, Cambridge, Mass.: MIT Press

1988b. "Sustainability and the Decline of the Dollar," in Bryant, Holtham, and Hooper (eds.), 82–99

1988a. "Louvre's Lessons – Let the Dollar Fall," *International Economy* 1, 76–82

1985. "Is the Strong Dollar Sustainable?," in Federal Reserve Bank of Kansas City, *The U.S. Dollar: Recent Developments, Outlook and Policy Options*, Kansas City, 103–33

1979. "A Model of Balance-of-Payments Crises," *Journal of Money, Credit and Banking* 11, 311–25.

1978. "Purchasing Power Parity and Exchange Rates: Another Look at the Evidence," *Journal of International Economics* 8, 397–407

Krugman, Paul and Richard E. Baldwin 1987. "The Persistence of the U.S. Trade Deficit," *Brookings Papers on Economic Activity*, 1–43

Krugman, Paul and Marcus Miller 1993. "Why Have a Target Zone?," *Carnegie–Rochester Conference Series on Public Policy* 38, 279–314

Krugman, Paul and Maurice Obstfeld 1991. *International Economics: Theory and Policy*, New York: HarperCollins

Kydland, Finn E. and Edward C. Prescott 1977. "Rules Rather than Discretion: The Inconsistency of Optimal Plans," *Journal of Political Economy* 85, 473–92

Kyle, Albert F. 1985. "Continuous Auctions and Insider Trading," *Econometrica* 53, 1315–36

Laidler, David 1992. "Bullionist Controversy," in Newman *et al.* (eds.), Vol. 1, 255–61

Lerner, Abba P. 1951. *Economics of Employment*, New York: McGraw-Hill

1944. *The Economics of Control*, New York: Macmillan

Levich, Richard M. 1985. "Empirical Studies of Exchange Rates: Price Behavior, Rate Determination and Market Efficiency," in Jones and Kenen (eds.), 979–1040

Lewis, Karen K. 1994. "What Can Explain the Apparent Lack of International Consumption Risk Sharing?," draft

1992. "Peso Problem," in Newman *et al.* (eds.), Vol. 3, 140–2

1989. "Changing Beliefs and Systematic Rational Forecast Errors with Evidence from Foreign Exchange," *American Economic Review* 79, 621–36

1988. "The Persistence of the 'Peso Problem' when Policy is Noisy," *Journal of International Money and Finance* 7, 5–21

Lindberg, Hans and Paul Söderlind 1994. "Testing the Basic Target Zone Model on Swedish Data, 1982–1990," *European Economic Review* 38, 1441–70

Lindberg, Hans, Paul Söderlind, and Lars E.O. Svensson 1993. "Devaluation Expectations: The Swedish Krona 1985–92," *Economic Journal* 103, 1170–9

Liu, Peter C. and G.S. Maddala 1992. "Rationality of Survey Data and Tests for Market Efficiency in the Foreign Exchange Markets," *Journal of International Money and Finance* 11, 366–81

Lizondo, José Saöl 1991. "Real Exchange Rate Targets, Nominal Exchange Rate Policies, and Inflation," *Revista de Análisis Económico* 6, 5–22

1983. "Foreign Exchange Futures Prices Under Fixed Exchange Rates," *Journal of International Economics* 14, 69–84

Lohmann, Susanne 1992. "Optimal Commitment in Monetary Policy: Credibility Versus Flexibility," *American Economic Review* 82, 273–86

Loopesko, Bonnie E. 1984. "Relationships Among Exchange Rates, Intervention, and Interest Rates: An Empirical Investigation," *Journal of International Money and Finance* 3, 257–78

Lotz, Walther 1889. "Die Währungsfrage in Österreich-Ungarn," *Schmollers Jahrbuch* 13, 34–5

Lucas, Robert E. Jr. 1982. "Interest Rates and Currency Prices in a Two-Country World," *Journal of Monetary Economics* 10, 335–59

1978. "Asset Prices in an Exchange Economy," *Econometrica* 46, 1429–45

Lyons, Richard K. 1993. "Tests of Microstructural Hypotheses in the Foreign Exchange Market," *Working Paper* 4471, National Bureau of Economic Research

MacDonald, Ronald and Mark P. Taylor 1992. "Exchange Rate Economics: A Survey," International Monetary Fund *Staff Papers* 39, 1–57

Macklem, R. Tiff 1993. "Terms-of-Trade Disturbances and Fiscal Policy in a Small Open Economy," *Economic Journal* 103, 916–36

Magee, Stephen P. 1973. "Currency Contracts, Pass-through, and Devaluation," *Brookings Papers on Economic Activity*, 303–23

Mankiw, N. Gregory 1993. "Symposium on Keynesian Economics Today," *Journal of Economic Perspectives* 7, 3–4

Mark, Nelson C. 1990. "Real and Nominal Exchange Rates in the Long Run," *Journal of International Economics* 28, 115–36

Markowitz, Harry M. 1959. *Portfolio Selection*, New York: Wiley

Marris, Robin 1984. "Comparing the Incomes of Nations: A Critique of the International Comparison Project," *Journal of Economic Literature* 22, 40–57

Marsh, Ian W. and Stephen P. Tokarick 1994. "Competitiveness Indicators: A Theoretical and Empirical Assessment," *Working Paper* WP/94/29, International Monetary Fund

Marshall, Alfred 1923. *Money, Credit and Commerce*, London: Macmillan

Marston, Richard C. 1993. "Interest Differentials Under Bretton Woods and the Post-Bretton Woods Float: The Effects of Capital Controls and Exchange Risk," in Bordo and Eichengreen (eds.), 518–38

1987. "Real Exchange Rates and Productivity Growth in the United States and

Japan," in Sven Arndt and J. David Richardson (eds.), *Real-Financial Linkages Among Open Economies*, Cambridge, Mass.: MIT Press

1985. "Stabilization Policies in Open Economies," in Jones and Kenen (eds.), 859–916

1976. "Interest Arbitrage in the Eurocurrency Markets," *European Economic Review* 7, 1–13

Masson, Paul 1995. "Gaining and Losing ERM Credibility: The Case of the United Kingdom," *Economic Journal* 105

Masson, Paul, Steven Symansky, and Guy Meredith 1990. "MULTIMOD Mark II: A Revised and Extended Model," *Occasional Paper* 71, Washington: International Monetary Fund

Masson, Paul and Mark P. Taylor 1992. "Issues in the Operation of Monetary Unions and Common Currency Areas," in Morris Goldstein *et al.*, "Policy Issues in the Evolving International Monetary System," *Occasional Paper* 96, Washington: International Monetary Fund, 39–72

Mathieson, Donald J. and Liliana Rojas-Suárez 1993. "Liberalization of the Capital Account: Experiences and Issues," *Occasional Paper* 103, Washington: International Monetary Fund

McCallum, Bennett T. 1994. "A Reconsideration of the Uncovered Interest Parity Relationship," *Journal of Monetary Economics* 33, 105–32

McCormick, Frank 1979. "Covered Interest Arbitrage and Market Turbulence," *Journal of Political Economy* 87, 411–17

McKibbin, Warwick J. and Jeffrey D. Sachs 1991. *Global Linkages: Macroeconomic Interdependence and Cooperation in the World Economy*, Washington: The Brookings Institution

McKinnon, Ronald I. 1981. "The Exchange Rate and Macroeconomic Policy: Changing Postwar Perceptions," *Journal of Economic Literature* 19, 531–7

1976. "Floating Exchange Rates 1973–74: The Emperor's New Clothes," *Carnegie–Rochester Conference Series on Public Policy* 3, 79–114

1969. "Portfolio Balance and International Payments Adjustment," in Mundell and Swoboda (eds.), 199–234

1963. "Optimum Currency Areas," *American Economic Review* 53, 717–25

McKinnon, Ronald I. and Wallace E. Oates 1966. "The Implications of International Economic Integration for Monetary, Fiscal, and Exchange-Rate Policy," *Princeton Studies in International Finance* 16, Princeton: International Finance Section, Department of Economics, Princeton University

Meade, James E. 1955. "The Case for Variable Exchange Rates," *Three Banks Review* 27, 3–28

1951. *The Theory of International Economic Policy Volume One: The Balance of Payments*, London: Oxford University Press

Meese, Richard A. 1990. "Currency Fluctuations in the Post-Bretton Woods Era," *Journal of Economic Perspectives* 4, 117–34

1989. "Empirical Assessment of Foreign Currency Risk Premiums," in Stone (ed.), 157–80

1986. "Testing for Bubbles in Exchange Markets: The Case of Sparkling Rates," *Journal of Political Economy* 94, 345–73

Meese, Richard A. and Kenneth Rogoff 1988. "Was It Real? The Exchange Rate-Interest Differential Relationship over the Modern Floating-Rate Period,"

Journal of Finance 43, 933–48

1983b. "The Out-of-Sample Failure of Empirical Exchange Rate Models: Sampling Error or Misspecification?," in Frenkel (ed.), 67–112

1983a. "Empirical Exchange Rate Models of the Seventies: Do They Fit Out of Sample?," *Journal of International Economics* 14, 3–24

Meese, Richard A. and Andrew K. Rose 1991. "An Empirical Assessment of Nonlinearities in Models of Exchange Rate Determination," *Review of Economic Studies* 58, 603–19

Mélitz, Jacques 1988. "Monetary Discipline, Germany and the European Monetary System: A Synthesis," in Giavazzi *et al.* (eds.), 51–79

Mendoza, Enrique G. 1992b. "The Terms of Trade and Economic Fluctuations," *Working Paper* WP/92/98, International Monetary Fund

1992a. "The Effects of Macroeconomic Shocks in a Basic Equilibrium Framework," International Monetary Fund *Staff Papers* 39, 855–89

Metzler, Lloyd A. 1951. "Wealth, Saving and the Rate of Interest," *Journal of Political Economy* 59, 930–46

1949. "The Theory of International Trade," in Howard S. Ellis (ed.), *A Survey of Contemporary Economics*, Philadelphia: Blakiston, 210–54

Mill, John Stuart 1894. *Principles of Political Economy*, Vol. II, New York: Collier & Son

Moggridge, Donald E. 1972. *British Monetary Policy 1924–1931: The Norman Conquest of $4.86*, Cambridge: Cambridge University Press

Montiel, Peter J. and Jonathan D. Ostry 1991. "Macroeconomic Implications of Real Exchange Rate Targeting in Developing Countries," International Monetary Fund *Staff Papers* 38, 872–900

Mundell, Robert A. 1969. "Problems of the International Monetary System," in Mundell and Swoboda (eds.), 21–38

1963. "Capital Mobility and Stabilization Policy Under Fixed and Flexible Exchange Rates," *Canadian Journal of Economics and Political Science* 29, 475–85

1962. "The Appropriate Use of Monetary and Fiscal Policy for Internal and External Stability," International Monetary Fund *Staff Papers* 12, 70–9

1961c. "Flexible Exchange Rates and Employment Policy," *Canadian Journal of Economics and Political Science* 27, 509–17

1961b. "A Theory of Optimum Currency Areas," *American Economic Review* 51, 657–65

1961a. "The International Disequilibrium System," *Kyklos* 14, Fasc. 2, 153–72

1960. "The Monetary Dynamics of International Adjustment Under Fixed and Flexible Exchange Rates," *Quarterly Journal of Economics* 74, 227–57

Mundell, Robert A. and Alexander K. Swoboda (eds.) 1969. *Monetary Problems of the International Economy*, Chicago: University of Chicago Press

Mussa, Michael 1993. "Discussion," in Blundell-Wignall (ed.), 23–8

1990. "Exchange Rates in Theory and in Reality," *Essays in International Finance* 179, Princeton: International Finance Section, Department of Economics, Princeton University

1986. "Nominal Exchange Rate Regimes and the Behavior of Real Exchange Rates: Evidence and Implications," *Carnegie–Rochester Conference Series on Public Policy* 25, 117–214

260   References

1984. "The Theory of Exchange Rate Determination," in Bilson and Marston (eds.), 13–78

1982. "A Model of Exchange Rate Dynamics," *Journal of Political Economy* 90, 74–104

1981. "The Role of Official Intervention," *Group of Thirty Occasional Papers* 6

1979. "Empirical Regularities in the Behavior of Exchange Rates and Theories of the Foreign Exchange Market," *Carnegie–Rochester Conference Series on Public Policy* 11, 9–57

1977. "A Dynamic Theory of Foreign Exchange," in Michael J. Artis and A. Robert Nobay (eds.), *Studies in Modern Economic Analysis*, Oxford: Basil Blackwell, 121–43

1976. "The Exchange Rate, the Balance of Payments, and Monetary and Fiscal Policy Under a Regime of Controlled Floating," *Scandinavian Journal of Economics* 78 2, 229–48

Mussa, Michael, Morris Goldstein, Peter Clark, Donald Mathieson, and Tamim Bayoumi 1994. "Improving the International Monetary System: Constraints and Possibilities," *Occasional Paper* 116, Washington: International Monetary Fund

Muth, John F. 1961. "Rational Expectations and the Theory of Price Movements," *Econometrica* 29, 315–35

Newman, Peter, Murray Milgate, and John Eatwell (eds.) 1992. *The New Palgrave Dictionary of Economics*, New York: Stockton Press

Nicholl, Peter W.E. and David J. Archer 1992. "An Announced Downward Path for Inflation," in Richard O'Brien (ed.), *Finance and the International Economy* 6, Oxford: Oxford University Press, 116–27

Niehans, Jurg 1968. "Monetary and Fiscal Policies in Open Economies Under Fixed Exchange Rates: An Optimizing Approach," *Journal of Political Economy* 76, 893–913

Nurkse, Ragnar 1945. "Conditions of International Monetary Equilibrium," *Essays in International Finance* 4, Princeton: Princeton University Press

1944. *International Currency Experience: Lessons of the Interwar Period*, Geneva: League of Nations

Obstfeld, Maurice 1995. "International Capital Mobility in the 1990s," in Kenen (ed.)

1994. "The Logic of Currency Crises," *Working Paper* 4640, National Bureau of Economic Research

1991. "Destabilizing Effects of Exchange-Rate Escape Clauses," *Working Paper* 3603, National Bureau of Economic Research

1990. "The Effectiveness of Foreign Exchange Intervention: Recent Experience, 1985–1988," in Branson *et al.* (eds.), 197–237.

1989. "Commentary," in Stone (ed.), 181–96

1986b. "Capital Mobility and the World Economy: Theory and Measurement," *Carnegie–Rochester Conference Series in Public Policy* 24, 55–104

1986a. "Rational and Self-Fulfilling Balance-of-Payments Crises," *American Economic Review* 76, 72–81

1985. "Floating Exchange Rates: Experience and Prospects," *Brookings Papers on Economic Activity*, 369–450

1982c. "Aggregate Spending and the Terms of Trade: Is There a Laursen–Metzler

Effect?," *Quarterly Journal of Economics* 9, 87–98

1982b. "Can We Sterilize? Theory and Evidence," *American Economic Review* 72, 45–50

1982a. "The Capitalization of Income Streams and the Effects of Open-Market Policy Under Fixed Exchange Rates," *Journal of Monetary Economics* 9, 87–98

Obstfeld, Maurice and Kenneth Rogoff 1995. "The Intertemporal Approach to the Current Account," in Grossman and Rogoff (eds.)

1994. "Exchange Rate Dynamics Redux," *Working Paper* 4693, National Bureau of Economic Research

1986. "Ruling Out Divergent Speculative Bubbles," *Journal of Monetary Economics* 17, 349–62

Obstfeld, Maurice and Alan C. Stockman 1985. "Exchange-Rate Dynamics," in Jones and Kenen (eds.), 917–77

Officer, Lawrence H. 1982. *Purchasing Power Parity and Exchange Rates: Theory, Evidence and Relevance*, Greenwich, Conn.: JAI Press

Ozkan, F. Gulcin and Alan Sutherland 1994. "A Model of the ERM Crisis," *Discussion Paper* 879, Centre for Economic Policy Research

Padoa Schioppa, Tommaso 1988. "The European Monetary System: A Long-Term View," in Giavazzi *et al.* (eds.), 369–84

Papell, David H. 1988. "Expectations and Exchange Rate Dynamics After a Decade of Floating," *Journal of International Economics* 25, 303–17

Pauls, B. Dianne 1990. "U.S. Exchange Rate Policy: Bretton Woods to Present," *Federal Reserve Bulletin*, 891–908

Persson, Torsten and Guido Tabellini 1993. "Designing Institutions for Monetary Stability," *Carnegie–Rochester Conference Series on Public Policy* 39, 53–84

1990. *Macroeconomic Policy, Credibility and Politics*, Chur, Switzerland: Harwood Academic Publishers

Polak, Jacques J. 1988. "Economic Policy Objectives and Policymaking in the Major Industrial Countries," in Guth (ed.), 1–25

1957. "Monetary Analysis of Income Formation and Payments Problems," International Monetary Fund *Staff Papers* 6, 1–50

Poole, William 1970. "Optimal Choice of Monetary Policy Instruments in a Simple Stochastic Macro Model," *Quarterly Journal of Economics* 84, 197–216

1967. "Speculative Prices as Random Walks: An Analysis of Ten Time Series of Flexible Exchange Rates," *Southern Economic Journal* 33, 468–78

Porter, Michael G. 1972. "Capital Flows as an Offset to Monetary Policy: The German Case," International Monetary Fund *Staff Papers* 19, 395–424

1971. "A Theoretical and Empirical Framework for Analyzing the Term Structure of Exchange Rate Expectations," International Monetary Fund *Staff Papers* 18, 613–42

Portes, Richard 1993. "EMS and EMU After the Fall," *The World Economy* 16, 1–16

Razin, Assaf 1995. "The Dynamic Optimizing Approach to the Current Account: Theory and Evidence," in Kenen (ed.)

Research Department, IMF 1993. "A Note on Macroeconomic Causes of Recent Exchange Market Turbulence," in Group of Ten Deputies, Annex V, 139–72

Rhomberg, Rudolf R. 1964. "A Model of the Canadian Economy Under Fixed and Fluctuating Exchange Rates," *Journal of Political Economy* 72, 1–31

262   References

Ricardo, David 1951. *On the Principles of Political Economy and Taxation* (1821), in Piero Sraffa (ed.), *The Works and Correspondence of David Ricardo* I, Cambridge: Cambridge University Press

Richardson, Peter 1988. "The Structure and Simulation Properties of OECD's INTERLINK Model," *OECD Economic Studies* 10, Paris: Organization for Economic Cooperation and Development

Riehl, Heinz and Rita M. Rodríguez 1983. *Foreign Exchange and Money Markets: Managing Foreign and Domestic Currency Operations*, New York: McGraw-Hill

Robinson, Joan 1947. "The Foreign Exchanges," in Robinson, *Essays in the Theory of Employment*, Oxford: Basil Blackwell, 134–55.

Rodríguez, Carlos A. 1980. "The Role of Trade Flows in Exchange Rate Determination," *Journal of Political Economy* 88, 1148–58

Rogoff, Kenneth 1992b. "Traded Goods Consumption Smoothing and the Random Walk Behavior of the Real Exchange Rate," Bank of Japan *Monetary and Economic Studies* 10, 1–29

1992a. "Monetary Policy Coordination and Monetary Convergence," in Newman *et al.* (eds.), Vol. 2, 748–50

1985b. "The Optimal Degree of Commitment to an Intermediate Monetary Target," *Quarterly Journal of Economics* 100, 1169–89

1985a. "Can International Monetary Policy Coordination be Counterproductive?," *Journal of International Economics* 18, 199–217

1984. "On the Effects of Sterilized Intervention: An Analysis of Weekly Data," *Journal of Monetary Economics* 14, 133–50

1980. "Tests of the Martingale Model for Foreign Exchange Futures Markets," in *Essays on Expectations and Exchange Rate Volatility*, doctoral dissertation, Cambridge, Mass.: Massachusetts Institute of Technology

Roll, Richard 1979. "Violations of Purchasing Power Parity and Their Implications for Efficient International Commodity Markets," in Marshall Sarnat and Giorgio P. Szego (eds.), *International Finance and Trade*, Vol. 1, Cambridge, Mass.: Ballinger, 133–76

Romer, David 1993. "Rational Asset-Price Movements Without News," *American Economic Review* 80, 1112–30

Roper, Don E. and Stephen J. Turnovsky 1980. "Optimal Exchange Market Intervention in a Simple Stochastic Macro Model," *Canadian Journal of Economics* 13, 296–309

Rose, Andrew K. 1994. "Exchange Rate Volatility, Monetary Policy, and Capital Mobility: Empirical Evidence and the Holy Trinity," Discussion Paper 929, Centre for Economic Policy Research

Rose, Andrew K. and Lars E.O. Svensson 1994. "European Exchange Rate Credibility Before the Fall," *European Economic Review* 38, 1185–216

Sachs, Jeffrey D. 1982. "The Current Account and the Macroeconomic Adjustment Process," *Scandinavian Journal of Economics* 84, 147–59

Salant, Stephen W. and Dale W. Henderson 1978. "Market Anticipations of Government Policies and the Price of Gold," *Journal of Political Economy* 86, 627–48

Salter, W.E.G. 1959. "Internal and External Balance: The Role of Price and Expenditure Effects," *Economic Record* 35, 226–38.

Samuelson, Paul A. 1964. "Theoretical Notes on Trade Problems," *Review of Economics and Statistics* 46, 145–54

Santaella, Julio A. 1993. "Stabilization Programs and External Enforcement," International Monetary Fund *Staff Papers* 40, 584–621

Sargent, Thomas J. 1982. "The Ends of Four Big Inflations," in Robert E. Hall (ed.), *Inflation: Causes and Effects*, Chicago: University of Chicago Press, 41–97

Scammell, W.M. 1965. "The Working of the Gold Standard," *Yorkshire Bulletin of Economic and Social Research*, reprinted in Eichengreen (ed.), 1985, 103–19

Schadler, Susan, Maria Carkovic, Adam Bennett, and Robert Kahn 1993. "Recent Experiences with Surges in Capital Inflows," *Occasional Paper* 108, Washington: International Monetary Fund

Schinasi, Gary and P.A.V.B. Swamy 1989. "The Out-of-Sample Forecasting Performance of Exchange Rate Models when Coefficients Are Allowed to Change," *Journal of International Money and Finance* 8, 375–90

Shiller, Robert J. 1978. "Rational Expectations and the Dynamic Structure of Macroeconomic Models: A Critical Review," *Journal of Monetary Economics* 4, 1–44

Shleifer, Andrei and Lawrence H. Summers 1990. "The Noise Trader Approach to Finance," *Journal of Economic Perspectives* 4, 19–33

Solomon, Robert 1991. "Background Paper," in *Partners in Prosperity: The Report of the Twentieth Century Task Force on the International Coordination of National Economic Policies*, New York: Priority Press Publications, 45–128

　1982. *The International Monetary System 1945–1981*, New York: Harper & Row

Spufford, Peter 1986. *Handbook of Medieval Exchange*, Bury St. Edmunds, Suffolk: St. Edmundsbury Press

Stallings, David A. 1993. "Increased Protection in the 1980s: Exchange Rates and Institutions," *Public Choice* 77, 493–521

Steiger, Otto 1992. "Cigarette Currencies," in Newman *et al.* (eds.), Vol. 1, 354–5

Stein, Jerome L. 1994. "The Natural Real Exchange Rate of the United States Dollar and Determinants of Capital Flows," in Williamson (ed.), 133–75

Stevens, Guy V.G., Richard B. Berner, Peter B. Clark, Ernesto Hernández-Catá, Howard J. Howe, and Sung Y. Kwack 1984. *The U.S. Economy in an Interdependent World*, Washington: Board of Governors of the Federal Reserve System

Stigum, Marcia 1990. *The Money Market*, Homewood, Ill.: Dow Jones–Irwin

Stockman, Alan 1988. "Real Exchange-Rate Variability Under Pegged and Floating Nominal Exchange-Rate Systems: An Equilibrium Theory," *Carnegie–Rochester Conference Series on Economic Policy* 29, 259–94

　1983. "Real Exchange Rates Under Alternative Nominal Exchange Rate Systems," *Journal of International Money and Finance* 2, 147–66

　1980. "A Theory of Exchange Rate Determination," *Journal of Political Economy* 88, 673–98

　1979. "Monetary Control and Sterilized Intervention Under Pegged Exchange Rates," draft, University of Rochester

Stockman, Alan and Linda Tesar 1990. "Tastes and Technology in a Two-Country Model of the Business Cycle: Explaining International Comovements," *Working Paper* 3566, National Bureau of Economic Research

Stone, Courtenay C. (ed.) 1989. *Financial Risk: Theory, Evidence and Implications*, Boston: Kluwer Academic Publishers

Summers, Lawrence H. 1994. "Shared Prosperity in the New International Economic Order," in Kenen (ed.), 419–26

Summers, Robert and Alan Heston 1991. "The Penn World Table (Mark 5): An Expanded Set of International Comparisons, 1950–1988," *Quarterly Journal of Economics* 106, 327–68

Svensson, Lars E.O. 1994. "Why Exchange Rate Bands? Monetary Independence in Spite of Fixed Exchange Rates," *Journal of Monetary Economics* 33, 157–99

   1993. "Assessing Target Zone Credibility: Mean Reversion and Devaluation Expectations in the ERM, 1979–1992," *European Economic Review* 37, 763–802

   1992b. "An Interpretation of Recent Research on Exchange Rate Target Zones," *Journal of Economic Perspectives* 6, 119–44

   1992a. "The Foreign Exchange Risk Premium in a Target Zone with Devaluation Risk," *Journal of International Economics* 33, 21–40

   1991. "The Term Structure of Interest Rates in a Target Zone: Theory and Swedish Data," *Journal of Monetary Economics* 28, 87–116

Svensson, Lars E.O. and Assaf Razin 1983. "The Terms of Trade and the Current Account: The Harberger–Laursen–Metzler Effect," *Journal of Policy Economy* 91, 97–125

Swan, Trevor W. 1963. "Longer-Run Problems of the Balance of Payments," in Heinz W. Arndt and Max W. Corden (eds.), *The Australian Economy: A Volume of Readings*, Melbourne: Cheshire, 384–95.

Sweeney, Richard J. 1986. "Beating the Foreign Exchange Market," *Journal of Finance* 41, 163–82

Takacs, Wendy E. 1981. "Pressures for Protectionism: An Empirical Analysis," *Economic Inquiry* 19, 687–93

Takagi, Shinji 1991. "Exchange Rate Expectations: A Survey of Survey Studies," International Monetary Fund *Staff Papers* 38, 156–83

Tavlas, George S. 1993. "The 'New' Theory of Optimum Currency Areas," *The World Economy* 16, 663–85

Taylor, John B. 1988. "The Treatment of Expectations in Large Multicountry Econometric Models," in Bryant, Henderson *et al.* (eds.), 161–79

   1977. "Conditions for Unique Solutions in Stochastic Macroeconomic Models with Rational Expectations," *Econometrica* 45, 1377–85

Taylor, Mark P. 1995b. "Exchange Rate Behavior Under Alternative Exchange Rate Regimes," in Kenen (ed.)

   1995a. "The Economics of Exchange Rates," *Journal of Economic Literature* 33

   1989. "Covered Interest Arbitrage and Market Turbulence," *Economic Journal* 99, 376–91.

   1987. "Covered Interest Parity: A High-Frequency High-Quality Data Study," *Economica* 54, 429–38

Taylor, Mark P. and Helen Allen 1992. "The Use of Technical Analysis in the Foreign Exchange Market," *Journal of International Money and Finance* 11, 304–14

Telser, Lester G. 1959. "A Theory of Speculation Relating Profitability and Stability," *Review of Economics and Statistics* 44, 295–302

Tesar, Linda L. and Ingrid M. Werner 1992. "Home Bias and the Globalization of Securities Markets," *Working Paper* 4218, National Bureau of Economic Research

Thomas, Alun H. 1994. "Expected Devaluation and Economic Fundamentals," International Monetary Fund *Staff Papers* 41, 262–85

Tinbergen, Jan 1952. *On the Theory of Economic Policy*, Amsterdam: North-Holland

Tobin, James 1992. "Money," in Newman *et al.* (eds.), Vol. 2, 770–9

    1991. "The International Monetary System: Pluralism and Interdependence," in Alfred Steinherr and Daniel Weiserbs (eds.), *Evolution of the International and Regional Monetary Systems: Essays in Honour of Robert Triffin*, New York: St. Martin's Press, 3–9

    1987. "Agenda for International Coordination of Macroeconomic Policies," in Paul A. Volcker *et al.* International Monetary Cooperation: Essays in Honor of Henry C Wallich, *Essays in International Finance* 169, Princeton: International Finance Section, Department of Economics, Princeton University, 61–9

    1967. "Liquidity Preference as Behavior Toward Risk," in Donald D. Hester and James Tobin (eds.), *Risk Aversion and Portfolio Choice*, New York: Wiley, 1–26

Tower, Edward and Thomas D. Willett 1976. "The Theory of Optimum Currency Areas and Exchange-Rate Flexibility," *Special Papers in International Economics* 11, Princeton: International Finance Section, Department of Economics, Princeton University

Triffin, Robert 1960. *Gold and the Dollar Crisis: The Future of Convertibility*, New Haven: Yale University Press

Tryon, Ralph W. 1983. "Small Empirical Models of Exchange Market Intervention: A Review of the Literature," *Staff Studies* 134, Washington: Board of Governors of the Federal Reserve System

Tsiang, S.C. 1959. "Fluctuating Exchange Rates in Countries with Relatively Stable Economies: Some European Experiences After World War I," International Monetary Fund *Staff Papers* 7, 243–73

Turner, Philip and Jozef Van 't dack 1993. "Measuring International Price and Cost Competitiveness," *BIS Economic Papers* 39

Ungerer, Horst, Jouko J. Hauvonen, Augusto López-Claros, and Thomas Mayer 1990. "The European Monetary System: Developments and Perspectives," *Occasional Paper* 73, Washington: International Monetary Fund

Van der Ploeg, F. (ed.) 1994. *The Handbook of International Macroeconomics*, Oxford: Blackwell

Végh, Carlos A. 1992. "Stopping High Inflation," International Monetary Fund *Staff Papers* 39, 626–95

Volcker, Paul A. 1978. "The Political Economy of the Dollar," reprinted in *Federal Reserve Bank of New York Quarterly Review* 3, 1–12

Volcker, Paul A. and Toyoo Gyohten 1992. *Changing Fortunes*, New York: Times Books

Wallich, Henry C. 1984. "International Cooperation in the World Economy," in Jacob A. Frenkel and Michael Mussa (eds.), *The World Economic System: Performance and Prospects*, Dover, Mass.: Auburn House, 85–99

Walmsley, Julian 1992. *The Foreign Exchange and Money Markets Guide*, New

York: Wiley

Walsh, Carl 1992. "Optimal Contracts for Central Bankers," *Working Paper* 92–07, Federal Reserve Bank of San Francisco

Wickham, Peter 1985. "The Choice of Exchange Rate Regime in Developing Countries," International Monetary Fund *Staff Papers* 32, 248–88

Williams, John H. 1947. "Economic Lessons of Two World Wars," in John H. Williams, *Postwar Monetary Plans and Other Essays*, New York: Alfred A. Knopf, cviii–cxxxvi

Williamson, John (ed.) 1994. *Estimating Equilibrium Exchange Rates*, Washington: Institute for International Economics

　1994. "Estimates of FEERs," in Williamson (ed.), 177–243

　1983. *The Exchange Rate System*, Washington: Institute for International Economics

Wilson, Charles A. 1979. "Anticipated Shocks and Exchange Rate Dynamics," *Journal of Political Economy* 87, 639–47

Wolff, Christian P. 1987. "Forward Foreign Exchange Rates, Expected Spot Rates, and Premia: A Signal-Extraction Approach," *Journal of Finance* 42, 395–406

Woo, Wing T. 1985. "The Monetary Approach to Exchange Rate Determination Under Rational Expectations," *Journal of International Economics* 18, 1–16

Working Group on Exchange Market Intervention 1983. *Report of the Working Group on Exchange Market Intervention*, Washington

Wren-Lewis, Simon 1992. "On the Analytical Foundations of the Fundamental Equilibrium Exchange Rate," in C.P. Hargreaves (ed.), *Macroeconomic Modeling of the Long Run*, Aldershot: Edward Elgar, 323–38

Wren-Lewis, Simon, Peter Westaway, Soterios Soteri, and Ray Barrell 1991. "Evaluating the United Kingdom's Choice of Entry Into the ERM," *Manchester School* 59, Supplement, 1–22

Yeager, Leland B. 1976. *International Monetary Relations: Theory, History and Policy*, New York: Harper & Row, second edition.

Index of authors

Index of subjects